HUNTING THE UNABOMBER

THE FBI, TED KACZYNSKI, AND
THE CAPTURE OF AMERICA'S MOST
NOTORIOUS DOMESTIC TERRORIST

LIS WIEHL WITH LISA PULITZER

NELSON
BOOKS

An Imprint of Thomas Nelson

Published in Nashville, Tennessee, by Nelson Books, an imprint of Thomas Nelson. Nelson Books and Thomas Nelson are registered trademarks of HarperCollins Christian Publishing, Inc.

Thomas Nelson titles may be purchased in bulk for educational, business, fund-raising, or sales promotional use. For information, please e-mail SpecialMarkets@ThomasNelson.com.

Any Internet addresses, phone numbers, or company or product information printed in this book are offered as a resource and are not intended in any way to be or to imply an endorsement by Thomas Nelson, nor does Thomas Nelson vouch for the existence, content, or services of these sites, phone numbers, companies, or products beyond the life of this book.

ISBN 978-0-7180-9234-4 (eBook)
ISBN 978-0-7180-9212-2 (HC)

Library of Congress Cataloging-in-Publication Data

Names: Wiehl, Lis W., author. | Pulitzer, Lisa, 1962-
Title: Hunting the Unabomber : the FBI, Ted Kaczynski, and the capture of America's most
    notorious domestic terrorist / Lis Wiehl with Lisa Pulitzer.
Other titles: FBI, Ted Kaczynski, and the capture of America's most notorious domestic terrorist
Description: Nashville, Tennessee : Nelson Books, [2020] | Includes bibliographical references
    and index. | Summary: "From Lis Wiehl, New York Times bestselling author and "storyteller
    extraordinaire" (Steve Berry), with New York Times bestselling crime writer Lisa Pulitzer, the
    definitive, gripping account of the longest pursuit in FBI history: the quest to find and capture
    the domestic terrorist Ted Kaczynski."--Provided by publisher.
Identifiers: LCCN 2019031034 (print) | LCCN 2019031035 (ebook) | ISBN 9780718092122
    (hardcover) | ISBN 9780718092344 (ebook)
Subjects: LCSH: Bombing investigation--United States. | Kaczynski, Theodore John, 1942- |
    Bombers (Terrorists)--United States. | Serial murder investigation--United States. | Terrorists--
    United States. | United States. Federal Bureau of Investigation.
Classification: LCC HV8079.B62 W54 2020 (print) | LCC HV8079.B62 (ebook)| DDC
    364.152/32092--dc23
LC record available at https://lccn.loc.gov/2019031034
LC ebook record available at https://lccn.loc.gov/2019031035

Printed in the United States of America

20 21 22 23 24 LSC 10 9 8 7 6 5 4 3 2 1

To the memory of FBI Special Agent Patrick Webb,
whose dedication to hunting the Unabomber made
the telling of this story possible.

CONTENTS

PART IV

PART V

PART VI

"My motive for doing what I am going to do is simply personal revenge. I do not expect to accomplish anything by it. . . . I certainly don't claim to be an altruist or to be acting for the 'good' (whatever that is) of the human race. I act merely from a desire for revenge. Of course, I would like to get revenge on the whole scientific and bureaucratic establishment, not to mention communists and others who threaten freedom, but, that being impossible, I have to content myself with just a little revenge."

—TED KACZYNSKI, APRIL 6, 1971

AUTHOR'S NOTE

Tracking down Theodore Kaczynski, aka the Unabomber, was one of the longest and most expensive manhunts in FBI history, spanning eighteen years and costing US taxpayers upward of $50 million. At the height of the task force's operation, there were more than five hundred people from three federal agencies working the case. Some dedicated a substantial portion of their careers to the investigation, while countless others rotated in and out of the effort to hunt down the elusive bomber who had millions of Americans fearing for their safety for nearly two decades.

The story has been the subject of countless articles, TV news programs, and books, as well as—most recently—a Discovery Channel docuseries, *Manhunt: Unabomber*. The Discovery program received nationwide attention, and some people have asked me why I chose to write a book on the topic when there is already a docuseries out there that many have watched. What some viewers may have missed is that the eight-part series was a *fictionalized* account of the case.

In condensing the decades-long investigation, the creators of the docudrama took extensive liberties with the facts, including the creation of a composite character loosely based on the work of FBI agent and criminal profiler James "Fitz" Fitzgerald. Producers turned Fitzgerald into a dramatic central figure and made it appear as though he spent many years on the case, was pivotal to the investigation, and played a key role in solving one of the nation's biggest mysteries.

But in the weeks and months after the docuseries aired, FBI agents and others came forward to say that Fitzgerald's character was absurdly widened to incorporate the work of many others who'd played pivotal roles. They say the miniseries left viewers with a gross misunderstanding of how the case played out, credited Fitzgerald for breakthroughs made by others, and made it appear that he was the one who ultimately solved the case. A handful of UNABOM task force members even published pieces faulting the miniseries and contending that its portrayal disrespects the group's achievements and leaves viewers with a "predominantly fiction-alized story" and one that is "more fiction than truth."

To be sure, Agent Fitzgerald played a role in the case, but he was just one individual in an enormous task force that at its peak spanned eight states, involved three federal agencies—the FBI; the Bureau of Alcohol, Tobacco and Firearms, now the Bureau of Alcohol, Tobacco, Firearms and Explosives; and the US Postal Inspection Service—and involved upward of five hundred agents. The biggest fabrication was Fitzgerald's supposed dramatic meeting with the Unabomber himself. In fact, Fitzgerald was never in Lincoln, Montana, where the Unabomber was finally identified and apprehended, and he never even met Kaczynski.

The Unabomber has steadfastly refused to speak about the case with anyone in the FBI; the only investigators Kaczynski talked to are the two members of the UNABOM task force (UTF) who pulled him out of his simple wood cabin on April 3, 1996, and ultimately placed him under arrest. The Discovery series also left viewers with the impression that Agent Fitzgerald had to fight against supervisors and others to pursue the case, when in fact those involved in the investigation argue that it was a cohesive team effort that ultimately led to the capture of Theodore J. Kaczynski.

As a third-generation federal prosecutor and the daughter of an FBI agent who played a role in the investigation of the assassination of President John F. Kennedy, I heard those stories and was disappointed by the liberties taken by the show's producers. In an era when Americans are questioning "the truth" and trying to distinguish facts from fiction, I am anxious to set the record straight and detail what really happened in those dark days when Kaczynski, a math genius and one of the youngest people to ever graduate Harvard University, turned his hatred of technology and inner rage into a decades-long bombing spree.

To help me chronicle the true story behind the eighteen-year investigation, I did a deep dive into the case with the aid of retired FBI Supervisory Special Agent Patrick J. Webb, someone who was uniquely positioned to tell the real story from the inside. While he never attempted to portray himself as a major player, he was, in fact, one of the longest serving members of the UNABOM task force.

For more than five years, Webb—a bomb technician and highly trained explosives expert—led the investigation out of the FBI's San Francisco office. He was in Lincoln, Montana, on the day investigators grabbed Kaczynski and placed him into custody. He was also one of the explosives experts who took part in the critical search of the primitive cabin where Kaczynski carefully crafted his homemade bombs—and was in the one-room dwelling when a live bomb was discovered under the suspect's bed, packaged, addressed, and ready to be mailed to an unsuspecting recipient.

From our first meeting, Webb and I hit it off and committed to work together to bring the incredible story behind this mammoth effort to light. I grew up with law enforcement, and I am proud of it. I heard stories from my father about the cases he worked on and the bad guys he helped put away. In a way, being the daughter of an FBI agent made me part of that broader family. FBI agents treat each other as family, and that bond includes extended family members such as wives, sons, and daughters. I understood Webb and what motivated him in a way that those outside law enforcement may never fully understand. There's a deep and unwritten bond among FBI agents and their families—one of truth, trust, and a commitment to pursue cases no matter the danger or duration. I also know that most of them have no desire to be in the limelight or publicly seek credit for their work. That's not what they do. That's why I am incredibly fortunate that former Supervisory Special Agent Webb was willing to step forward and help me tell this story. And it is with great sadness that I report his passing during the writing of this book.

He was undergoing chemotherapy for liver cancer when we first connected in late spring of 2018. As ill as he was, he graciously opened his home and his heart, and his assistance and input cannot be overstated. He also pointed me to other key players whose participation in this project has proved invaluable: Terry Turchie, a former deputy assistant director of the FBI's Counterterrorism Division, whose leadership of the UNABOM task force beginning in 1994 was the driving force behind Kaczynski's apprehension; US Postal Inspector Paul Wilhelmus, also a member of the UNABOM task force and one of only two members of law enforcement to have ever interviewed Kaczynski; and FBI Special Agent Kathy Puckett, who was a member of the behavioral analysis program in the bureau's National Security Division when she was tapped to join the UTF and has been lauded for her multijurisdictional study concerning lone domestic terrorists—including Unabomber Ted Kaczynski, Oklahoma City Bomber Timothy McVeigh, and Olympic Park Bomber Eric Rudolph. Others, including several former members of Webb's counterterrorism squad in San Francisco, have also shared their recollections and stories for this publication. I am grateful to each of them.

PART I

CHAPTER 1

IT'S UNABOM

December 1992
San Francisco, California

California was experiencing one of the longest droughts in its recorded history. The state had not seen any significant precipitation in six years, and the gray, rainless skies looming over much of the area seemed an ominous reminder that there was no relief in sight. Newly enacted water-conservation rules barred residents from washing their cars or watering their lawns. Every household had a rationed amount of water use per person, and there were no exceptions for anyone, rich or poor. The penalties were harsh; they started with fines for first-time offenders and ranged all the way up to a total shutdown of water service for a home or business for those who continued to violate the rules.

In Marin County, which is 90 percent dependent on rainwater runoff to fill its lakes and reservoirs, FBI Supervisory Special Agent Patrick Webb, a bomb technician with the bureau's San Francisco office, and his wife, Florence, had come up with all kinds of ingenious ways to conserve and reuse what water they had. They put bricks in the toilet tanks to save water on every flush, collected gray water as it came out of the washing machine, and placed buckets under downspouts to save rainwater. They even put plastic milk jugs in the shower to catch water while it was heating up—which they'd use to flush the toilets and water the plants. The couple and their two teen daughters had slowly adjusted to the water rationing, although Patrick's practice of pounding on the bathroom wall whenever one of the girls was taking a "long" shower had made him somewhat unpopular. So news that he would be away for a couple of days attending an FBI major case conference had both girls envisioning an extra minute or two, uninterrupted, in the shower.

Since joining the bureau's San Francisco office in 1974, Webb had worked mostly counterterrorism cases. San Francisco was a hotbed of bombing activity, with anti-government groups operating through the Bay Area and responsible for hundreds of attacks dating back to the early 1970s. Back then, anarchist groups were protesting the United States' involvement in Vietnam; and while their activities had tapered off in much of the rest of the country, San Francisco had remained a mecca for defiance. Bomb techs could barely finish processing evidence at one crime scene when they got word of another attack somewhere else in the city that needed their attention. Protest bombings were commonplace, with radical groups like the New World Liberation Front, the Red Guerilla Family, the Emiliano Zapata Unit, the Symbionese Liberation Army (SLA), and the Weather Underground operating with alarming frequency.

From the midseventies into the early eighties, there seemed to be a bombing every eight days on average, and sometimes even two in one week, prompting one FBI spokesman to dub the city "the Belfast of North America." The remark immediately caught the attention of someone at headquarters in Washington, DC, who called the agent to deliver a stern reprimand. "Don't ever say that again," he was told. "It makes America look unsafe."

One of the first cases Webb worked on was the SLA's kidnapping of newspaper heiress Patricia "Patty" Hearst, who made headlines when she was caught on CCTV participating in a bank robbery alongside her captors. Although Webb was not there for her actual arrest, he did escort her to her initial appearance before the magistrate (along with thirty-plus other agents).

Over the years, Webb and his squad had fallen into a groove, working as a tight-knit team conducting complex crime scene investigations and follow-up work in an efficient and methodical fashion. It wasn't the sort of work that just anyone could do. Bombs, by their very nature, left large and messy crime scenes that required experienced investigators who knew what they were looking for.

Most of the cases they had been dealing with were pretty straightforward. They'd go out to the crime scene; photograph, collect, and diligently label each piece of evidence; and then head back to the office located in the federal building at 450 Golden Gate Avenue in downtown San Francisco, where they'd lay everything out on big tables and examine each and every item in great detail before sending it all off to the explosives unit at the FBI laboratory. They had probed bombings in office buildings, trailers, and Safeway supermarkets; the San Francisco opera house and the Berkeley office of the FBI had also been targets. Many of the devices were accompanied by letters in which one or another of the organizations would claim credit for the violence, which quickly narrowed the list of likely suspects.

Major case conferences are common in the FBI, held to coordinate activities in various field offices where agents collaborate on crimes that appear to be linked. The case on the agenda for the upcoming conference was one that had been vexing Agent Webb and his team—along with their associates in multiple FBI offices across the US—for more than a decade.

To this point, the bureau had linked twelve explosive devices to an elusive bomber who appeared to be targeting universities and airlines. With no name or other identifying evidence to go on, the agents had started referring to their unknown perpetrator with the code name UNABOM—"UNiversity and Airline BOMber." (Years later, the media picked up on the acronym and started referring to the perpetrator as the "Unabomber.")

The attacks had begun in 1978 and had occurred in five different states—Illinois, Michigan, California, Tennessee, Washington—and in the District of Columbia. In all, the devices had killed one individual and injured twenty others, some severely. The bomb making was expert and demonstrated a meticulous level of craftsmanship. There were no letters from organizations claiming credit, and no eyewitnesses to any of the activity. Investigators had managed to collect some evidence over the years, but this bomber was still in the wind, and no one in the FBI knew if they'd ever be able to bring him to justice.

San Francisco had become the "office of origin" in the investigation in July 1982, five years into the investigation, when a package found in a break room at the University of California, Berkeley, detonated on a professor who attempted to move it. Because San Francisco was leading the investigative effort, and Webb was now the supervisory special agent in charge of the case, he had been tasked with organizing the two-day event. A major case conference on UNABOM, aka "Major Case 75," was long overdue, and Special Agent Christopher Ronay, the explosives unit chief at the FBI laboratory in DC, had reached out to ask that Webb get one on the calendar.

Ronay had played a pivotal role in the case years earlier when he was a newly arrived examiner in the explosives unit. He was the one who'd recognized some similarities in the construction of the first few devices and first suggested that the FBI might be dealing with a serial bomber. As a result, in 1979, the FBI took over investigative coordination and also brought in, when needed, investigators from the ATF and US Postal Inspection Service.

Webb decided to hold the multi-agency meeting in a no-frills conference room at the Holiday Inn Union Square on O'Farrell Street, about a block from the historic square for which it was named. The hotel was a favorite of the Bureau and had been the site of a number of past meetings; it had a big conference room and "rack rate" rooms to accommodate the large gathering. Twelve task force members were flying and driving in to San Francisco for the meeting. Even those who lived in the Bay Area would be spending the night. Webb and his case agent, John Conway, were attending from the San Francisco office, along with field agents from Chicago, the site of the first three bombings; Salt Lake City, the target of bomb number five; and Sacramento, where the Unabomber had claimed his first victim; as well as investigators from the ATF and US Postal Inspection Service. The Sacramento County Sheriff's Department had also sent a representative, Lieutenant Ray Biondi, commander of the homicide bureau. Sacramento was involved because that agency was initially responsible for investigating the one fatality so far, that of thirty-two-year-old Hugh Scrutton, who died from shrapnel injuries he sustained opening a package sent to his computer rental store, RenTech, on December 11, 1985.

Everyone involved in the UNABOM case had grown frustrated by the lack of leads—and their lack of progress in identifying potential suspects. The investigation was now in its fourteenth year, and despite countless man-hours and hundreds of thousands of dollars in federal funds, members of the UNABOM task force were no closer to solving the case than they had been a decade earlier. The leads had all dried up, just like California's landscape.

As the conference got underway, various individuals floated ideas for jumpstarting the investigation, but there was nothing that people hadn't thought of before. That was perhaps the most frustrating element of the whole investigation: the case had plodded along for so many years that just about all the agents had had at least one opportunity to pursue some different direction, but none of the leads had gone anywhere.

For all intents and purposes, the case had gone cold six years earlier when the media obtained a police sketch of the Unabomber suspect outside a Salt Lake City computer store. A woman claimed to have seen a mustachioed man in a gray hooded sweatshirt pull a wooden object from a laundry bag and place it next to a parked car that detonated when Gary Wright, the owner of CAAMS Incorporated, a computer store not far from the University of Utah, spotted it and attempted to kick it out of the way of his designated parking space, detonating the pipe bomb hidden inside a hand-carved wooden box. The bombings had stopped immediately after the sketch was circulated, and authorities assumed that the suspect may have gone deep underground.

For six years, no one heard anything more from him, leading to even more suspicions from investigators that the suspect was either dead or in prison serving time for some other crime. The only tips the FBI was getting at this point were from readers of an old *Reader's Digest* article about the Unabomber, copies of which were still lying around doctors' office waiting rooms.

Agent Webb was forever the optimist; he hoped that by bringing the agents together and doing yet another deep dive into the case, they'd be able to make progress.

"Where can we go with this case?" he asked after the usual round of introductions from the men in suits and ties sitting around the conference-room table. There was only one new face in the group that Webb and the others didn't recognize—a guy named Robert "Bob" Pocica, a desk supervisor from the FBI's Criminal Investigative Division who had accompanied Ronay from DC.

From the start, Pocica seemed skeptical about the FBI's continued involvement in the investigation. The Criminal Investigation Division oversaw the entire investigation, and Pocica had come as its representative. As the meeting progressed, Webb was growing frustrated that a good deal of time was being spent answering his inquiries. Pocica was questioning all the moves the team had made up to now and hammering away at the agents for pursuing leads that had yielded no results. He wanted to know, "Why do you do *this* if *this* doesn't bring you a return?"

To Webb and the others, it soon became apparent that Pocica had been sent by headquarters to play the role of devil's advocate, and nobody knew why.

After an hour or so, Webb called for a break in the meeting, and he and Special Agent Ronay took Pocica aside.

"You are being kind of a jerk," Ronay told him. "What's your angle here?"

Pocica's response blindsided both men. He said that headquarters no longer had any appetite for this case; either they felt they had bigger fish to fry or they saw it as unsolvable.

When the meeting reconvened, Pocica's pessimism continued. He told the larger group about his—and his superiors'—frustrations, eventually admitting that his section chief had sent him from headquarters to close the investigation down. "Unless you can show us a compelling reason not to, we are prepared to kick the case back to the locals," he said. This meant turning the case over to the Sacramento County Sheriff's Department, where the only murder linked to the Unabomber—the death of computer store owner Hugh Scrutton—had occurred.

This was the first time task force members had even met Pocica, and no one knew what to say next. It was almost as if there was no reason to even continue with the conference. A dark silence hung over the room.

Sheriff's Lieutenant Ray Biondi pushed his chair away from the table, stood up, and launched into an impassioned speech. "Fine—you guys can close it; we will take it gladly. But we need the strength of the FBI behind us." Biondi didn't make explicit his concern, but everyone in the room heard what he was really saying: The Sacramento County Sheriff's Department could take the case back—but there was no way the department was going to be able to make progress or come closer to solving the case with its relatively meager resources. The department needed the FBI's involvement at some level—either out in front or through the back door. Without the FBI, the case was going nowhere—and Biondi and his department weren't going to be taking responsibility if something went seriously awry.

Biondi was an honest and sometimes abrasive homicide detective, and his remarks were met with a collective gulp from those seated around the table.

"And who is going to deal with my monthly phone call from Mrs. Scrutton?" Biondi continued. "Every month she calls me. 'Lieutenant Biondi,' she asks, 'what have you done to solve the case this month? Do you have any leads to find out who killed my son?'"

No one had any response, and Biondi knew that he'd be the one fielding her next call. The meeting didn't seem to have much direction after Pocica's remarks. Everyone there knew that what mattered most was what was going to happen thousands of miles away at the FBI headquarters in Washington, DC.

By midafternoon, everyone was disheartened and ready for a drink. A lot of the guys were from out of town, and San Francisco being a tourist city, most of them headed to Fisherman's Wharf to do some sightseeing and grab a bite to eat.

Webb and Conway were determined to persuade Pocica that the bureau was making a huge mistake in closing down the investigation, so they invited him to join them and their longtime colleague Chris Ronay at Liverpool Lil's, a steakhouse on Greenwich Street, right next to the Presidio. After a few drinks, the discussion turned to UNABOM. Webb knew that Pocica was a bright young agent who wanted to move up through the FBI's ranks; it was a reasonable career goal, and one shared by hundreds of other men and women in the FBI. But he and Conway also knew that it would be a serious mistake if Pocica convinced their superiors to abandon the UNABOM case now.

After sharing a meal and drinks, Webb and Conway cornered Ronay and, out of earshot of Pocica, threw out a bunch of reasons why the FBI should continue to support the investigation. Ronay was now head of the explosives unit, and he was a big UNABOM fan. He knew all about the case, having examined the various devices, and he was convinced it could be solved. So he was best positioned to sway opinion of higher-ups back at headquarters in DC.

Webb and Conway pointed to the burden of all the unsolved cases; the Unabomber had sent devices to Boeing and Vanderbilt University, the University of Michigan, the University of Chicago, Northwestern, the University of Utah, and UC Berkeley. He'd been pretty active over the long term, and he had killed a man. Just because he had stopped for six years didn't mean he wasn't going to come back.

"We are going to be the scorn of the world if we walk away from the case and he resurfaces and harms more people," Agent Conway argued. "Do you want to take that kind of hit when he strikes again?"

Deep down, Webb felt that too much was hinging on the investigation to stop at this point. Sure, there were the monthly calls from Hugh Scrutton's mother, but that was something that lots of law enforcement officials had to deal with; some relatives would always push for justice, no matter what.

More importantly, Webb and Conway both had a gut feeling that the UNABOM suspect was still alive and well, and that the bombings would resume at some point. There hadn't been any evidence of action from the suspect in six years—a long time, indeed. But there was no indication either that their suspect had died or otherwise permanently disappeared. They also knew that if the FBI dismantled the investigation and the Unabomber returned, there would be no way to immediately set up a task force, so valuable time could potentially be lost.

"Just give us a chance to play this thing out," Conway implored.

Ronay was now a unit chief, which meant he had some power at the bureau, and both Webb and Conway were heartened when he agreed to lobby Pocica and his superiors on their behalf. He would talk to the assistant director responsible for the FBI's laboratory about the CID's efforts to close the case down, hoping to convince him to advocate against it with higher-ups at the bureau.

Within days, the decision came down from headquarters: the investigation would continue for one more year. The team was both relieved and elated; a sense of justice and determination had prevailed.

But the clock was ticking.

———

Exactly six months after the UNABOM conference in San Francisco, Agent Webb and members of his counterterrorism squad were called to the scene of a bombing at a private home in Tiburon, a town just north of San Francisco in Marin County. Dr. Charles Epstein, a geneticist at the University of California San Francisco, had received a package in the mail, a padded envelope about the size of a paperback book.

Earlier that day, Epstein's teenage daughter, Joanna, had found the package outside and brought it into the house, placing it on the kitchen table. She later went out, leaving her dad alone in the residence. The bomb went off as soon as Dr. Epstein started to remove the packaging, causing him severe injury. The blast was so powerful it blew out the kitchen windows, ripped the legs from the table, tossed dishes and glasses off the shelves, and tore cabinets wide open. The bomb ripped apart Epstein's hand, and left shrapnel in his abdomen and forever impaired his hearing.

An initial walk-through of the crime scene was all Webb needed to confirm what he and the others already suspected.

"It's UNABOM," he told the agents at headquarters the following morning after comparing the components from this bomb to images of previous devices.

Two days after the Epstein bomb, Webb was driving to work along the San Francisco Marina when his cell phone rang. It was FBI headquarters, so he pulled over to take the call. "There's been a bombing at Yale," the supervisor told him. "They think it's UNABOM."

The Unabomber was back, just as Agents Webb and Conway long suspected.

CHAPTER 2

FC STRIKES AGAIN

FBI Supervisory Special Agent Patrick Webb toiled fourteen years on the Unabomber case. He was one of the longest-serving members in the painstaking and exhaustive effort to track down the elusive individual who had struck terror into Americans with his mysterious and seemingly random attacks across the nation.

A highly trained bomb technician and explosives expert, Webb had led a dangerous and often unpredictable life. For much of his career, he carried a Glock, an MP5 machine gun, a lightweight bomb suit, a huge spool of detonating wire, and a Percussion Actuated Nonelectric (PAN) Disruptor (a remote bomb-disabling device) in the trunk of his clunky, unmarked black four-door sedan.

During my first conversation with him, the seventy-two-year-old man with salt-and-pepper hair and a gentle demeanor told me about a box of "treasures" he'd saved from his fourteen years on the Unabomber case. The banker's box, which contained three-ring binders, yellowing Polaroid photographs, and assorted loose papers Webb had saved over his long service, were something of a metaphor for the case itself. The FBI investigation was conducted long before the Internet became the

13

everyday tool it is today. Smartphones were little more than a dream at the time, and there was no instant communication between agents in the field when Webb oversaw the UNABOM task force. It was a time of letters, fax machines, and investigative reports—hard copies on paper—that were sent via snail mail to agents in the field. To be sure, Webb and the team of agents he supervised used the latest technology available at the time—and even broke some new ground with the uploading of thousands of pages to computers for analysis. But it was a simpler time, and some elements of criminal investigations just took longer than they do today.

Webb reminded me of my father, a former FBI agent. I grew up surrounded by members of the legal system. My great-grandfather was a sheriff in White Bluffs, Washington, and his sons all grew up to be lawmen. Webb struck me as a consummate lawman, and not all that different from my family members. Like my father, Webb was reserved and proud, with a deep respect for God and country. Perhaps that sense of quiet self-assurance comes naturally after spending years as an agent in the FBI. You learn to trust your instincts and keep the idle chatter to a minimum. And, for most in law enforcement anyway, you follow the letter of the law. The last thing you want to do is make some small mistake that could cost you the trust of others, or perhaps a court conviction.

I'd heard that Webb was such a straight arrow that he never even took civilians for a ride in his bureau-issued sedan. My father never took civilians in his bureau car either, and that included me and my mom. (I remember my mom saying that J. Edgar Hoover counted paperclips at the end of the day to make sure agents weren't taking off with extra ones for home.) To be sure, the cars were perfunctory domestic-built vehicles with few frills. But some folks invariably yearn for a drive in a law enforcement vehicle, and for Webb even that was unacceptable. In all our conversations, he always sought to emphasize the teamwork that went into the Unabomber investigation and the efforts of the hundreds of people who worked on it.

Webb's job as a bomb tech was in stark contrast to his quiet, Catholic, all-boys-school upbringing in Seattle, Washington. He joked that being in the presence of so many girls his freshman year of college had him so distracted he failed out and, discouraged, he decided to take a year off to figure out what to do next. A friend's mother was a secretary at the FBI's Seattle field office, so on her advice he applied to the agency and was hired as a clerk, a post he enjoyed. In 1965, in the midst of it all, he received a draft notice. Unsure how to respond, he sought the advice of some of the agents in the office. They advised him to enlist in the US Army as an intelligence analyst; not only would he save himself a lot of time, it could also save his life.

To pass muster, he would need to take a test and be interviewed by a local intelligence officer. A recruiter took him to San Francisco's Pier 59, where he was approved for duty and sent on to basic training at Fort Ott in Greensburg, Pennsylvania, then to a base in Maryland, and finally to Orléans, France, about seventy miles southwest of Paris, where he underwent intelligence training.

It was in France that Webb worked on his first espionage case. He was there for about six months before being transferred to West Berlin, Germany, at the height of the Cold War, where he shared a house (more like a mansion) with four young men who were also in the service. In West Berlin, he worked in civilian clothes, a suit and tie, and was sent on all kinds of missions.

The enlistment ended in 1968, and he was offered a job as a clerk for the Central Intelligence Agency. But he didn't want to stay in Germany; he wanted to return home to Seattle. So he rejoined the FBI and moved in with his mother and grandmother. In Seattle, a posting came through for a job in Anchorage, Alaska. "You are going to be bored silly," the interviewer warned him. "You need to go to college."

Once in Anchorage, Webb was accepted at Alaska Methodist University (now Alaska Pacific University), where he met his wife, Florence Rynkiewicz, a bright young English major from New Hampshire. For the next three years, Webb worked the midnight to 8:00 a.m. shift, slept for three hours, then headed to class. Upon graduating in 1973, he took the FBI exam to become a special agent, and within two weeks he got his first appointment to go to headquarters in Washington, DC, for new agent training.

Webb then was assigned to the San Francisco field office, and in 1974 he joined the bomb squad. He was in the post about six months when the Weather Underground bombed the Berkeley field office of the FBI. With no formal bomb crime scene training, he couldn't contribute much. As the duty officer in charge, his job was to man the only stairway to the third floor (the elevators had been blown out in the explosion) and log everyone who went into the crime scene. Junior agents always get the plum jobs, he joked. When the agent in charge, Charlie Bates, arrived on the scene, he wanted to know why he was standing there.

"If we had bombing crime scene school, I would be upstairs helping like everybody else," Webb replied.

Taken aback, Bates shot him a stunned look, then demanded to know his name. Webb gave it to him. The agent's statement was edgy for someone in the FBI, which has a very clear chain of command—along with rigid policies and procedures. But Bates had heard him and remembered his name. The following week, Webb and three others from the San Francisco field office were on their way to the FBI Academy in Quantico, Virginia, to attend bombing crime scene school.

In spring 1982, Webb became qualified as a special agent bomb technician, having completed further training at the FBI's Hazardous Devices School at Redstone Arsenal, the National Center for Explosives Training and Research, in Huntsville, Alabama.

At the time, the United States Army ran the training at Redstone; and according to Webb, it encompassed "blowing up everything." His first day there, he "blew himself up" four times (as in failed to deactivate the device before the timer sounded) trying to disarm a package in one of the facility's training rooms and returned to his quarters that evening slightly shaken. Learning proper techniques to disarm a variety of different types of bombs was literally a matter of life and death—and Webb knew that the training demanded all his attention. He was sent into a variety of "scenario" rooms—an aircraft cabin, a school classroom, a medical lab, a movie theater—and instructed to "take care of a suspicious package." The package was armed with a buzzer set to go off if you didn't complete the task in time; if it went off, "bang," he was dead! By the end of the course, Webb was so proficient he could disarm a live device with a toothpick and was certified to handle live explosives, detonate bombs, and render devices safe.

The UNABOM attacks had been going on for four years when Webb and members of the San Francisco Division's counterterrorism squad first got involved with the case in the summer of 1982. Special Agent Webb was a junior member of San Francisco's counterterrorism squad when the Unabomber struck for a seventh time at the campus of University of California, Berkeley, on July 2, 1982.

In the FBI, every field office has an agent in charge, called the SAC (special agent in charge), who is responsible for all the programs in his or her office. Each program is headed up by an assistant agent in charge, or ASAC. ASACs run various programs within the office. In the San Francisco Division, one of the largest offices in the bureau, there is a drug ASAC, a counterterrorism ASAC, a violent crimes ASAC, a counter-intelligence ASAC, an intelligence ASAC, and so on. Underneath them are squads, so in the more active field offices you might have three drug squads, one or two counterterrorism squads, four violent crime squads (which handle bank robberies and extortion cases), and two or three counterintelligence squads. San Francisco had two counterintelligence squads, a Russian counterintelligence squad (back then there was a Russian consulate in San Francisco that has since closed), and a Chinese counterintelligence squad. There was also a foreign squad that looked at other countries posing potential threats to national security.

On the day the Unabomber struck, Webb was at his desk on the seventh floor of the federal building at 450 Golden Gate Avenue in down-town San Francisco discussing plans for the upcoming Fourth of July weekend with colleagues. Since he was the duty officer in charge of the office that day, the call about the bombing at the UC Berkeley campus was directed to him. Upon joining the San Francisco Division in 1974, Webb had been assigned to the counterterrorism squad, also known as the "bomb squad." Webb and his squad members were pretty used to bombings, and within minutes they were boarding the equipment truck in the underground garage and heading for the Bay Bridge.

As a junior agent, Webb's role was still that of a helper to the senior bomb personnel on his squad. But he was approaching the Berkeley crime scene with a keener focus and perhaps a slightly different optic following his recent experience at bomb school. No one knew that the incident had any connection to the UNABOM investigation; agents only pieced that together afterward.

Until that point, the Unabomber had struck six times at university campuses in Chicago, Utah, and Tennessee; he had planted a bomb aboard an American Airlines jet, and he had mailed a device to the president of United Airlines. At first, various field offices within the FBI and other federal agencies had investigated the attacks as unrelated incidents. But then there'd been a breakthrough in the late seventies when lab tech Chris Ronay realized that the bombs were all constructed in a similar fashion—and that the bureau very likely had a serial bomber on its hands.

The University of California, Berkeley, had its own police force (which even included a bomb squad) and the head of the unit, Captain Bill Foley, was waiting for the team outside the Student Technology Services building, Cory Hall, where the device had detonated. Webb recalled that the building was located in the northeast quadrant of the campus just off a side street and not far from Shattuck Avenue, one of the main streets through Berkeley.

Shattuck was busy not just with vehicular traffic but with lots of pedestrian traffic too. That meant just about anyone could have easily walked onto the campus without attracting any attention. But the location of the bomb—in a coffee room on the building's fourth floor—suggested that the perpetrator likely knew the campus in some detail, Webb thought to himself as Foley led them into the building and they crowded into the elevator.

The coffee room where the explosion had occurred was part of the school's Electronic Engineering and Computer Sciences Department. Whoever placed the bomb there had to have known his or her way around the building. The victim had already been transported to the hospital when the team arrived at room 411. Blood and broken glass were everywhere, and the smell of gasoline hung in the air. The Venetian blinds had been tossed aside and hung at odd angles from the windows, and the walls were pocked with holes from the shrapnel created by the improvised explosive device.

Captain Foley told the agents that the victim, Diogenes Angelakos, a professor of electronic engineering and director of the university's electronics research laboratory, had visited the coffee break room at around 7:45 that morning, where he'd spotted an odd gadget on the floor in front of a Mr. Coffee machine that just about everyone used. There was remodeling work going on in the building, and Angelakos assumed it was some piece of test equipment that likely belonged to a member of the construction crew.

According to Webb, the bomb was a peculiar-looking and relatively small homemade device—he'd never seen one like it—that probably wouldn't have appeared at all dangerous to the professor. It included a one-gallon gasoline can like you might find at a local Pep Boys auto parts store. The bomb maker had disguised the gas can by covering portions of it with electrical and filament tape to give it the appearance of a wooden box. The perpetrator had removed the gas can's metal handle and replaced it with a piece of wood that had been painted with green enamel paint. Glued to the piece of wood was a crude gauge, or measuring device, made from a piece of blue-lined paper with typed numbers. The device had been wrapped with brown paper, basically a glued-on grocery bag, using homemade glue.

Taped to the top of the device was a typed note that read: "Wu, it works. I told you it works. I told you it would . . . FC."

Clearly the note was meant to elicit curiosity. Based on Professor Angelakos's actions, it appeared that he had indeed been intrigued and curious to learn more. He leaned down to lift the handle, triggering the wires affixed to the sides of the gas can, causing the pipe bomb suspended inside to detonate. The explosion sent gasoline spraying all around the room and drenched the professor from head to toe. For whatever reason, the gasoline didn't ignite, sparing Angelakos more serious injury or even death. Still, he sustained severe damage to his face, and the force of the explosion ripped several fingers from his right hand. For Webb and the others who were investigating, it was a kind of mystery bombing. There had been no warning, no demand, and no claim letter.

The investigation took a startling turn when FBI Case Agent Don Ulrich, one of the bomb techs on the scene, suggested that the incident may be linked to others in the agency's records.

"I think this is UNABOM!" Ulrich declared, drawing a moment of stunned silence from the team as the impact of his remark sank in. They all knew that his declaration changed everything.

While everyone in the FBI was aware of the case, Ulrich was more familiar with it than most—and especially with the bomb-making handiwork of the terrorist known as the Unabomber. Ulrich had attended a series of meetings at headquarters in DC where the UNABOM investigation had been discussed. He noted that some of the components at the crime scene appeared consistent with those used in earlier attacks. His observation was immediately confirmed by Bennett Cale, a bomb tech from the Oakland field office who was among the dozen or so agents present that day. The team wouldn't know for sure if the forensics matched until the examiners at the FBI lab in DC had reviewed all the evidence—but preliminarily, at least, the suggestion was compelling.

Agents spent two full days processing the crime scene, and they observed a number of inconsistencies and other elements that warranted follow-up by the team. For one, the device had been found in the

Engineering and Computer Sciences Department, which had a high-tech lab. Nobody was making devices with phony wooden dials like the one left in the coffee room.

Because the typewritten note attached to the device had referenced someone with the name "Wu," agents set out to find this mystery person, and Asian students, faculty members, and visitors to Cory Hall were interviewed. At UC Berkeley, where the student population is heavily Asian, this meant hours of legwork that ultimately led nowhere.

There were at least a couple of facts in the case to suggest that the professor wasn't the actual target: the bomb had been left in a public area of Cory Hall, and the attached note had not been addressed to anyone in particular. It appeared to investigators that the professor had just been in the wrong place at the wrong time—and the *real* target was the university itself. To date, five of the Unabomber's seven attacks had been directed at universities and, more specifically, at technology centers at the campuses.

Before packing up all the materials for the lab, the team attempted to reassemble the bomb back in the San Francisco office so they could learn how it worked. Having just returned from his course at Redstone, Webb was really attuned to the bomb's construction and was fascinated by the bomber's meticulous craftsmanship. It took the group two days to rebuild the device, which Webb described as "elementary, yet cunning." Inside the homemade wooden box that had been secured to the top of the gas can were batteries and two toggle switches, which were important because it meant the bomber could construct the device in one location, then transport it to the scene, where it could be initiated by turning on the toggle switches, basically arming the bomb. By pulling on the handle, Angelakos closed the circuit (two metal wires at the base of the device), causing it to detonate.

Analysis of the components by examiners in DC concluded the device was similar to those recovered several months earlier at a bomb crime scene at Vanderbilt University in Nashville, Tennessee, right down to the initials FC scratched into the galvanized pipe. Like all the Unabomber's past devices, this one had employed wood, batteries stripped of their outer casings and wrapped in filament tape, a galvanized pipe, and various lengths of wire. Some components were new to investigators: two flashlight bulbs, alligator clips, and the two on-and-off Leviton toggle switches. The initials FC—the same signature found on the typewritten note—had been scored into the bomb's steel pipe. Examiners determined the note had come from a Smith Corona 1925 to 1930 typewriter with 2.54 spacing—the same typewriter that had been used in previous attacks. There was also a second set of letters, B and W, etched into the device's wood handle. But no one knew what significance they held.

To be sure, this was a key moment in the case for Webb and the entire San Francisco team: the UC Berkeley bombing—officially known as Bomb Number Seven—was positively connected to others linked to the Unabomber. But it also left the team in something of a quandary. This was no longer their case to work—and potentially solve—on their own. The San Francisco Division had now become part of a much larger, multijurisdictional investigation encompassing six other attacks on targets with little to no obvious connection. The team's path forward was anything but clear.

CHAPTER 3

A SERIAL BOMBER?

To this point, three different agencies had been involved in the UNABOM case—the Bureau of Alcohol, Tobacco and Firearms (ATF); the US Postal Inspection Service; and the FBI. Each agency had its own specific jurisdiction. The FBI had authority over bombs placed on college campuses and aboard aircrafts; the Postal Inspection Service was responsible for investigating bombs that had gone through the US mail; and ATF's prime jurisdiction was bombs that had been found out in the general public. Because of these jurisdictional divisions, each of the agencies was empowered to commence its own independent inquiry. There was no policy or procedure in place at the time for keeping other agencies informed of that ongoing work.

In the absence of interagency coordination, multiple law enforcement offices were conducting their own independent investigations—and none of them had a full understanding of what other investigators across the United States were doing. The FBI, ATF, and US Postal Inspection Service were all probing bombings at various locations. And none of them were coordinating their work with each other or sharing investigative findings in a manner that could advance the case. The investigation was proceeding in a helter-skelter fashion with no centralized oversight or administration, with investigators from different agencies all off pursuing their own leads.

To further complicate matters, ATF had been given jurisdiction over the first two bombings, even though they had both detonated on college campuses. In theory at least, those investigations should have been handled by the FBI, as campus attacks were in its bailiwick. But that wasn't the case when the Unabomber first announced himself with a bomb that exploded at Northwestern University in Evanston, Illinois in 1978.

That first bomb—Bomb Number One—came to Northwestern by a circuitous route. A woman cutting through a parking lot at the University of Illinois Chicago Circle Campus on May 24, 1978, spotted a rectangular package wrapped in brown craft paper on the ground next to a car. The sender had applied a white, gummed mailing label to the parcel and written out the address using a blue ballpoint pen. It was to "Professor E. J. Smith" in the Department of Mechanical, Aerospace, and Nuclear Engineering at Rensselaer Polytechnic Institute's School of Engineering in Troy, New York. The woman noticed that the package did not have a postmark, indicating it hadn't gone through the US mail system. Rather than take the box to a post office—the main branch was just two blocks away—she opted to take it to her apartment, which was just steps from the campus. From the apartment, she tried to contact the sender—one "Buckley Crist," a materials science professor at Northwestern University in nearby Evanston.

Professor Crist insisted he was not the sender of the parcel and told the woman that he didn't know anything about it. Suspicious, he contacted campus police. Some phone calls later, campus police went to the woman's apartment where they picked up the parcel and delivered it to Northwestern's Evanston campus, where officials intended to sort out what it was and where it was supposed to go. But things didn't go the way they'd planned.

When it arrived at Northwestern, it was delivered to the Technological

Institute, also known as the "Tech" building, where Professor Crist had an office. Then, on May 25, a public safety officer attempted to open it. As he fiddled with the packaging, the pipe bomb went off. Fortunately for the officer, the blast went out to the side and away from him, and he suffered only minor injuries.

Under normal circumstances, the FBI would have been called in to investigate and the evidence would have been sent to the FBI lab in Washington, DC, for analysis. Back in my day as a prosecutor, FBI agents had to send their handwritten notes of witness interviews to Salt Lake City or Quantico for typing; several central locations were available depending on where the agent was stationed, but the notes were shipped out nonetheless. This process could take up to four weeks. The FBI agents I worked with structured their written notes in the form of documents known as 302s. Those 302s were dictated and then sent to a central source, most often Quantico, for typing. In prioritizing typing, the typists at Quantico looked at the urgency or immediacy of the case in question. So, if an agent's case was deemed not urgent, or, worse, a cold case, that agent could wait for many weeks to receive the typed 302s. Meanwhile, the prosecutor waited for the notes.

Of course, I would speak with my agents without the benefit of the notes, but it shows how Byzantine the hunting process could be. And each agent wants to get credit for the apprehension and conviction of high-profile targets because, along with the ceremonial plaques that are awarded, promotions within the ranks often hinge on the number of high-visibility convictions an agent has under his or her belt.

These factors result in a startling lack of coordination between agencies, and that lack of communication can be dangerous. As is now well-known, there is good evidence that the CIA did not inform the FBI of what it knew about the potential of the 9/11 attacks, as cited in the 9/11 Commission Report, a scathing critique of the two agencies released in July 2003. According to the report, prepared by a joint committee of the House and Senate intelligence panels, communication between the two agencies had failed in the months leading up to the terror attacks. Like others, I often wonder if the course of history would have changed had the agencies been coordinating their efforts.

In the case of the Unabomber, no one at Northwestern or at the University of Illinois could explain how the case wound up with ATF rather than the FBI. But ATF took the lead, then sent the components to its own lab for evaluation. ATF's experts concluded that the bomb had been cobbled together with generic parts that could be found just about anywhere. The bomb maker had used match heads and smokeless powders to fashion a primitive initiator. Despite its simple components, ATF determined that the device was powerful enough to maim or kill someone if it had detonated as the bomber had intended. The lab analysis was then shared with others within the ATF.

Professor Crist told ATF investigators he didn't know the addressee, Professor Smith, although he pointed out that someone unfamiliar with the nuances of the two men's work might confuse their areas of research and expertise. Perhaps this angle was a motive that warranted exploration? Professor Smith, too, had never met Professor Crist and had no knowledge of the parcel and no information about who may have built and delivered the explosive device.

The following spring, a second package bomb detonated in the Tech building at Northwestern University, and again the case was referred to ATF for investigation. The package was also wrapped in brown craft paper but carried no address, so it was unclear who the intended recipient might have been. It was found on a table near a cabinet with multiple mail slots—the sort used for delivering letters and packages to people in an office complex. Most of the slots were assigned to graduate-level students and faculty members in the mechanical and civil engineering disciplines. Several people remember seeing it on the table the morning of May 9, 1979, but it didn't explode until midafternoon, when graduate student John Harris, a member of the Civil Engineering Department, tried to open it. This device was housed in a Phillies brand cigar box. Its main charge consisted of match heads and a fusing system, made up of two independent circuits, each of which could detonate the bomb. Harris

26

was transported to the local hospital where he remained overnight to be treated for numerous burns and lacerations.

To this day, it remains unclear why the FBI was not alerted; perhaps it was because no one was seriously hurt in the incidents. Even more frustrating, the ATF agent who had been assigned to look into the two bombings was transferred shortly after assuming responsibility for the cases, and the investigations were dropped and basically forgotten once he left his post, as neither incident had been logged into any formal data system.

The third attack occurred in fall 1979, and I remember hearing about it on the news. On November 11, 1979, a package bomb exploded in the cargo hold of an American Airlines jet carrying ninety-two passengers and crew members from Chicago's O'Hare International Airport to Reagan National Airport, just outside of Washington, DC. The bomber had created a primitive barometer for the device, which was designed to explode when the aircraft reached a cruising altitude of 34,500 feet. While the bomb had gone off as intended, the explosion was nowhere near as powerful as its builder had hoped. Passengers heard a loud thud and heavy smoke engulfed the cabin, prompting the pilot to make an emergency landing at Washington's Dulles International Airport, where approximately eighteen passengers were treated for smoke inhalation by paramedics on the runway. Webb noted that the plane had touched down just in time. If the fire had continued to burn for just a few more minutes, the plane could have lost its hydraulics system, making it impossible for the pilots to control the craft. The fire damaged the baggage compartment and the luggage inside it.

While most people outside the Chicago area had not heard about the two previous attacks at Northwestern University, this one had the nation's attention. Because the attack had occurred aboard an aircraft, the FBI responded and commenced an investigation, joined by inspectors from the US Postal Inspection Service, who had jurisdiction over items that had gone through the mail. The airmail package was placed into a cargo pod, number 7021, between 3:00 a.m. and 6:00 a.m., which was then loaded onto American Airlines Flight 444, a 727 destined for Reagan Airport outside DC.

Evidence collected from the aircraft was sent to the FBI lab in DC for analysis. Lab technicians determined the bomb had been built using a large tin juice can that housed an explosive main charge comprised of smokeless powder and a variety of chemicals commonly used in the manufacture of pyrotechnics, such as firecrackers. The device was hidden inside a homemade wooden box measuring seven and a half inches by nine and five-eighths inches with a lid hinged at the rear. The box had been wrapped in about five layers of brown craft paper. The primitive pipe bomb inside had been assembled using a wooden dowel, four C-cell batteries, and various types of tapes, solder, and wire. Examiners were not able to determine to whom the package had been addressed because part of the wrapping had been destroyed by the explosion and subsequent fire. All that was left were the letters "R Lines NW" stenciled in green ballpoint ink and $8.00 worth of postage: three $1.00 America's Light Fueled by Truth and Reason stamps; one $1.00 Eugene O'Neill stamp; five fifty-cent Lucy Stone stamps; and six twenty-five cent Fredrick Douglass stamps.

Investigators from the US Postal Inspection Service determined the package had been sent through Chicago's massive north suburban Illinois postal facility, which handled some three million pieces of mail a day, making it virtually impossible to trace it back to its sender.

The following June, United Airlines president Percy A. Wood was severely injured when a fourth device that had been inside a package sent to his Chicago-area home detonated, causing him significant injury. Wood told investigators that a few days before the attack, he had received a letter in the mail signed by one "Enoch W. Fisher" of 3214 N. Ravenswood, Chicago, Illinois, 60657. Fisher was writing to alert him to a package that would be arriving in the coming days that contained a book of "great social significance." The book, the letter noted, was also being sent to a number of "prominent individuals" in the Chicago area and should be read by those "making important decisions affecting the public welfare." Fisher went on to acknowledge that Wood was a "busy man" who might not have time to read it but insisted it would be "well worth his time" to at least "glance" through it, "since it was as entertaining as it was significant."

Four days later, on June 8, 1980, a package arrived at Wood's home in Lake Forest, Illinois. But Wood worked late that day and so didn't open it until the following afternoon. Inside, he found what appeared to be a book, a copy of *Ice Brothers*, written by Sloan Wilson and released on September 1, 1979, by Arbor House Publishing Company. But when he looked at it more carefully, he realized that it wasn't a book at all—that it was "unusual-looking," and "similar to a candy box painted to look like a textbook." When he opened the lid of the "book," the device exploded. The box contained a pipe bomb that was triggered when he lifted the cover, blanketing the kitchen with shrapnel that embedded itself into the walls and cabinets. Wood was subsequently treated for severe lacerations to his left leg and face.

This time investigators from both the Bureau of Alcohol, Tobacco and Firearms and the US Postal Inspection Service launched inquiries. Curiously, investigators found no postage on the package, suggesting it had been hand delivered. They also determined there was no such person as Enoch W. Fischer; and while Ravenswood is a real street in Chicago, the address on the package, 3414 North Ravenswood, was fictitious. And there were other things in the package too—a copy of a story from the *Chicago Sun Times* dated June 3, 1980, that expressed concern about genetic engineering and a John Fischetti cartoon portraying an unemployed person feeding pigeons in the park. To be sure, this was an odd assortment of items, and authorities were left wondering what it all meant. Lab examiners determined the letter had been typed on a Smith Corona typewriter manufactured between 1925 and 1930 with 2.54 spacing.

The attacks, first aboard flight 444 and then targeting the president of United Airlines, prompted investigators from ATF and the Postal Inspection Service to start poking around and querying other agencies and jurisdictions about previous bombings with comparable characteristics.

The inquiry uncovered the two bombings at Northwestern University that were being handled by a local office of the ATF in the Chicago area—and hadn't garnered much attention. Arrangements were made to have the evidence from those attacks sent to the FBI lab in DC for review. In examining the debris, Christopher Ronay, then an examiner at the famed FBI lab in Washington, DC, made a startling discovery: the components from this latest device were strikingly similar to those of earlier bombs that had detonated at Northwestern University. The C-cell batteries, the various types of tape, the hand-carved wooden box, the brown craft paper, the homemade initiator—it all matched what he'd seen in prior IEDs. Ronay suddenly realized that the FBI almost certainly had a serial bomber on its hands. His suspicion would be confirmed eighteen months later when the FBI was called to Vanderbilt University in Nashville, Tennessee, where a bomb had gravely injured a secretary on campus, and his revelation immediately broadened the investigation and moved it in a totally new direction.

The Vanderbilt device had initially been sent to Pennsylvania State University, where it was moved from one mail room to another for several weeks because the person it was addressed to—scientist Patrick C. Fischer—was no longer employed there. Fischer was considered a leader in the computer science community for his work in database theory; it was his theoretical work that helped make Internet searches possible. He'd held a faculty position at Penn State until 1980 when he accepted a post at Vanderbilt to help grow the university's Computer Science Department. Fischer was lecturing in Puerto Rico when the small package finally arrived at his Vanderbilt office on May 5, 1982, with a return address from one Professor LeRoy W. Bearnson at Brigham Young University in Provo, Utah. With Fischer out of town, his secretary, Janet Smith, opened the enclosed cigar box–shaped container and was badly hurt in the ensuing pipe-bomb explosion. Her injuries were severe and required a three-week hospital stay, followed by a lengthy recovery period at home.

Because the bombing had occurred on a college campus, police in Nashville alerted the FBI. They also brought in the US Postal Inspection

Service, since the package had been sent through the US mail, and both agencies commenced parallel investigations. It was determined the mailing label had been typed using a 1925 to 1930 Smith Corona typewriter, Pica-style type, with 2.54 spacing—the same typewriter the Unabomber would use for the rest of his career, including on his manifesto. Investigators were constantly looking for that typewriter.

Postal inspectors were able to determine that the parcel had been mailed from a facility at Brigham Young University (BYU) in Provo, Utah; they immediately dispatched a team to interview employees there. People in the mailroom remembered seeing the odd, cigar box– shaped package when it first came in. Postal inspectors also met with an investigator at BYU, Brian Andreessen, and carefully described the package and its contents to him—including the "FC" tag found scratched into the Vanderbilt device. Investigators were convinced the bomber had begun putting the small metal tag inside his bombs due to frustration at not getting credit for his earlier devices.

"Hmm, that sounds just like that bomb that was found up at the University of Utah last year," Andreessen remarked—stunning investigators who had been unaware of the bomb at the Salt Lake City campus.

Until that point, none of the federal agencies investigating the various bombings had heard of the incident at the University of Utah. Suddenly, investigators had yet another trail to follow. That attack had occurred on October 8, 1981, in the University of Utah's College of Business. A maintenance worker, Robert Lockyer, was cleaning a third-floor classroom when he came across a package that had been left on one of the desks. The parcel was wrapped in brown craft paper and tied with a string. Lockyer wisely decided that the package was suspicious in nature and alerted campus security. While waiting for officers to arrive, a student tilted the package, causing a stick to slide out from the bottom. Fortunately, the device did not detonate, and both the maintenance worker and the student escaped unharmed.

Once again ATF—and not the FBI—was called to respond, along with members of the bomb unit from the nearby Fort Douglas US

Army Base. The army officers took the device—a gasoline bomb—into a women's restroom and successfully rendered it safe. Not until years later, during the UNABOM investigation, did investigators learn that the device had been rendered safe in a public bathroom, thus nullifying the potential for DNA evidence to directly solve the crime.

Like the bomb that would later be recovered at UC Berkeley—Bomb Number Seven—this device also incorporated a one-gallon gas can on top of which was a homemade wooden box containing two D-size batteries, stripped of their aluminum cases and wired in a series to increase their voltage. One of the wires had been connected to a General Electric household on/off switch, which was then mounted to the box. Inside the gas can, the bomber had secured a steel pipe filled with smokeless powder, a flammable liquid believed to be gasoline and flash powder. Wooden plugs had been affixed to either end of the pipe with epoxy-type glue to create a seal.

Components from the bomb were forwarded to the ATF lab in Treasure Island, San Francisco, where examiners recovered a single strand of red hair. However, they could not rule out the possibility that it had been picked up in the women's room while bomb techs were deactivating the device. The hair had no root, so lab technicians were unable to extract any DNA.

Ultimately, the lab techs concluded the device was "non-functional" and therefore ruled the incident a "hoax." No one was hurt, so at the conclusion of their analysis, examiners at ATF's regional laboratory in San Francisco had returned the bomb components to the University of Utah, where they were filed away on a shelf and left to gather dust.

After making the connection to the Vanderbilt University incident, postal inspectors traveled to the Salt Lake City campus, met with administrators, and left carrying the debris from the exploded device. That evidence, too, was submitted to the postal inspector's laboratory for further testing. The alleged sender, Dr. LeRoy Bearnson, a professor of electrical engineering at Brigham Young, was interviewed and told investigators that he had no knowledge of the package or its intended recipient.

In yet another weird twist, the experts in the postal inspector's lab strongly disagreed with the earlier findings from ATF's investigators. The postal inspector's laboratory concluded that the device had indeed been a fully functioning gasoline bomb. Had Lockyer attempted to move or open the package in that university classroom, the results could have been far worse—and potentially tragic.

The contradictory results prompted the two agencies to seek a third opinion from examiners at the FBI lab in DC, where it was determined that not only was the Utah bomb functional, but it had been constructed by the same individual responsible for five other attacks.

For a time, postal inspectors had been somewhat casually referring to their elusive suspect as the "Junkyard Bomber" because of his tendency to craft his devices from discarded items and scrap materials that could be found in a pile of demolition and construction debris, rather than store-bought items that could likely be traced back to him. That moniker would officially change once the crimes were linked, and the casual term "Junkyard Bomber" would be replaced as the FBI declared this to be major case 75, code-named UNABOM—which stood for "UNiversity and Airline BOMber."

CHAPTER 4

MAJOR CASE CONFERENCE

After the July 2, 1982, bombing at UC Berkeley—Bomb Number Seven—the event that had first brought Special Agent Webb and members of his squad into the investigation—a major case conference was held in San Francisco to discuss the latest developments in the investigation and to sketch out a path forward for the dozen or so in attendance. Participants included agents from FBI field offices in Chicago, Utah, Tennessee, and now the local San Francisco group. Investigators from the US Postal Inspection Service and the Bureau of Alcohol, Tobacco and Firearms were also on board. And there was a new member of the team: a representative from the US attorney's office in San Francisco who would be responsible for taking any legal action needed to support the investigation, including procuring search warrants and subpoenas on a moment's notice.

From my time in the US attorney's office in Seattle, I understand the value in having a prosecutor involved in a case even as the investigation is ongoing. Time is critical, and having access to an attorney who is being kept current on the case—and knows all the key elements—enables authorities to move quickly in the event of a break in the case.

Webb told me that having a prosecuting attorney on the team was critical to its work, ensuring that agents didn't lose time or miss an opportunity to make a collar.

As we talked, I marveled at the differences between the lightning-fast work done by investigators in the MAGA Bomber case that rocked the nation in 2018 and the painfully slow work done by investigators in the UNABOM case. A former pizza deliveryman, strip-club worker, and outspoken supporter of President Donald J. Trump was suspected of sending more than a dozen mail bombs to targets around the country as part of a terror plot aimed at Democrats and vocal critics of President Trump such as former president Barack Obama, Hillary Clinton, liberal billionaire donor George Soros, former CIA director John Brennan, and CNN's Manhattan headquarters.

Webb was quick to acknowledge the wildly different pacing in the two cases. At a superficial level at least, they were similar because both cases involved a series of mail bombings at various locations across the US committed by one or more unknown suspects. But he forcefully argued that the similarities between the cases ended there—and that there were some very good reasons for the slow progression of the work in the UNABOM case. For one, Ted Kaczynski was very intelligent—he was a young man with a genius IQ and, at the age of sixteen, among the youngest students to attend Harvard University. He'd read books describing investigative techniques and was extraordinarily careful to avoid leaving any DNA on his bombs. He made sure there were no fingerprints on anything he produced. Serial numbers, production codes, and other identifying characteristics were removed from batteries and other items he utilized. And none of his components were store-bought, rendering them untraceable. He was painstakingly careful not to lick any of the stamps he used to mail his packages. And he abhorred technology. There was no Internet at the time—but even if there had been, Kaczynski would have been perhaps the last person in the US to consider using it. The Unabomber lived totally off the grid, making his life in a remote cabin in the woods.

The suspect in the MAGA Bomber case, by comparison, doesn't appear to have the Unabomber's intellect, and he left behind extensive evidence, including Internet searches, his DNA on stamps, various YouTube videos, and a van that was a moving billboard. The MAGA Bomber lived anything but a quiet life in the woods.

In the MAGA Bomber case, the prosecutor was able to act immediately when investigators turned up new pieces of evidence. For example, when a single fingerprint taken from a mail bomb sent to the DC office of US Representative Maxine Waters yielded a possible match to someone already in the national database—fifty-six-year-old Cesar Altieri Sayoc Jr. in Florida—authorities conferred with their prosecuting attorney and moved with lightning speed to track down the perpetrator. One subpoena and two court orders were promptly obtained—all with the goal of building a case that would hold up in court and lead to a potential conviction. Ultimately, his cell phone enabled police to track him down.

Just ninety-six hours after a pipe bomb was discovered inside a package delivered to the Katonah, New York, home of George Soros, Sayoc was in custody, charged by prosecutors in the US attorney's office for the Southern District of New York (SDNY) with five federal crimes, including "interstate transportation of an explosive," "illegal mailing of an explosive," "threats against former presidents and certain other persons," "threatening interstate communications," and "assaulting federal officers." Kaczynski was no Cesar Sayoc.

Webb and other agents were frustrated that the Unabomber, whoever he was, took pains to ensure that he was not using materials that could be traced back to him or even reveal a partial fingerprint. Every step he took was designed to confound investigators. He even went so far as to remove the aluminum exterior from the batteries so he could strip off the plant codes.

Still, lab examiners were able to determine that the batteries used in most of the devices were Duracell brand. Agents from the FBI and the US Postal Service traveled to a Duracell manufacturing plant where they were shown an automated assembly line where batteries were rolling out at more than a thousand per minute. With so many coming off one production line in one plant, they realized that trying to track back the Unabomber's batteries to the point of manufacture would be virtually impossible. Attempts to trace a piece of lamp cord recovered from his sixth device (the Vanderbilt bomb) proved more promising, as it could be traced regionally based on a manufacturer's code printed on the wire. General Electric was able to determine that particular section of wire was made for distribution west of the Mountain States, so it was clear the Unabomber wasn't buying it at a Kmart in Cincinnati.

———

Supervisors in the San Francisco FBI field office assigned one case agent, Don Ulrich, to work full-time on the UNABOM investigation under the supervision of SSA Webb. Don was a bomb tech and visited all the UNABOM crime scenes, so he knew the case better than most. Still, progress was slow, and eventually Webb and the others turned their focus to new investigations coming in. Every once in a while a tip would arise, stirring up new hope that the case could be solved. But inevitably they all led nowhere, and a sense of frustration prevailed.

More than two years passed without another bombing after the attack at UC Berkeley, and supervisors back at FBI headquarters in DC had begun to wonder if perhaps they'd heard the last of the Unabomber. They'd soon learn that their elusive suspect had been using the time to perfect his devices with an eye to causing maximum damage.

Most of the devices had been pressure released and rigged to detonate upon opening. Many incorporated tiny springs and little pieces of metal the bomber had cut and forged himself. A number of them had gone through the mail service, where they were tumbled and sorted and picked up by the mail carrier without detonating, indicating whomever had constructed them was meticulous and had done a lot of testing to ensure they functioned as designed.

He'd manufactured the first few devices utilizing match heads and rubber bands to create an explosive charge. Starting with Bomb Number Four, the device sent to United Airlines president Percy A. Wood, he had begun sourcing different types of smokeless powder from bullets, perhaps in response to the malfunction of his third device, which failed to fully detonate aboard the American Airlines jet. The crudeness of his earlier devices indicated he wasn't somebody with military training or a background in explosives. An examination of the evidence from the Vanderbilt device revealed he had changed up his bomb-making formula. He had replaced his gunpowder-matchheads combination with a potent mix of ammonium nitrate and aluminum powder, telegraphing to investigators that his techniques were improving, and his devices were becoming more lethal.

The device found at the University of Utah—Bomb Number Five—had been designed utilizing an anti-motion device rigged to fall out of the bottom of the bomb, complete a circuit, and detonate when it was lifted. Thankfully it hadn't function as intended, which is why maintenance worker Robert Lockyer had not been blown to smithereens when he picked it up.

Webb explained that the Cory Hall device at UC Berkeley was almost an exact replica of the one at the University of Utah; instead of having an anti-motion device falling out of the bottom to complete the circuit, this one had the device built into its handle, so when the victim, in this case Professor Angelakos, lifted it, it would complete the circuit and detonate the bomb. The gasoline in the can was meant to ignite upon detonation; however, what the Unabomber failed to understand is that gasoline doesn't burn beneath the surface. So when the pipe bomb blew up, it didn't ignite the gasoline, although the ensuing explosion still caused Angelakos to suffer horrific injuries.

When the Unabomber did finally resurface thirty-four months after Bomb Number Seven, the device that had gravely injured Professor Diogenes Angelakos, he chose to return to the same target—the Student Technology Services building at the University of California at Berkeley, Cory Hall. Special Agent Webb was in his seventh-floor office when the call came in that Wednesday afternoon, May 15. It was finals week at UC Berkeley, and graduate student and Air Force captain John Edmond Hauser had popped into the computer room on the second floor to do a few last-minute calculations using one of the student terminals before heading off to class.

The year was 1985, and personal computers were still in their infancy. Just three years earlier, IBM had introduced the PC, with the DOS operating system, at a cost of $2,000. Apple's revolutionary Macintosh computer followed in 1984, but laptops were still years away. So graduate students like Hauser routinely used the computer terminals available to them on campus.

Hauser noticed a black three-ring binder atop one of the plastic file boxes students used to hold computer key cards on a desk in front of one of the terminals. He needed to move the box to get to the computer. The graduate program was small, so he attempted to pick up the notebook to see if perhaps it belonged to one of his classmates. What he had no way of knowing was that the binder had been rigged as part of an improvised trigger for a pipe bomb. By lifting it up, he detonated it. The bomber had used a rubber band to attach the binder to the file box, ensuring the device would go off as intended.

Remarkably, Diogenes Angelakos, the professor who had been injured in the first Berkeley bombing, was in the building that afternoon; and upon hearing the explosion, he rushed to Hauser's aid. The man was bleeding profusely from his right arm, and it was clear that he was going to die unless someone stanched the wound. Pulling the tie from around his neck, Angelakos created a tourniquet for Hauser's arm to stop the bleeding until help arrived. Hauser suffered severe nerve damage to his right arm and lost four of his fingers on his right hand in the blast, thwarting his dream of becoming an astronaut.

By now, Webb had been trained as a special-agent bomb technician (SABT), which meant his role in the UNABOM investigation had increased. That afternoon, he and his squad arrived at the student carousel area on the second floor to find one of Hauser's fingers stuck to the wall, his Air Force Academy ring still intact. The force of the blast had been so great that the ring left an imprint of the class crest in the sheet-rock wall. Everyone on the squad knew right away it was UNABOM. Still, the administrators at UC Berkeley had to figure out a narrative. As Webb pointed out, they couldn't very well just say, "He's back . . ."

The FBI team spent days at the campus crime scene combing through the debris, collecting evidence, and interviewing students, professors, staff members, and visitors, hoping to find someone who might have seen something. They reasoned that whoever had been building the bombs felt quite comfortable on a college campus, and that he was familiar and fit in with the UC Berkeley scene. He also knew how to fashion an explosive device that would appear harmless and wouldn't draw unwanted attention; his file box–binder combination fit perfectly into the student environment.

Through their interviews, Webb and the others learned that the explosive device had first been seen in the computer terminal room on May 13—two days before it was handled and then exploded. But they weren't able to find anyone who could describe who may have dropped it off. One thing was clear: the UNABOM subject had most likely visited the campus himself, left the device behind, and then waited for the inevitable explosion to occur. The information wasn't good news; no one felt quite as safe being a student on campus as they had previously.

Construction was underway at Cory Hall, so campus police looked at the contractors working on the project. They also combed through the university's files, flagging anyone who may have been denied admission or employment or had left the college on less than desirable terms. They even cross-referenced the Berkeley files with those of the other universities that had been targeted, eager to identify anyone who may have attended or taught at one or more of these schools. Officers reviewed all parking citations issued by campus police and officers from the local Berkeley force around the time of the 1982 and 1985 attacks, hoping to identify any suspicious vehicles that may have been in the area. Investigators also checked into whether the bomber could be a disciple of an anarchistic group, perhaps the Weather Underground or the Symbionese Liberation Army, that had operated with impunity in and around the Bay Area during the 1970s and 1980s. But the theory was eventually discounted, as members of those groups typically had demands that coincided with their attacks; the Unabomber, however, had failed to reach out at all.

SSA Webb and members of the counterterrorism squad in San Francisco were still following up on leads from the most recent incident at Berkeley when they got a call from headquarters that another device had been found at the fabrication division of the Boeing Company in Auburn, Washington, and members of the local bomb squad were on the scene.

An employee in the mailroom of the aircraft company had partially opened a package that had come in by mail and discovered what appeared to be a bomb. With technicians already on the scene, there was no need for anyone from the San Francisco office to go up there, but investigators agreed to stay in close contact about any developments.

What prompted the employee to look inside was that the parcel was simply addressed to the "Boeing Company Fabrication Division." There was no indication of what it contained or who at the company it was being sent to. It was postmarked May 8, 1985, from Oakland, California, and delivered to the company on May 16.

But because it was not addressed to a specific individual or department, it sat on a shelf in a parts warehouse for almost a month before an employee grew curious and decided to open it on June 13. He had looked up the name of the company that had supposedly sent the package and learned that Boeing had no record of ever doing business with "Weinberg Tool and Supply" of Oakland, California, and that the address provided for the company did not exist. Concerned, he called the police and reported the suspicious package.

Members of the King County Sheriff's Office bomb squad responded to the scene, and after x-raying the package, they determined it contained a live bomb. When they attempted to deactivate the device, they realized the batteries had gone dead.

Like so many of the Unabomber's previous devices, this one was also constructed of a homemade wooden box measuring four by fourteen inches containing a pipe bomb holding ammonium nitrate and aluminum powder, the same potent mixture that had been found in the UC Berkeley device.

Lab examiners later concluded that the Boeing device—and not the Berkeley bomb—was, in fact, the first to use the ammonium nitrate-aluminum powder combination, as the package addressed to the Boeing Company had been postmarked May 8, seven days before the craftily disguised IED had turned up at the UC Berkeley campus.

Because this attack had again targeted an airline, the National Transportation and Safety Board was also involved. Though the Boeing Company was known worldwide, few people were aware of a "Fabrication Division" within the company. A report released by the NTSB described the division as "obscure" and "unknown" to most people—with the possible exception of some structural technicians and sheet-metal workers. It was yet another lead for investigators, but one that never got them closer to the Unabomber.

Examiners at the FBI lab in DC determined the return label had been typed on that same 1925 to 1930 Smith Corona typewriter with the Pica-style type and 2.54 spacing. There was no question of who had sent it.

———

Ironically, that summer, the summer of 1985, I was in San Francisco clerking at a law firm in the heart of the downtown area, and I could sense an uneasiness among local residents in the wake of the latest bombing to hit the Bay Area. Since graduating from high school in 1979, I'd been traveling around the US and abroad. I'd completed my studies at West Valley High School in Yakima, Washington, early, finishing in three years, and I spent my senior year in Finland on a Rotary scholarship. There, I attended a local high school and took classes at the University of Helsinki. And I still had time to learn how to cross-country ski!

After that, I returned to Washington State, where I spent my freshman year at Yakima Valley Community College before transferring to Barnard College in New York City in the fall of 1980. From Barnard, I went straight to Cambridge, Massachusetts, to begin Harvard Law School. Being accepted to Harvard seemed like a miracle to me after spending most of my childhood in a small town in eastern Washington State.

Ironically, forty dollars almost kept me from ever seeing the inside of Harvard Law School. The application fee to Harvard was forty dollars, and at that point I'd been offered a job in New York City as an assistant editor with *Ladies' Home Journal* after a summer's internship with the magazine. I knew I wanted to be a writer, so a job as an editor with a national magazine seemed like a dream job, especially coming right out of college. But having grown up surrounded by stories about cops and robbers, sheriffs and villains, I felt the pull of law school, so I took the law school entrance exams. But the forty dollars hurt. And who was I to think I had a shot at Harvard? The mystique of that elite school was beyond me. I was a kid from Yakima, Washington, after all.

It took a dare from my boyfriend at the time to push me into spending the precious fee and actually sending my application in, knowing I'd make a tidy profit on the bet. When I received a fat envelope from Cambridge, Massachusetts, in the return mail, my first thought was that the institution was sending my application back because I'd done something dumb like forgotten to sign it.

Shock is not a strong enough word to describe how I felt when I opened the envelope and began reading, "Dear Ms. Wiehl, We are delighted to inform you that . . ." Still in disbelief, I called home and told my parents, who were equally surprised. And as our surprise turned to excitement, mixed with some trepidation, I remember my father asking, "Are you ready for that world?"

"Of course," I replied, not having a clue.

Everyone knew of Harvard's reputation, but getting in seemed like nothing more than a dream. At the time, Harvard was still accepting mostly men to the program, and so as a woman I was especially pleased.

I knew I wanted to be a federal prosecutor at some point after graduation, to be like my dad and "wear the white hat." I was fortunate to land summer law jobs in both Seattle and San Francisco, because they provided me with valuable experience and helped me pay off a portion of my significant law school expense.

I loved San Francisco, but the Unabomber brought a certain level of omnipresent fear. As a young woman living alone, I felt that fear perhaps more so than some others. One thing was clear: I wasn't at all anxious to open any packages that arrived at my door.

CHAPTER 5

MOVING WEST

The two bombings at the Berkeley campus and the discovery of a third device at the Boeing warehouse in Washington State seemed to indicate that the Unabomber was changing his focus and moving west. The geographic shift in his targets prompted supervisors at FBI headquarters in DC to transfer its "office of origin" designation from Chicago, the site of the first three bombings, to San Francisco—meaning Webb and his squad would now take the lead in the investigation. Somebody from the San Francisco Division traveled to Chicago to retrieve all their files.

That year, 1985, would prove to be a particularly prolific one for the Unabomber. In addition to his bombings at UC Berkeley and the Boeing Company, he would launch two more attacks. Up to then, he'd sent out a total of seven bombs over five years. That year he struck four times in just seven months. For whatever reason, he was bumping up the cadence of his attacks.

On November 15, just thirteen days before Thanksgiving, Dr. James McConnell, a psychology professor at the University of Michigan, received a package. Oddly, the parcel had been delivered to McConnell's home—not his office at the university. Webb recalled it was about a foot long, eight inches wide, and three inches high, and it weighed about as much as a bag of sugar. Attached to the outside was a one-page type-written letter dated November 12, 1985, and signed by one "Ralph C. Kloppenburg," claiming to be a PhD candidate at the University of Utah and requesting that the professor review the enclosed dissertation on the development of the behavioral sciences:

Dear Dr. McConnell:

I am a doctoral candidate in History at the University of Utah . . . and I am writing my dissertation on the development of the behavioral sciences during the twentieth century . . .

I have now prepared an initial version of the dissertation . . . and I am asking several distinguished researchers . . . for their comments . . .

I realize that you may not have time to read it in its entirety, but I would appreciate it very much if you could at least look over Chapters 11 and 12 . . .

Very truly yours,

Ralph C. Kloppenburg

Professor McConnell had a reputation as an unconventional scientist. He was a biologist and an animal psychologist and had written a textbook, *Understanding Human Behavior*, which had earned him some notoriety. Its publication in 1974 was met with wide success, and it quickly became required reading on all college campuses for the basic psychology course, Psych 101. So receiving an unsolicited thesis from a PhD candidate at another university didn't seem all that unusual.

It was just after 3:00 p.m. when McConnell's research assistant, Nicklaus Suino, attempted to open the package, causing the device inside to immediately detonate. The sender had hidden it inside a ream of white paper, the middle of which had been hollowed out to make room for a homemade pipe bomb filled with ammonium nitrate and alumi-num powder. Fortunately, neither the researcher nor the professor was seriously injured; Suino sustained burns and shrapnel wounds to his arms and abdomen, and McConnell suffered slight hearing loss.

Postal inspectors Tony Mulijat and Dennis Piel, both members of the UNABOM task force, had been in Salt Lake City the previous week following up on leads related to the 1981 attack at the University of Utah. They immediately returned to the city to join the investigation. They learned the Unabomber had been in Salt Lake City on Tuesday, November 12, as evidenced by the postmark on the letter to Dr. McConnell. But their investigation turned up no eyewitnesses, and an examination of the evidence yielded no new clues.

About a month later, the Unabomber struck for a fourth time that year, and his final bomb of 1985 would turn out to be his deadliest. Around noontime on December 11, thirty-two-year-old Hugh Campbell Scrutton walked out the back door of his computer rental company on Howe Avenue in Sacramento, California, on his way to a computer show. As he strode to the parking lot, he noticed a dangerous-looking jumble of lumber, basically a couple of wooden boards hammered together with five sharp, protruding nails, on the ground near his car. Not wanting to run over it and puncture a tire, he attempted to move it out of the way, detonating the pipe bomb hidden inside.

Two members of the US Air Force were in the parking lot and raced over to help—only to realize that there wasn't anything they could do; Scrutton was still alive but his chest had been ripped open by the blast, and his heart was visible to the servicemen. It was impossible for them to do normal CPR, so they did what they could—comforting the dying man until the ambulance arrived.

"Excellent!" Kaczynski would later write of Scrutton's death. "Humane way to eliminate someone. He probably never felt a thing."

Like his previous devices, this one was fitted with a homemade wooden box that housed a bomb, constructed from three pipes, and filled with aluminum powder and ammonium nitrate.

Task force members were still struggling to ascertain what universities, airlines, and an airline manufacturer might have in common.

To date, several profilers at the FBI had offered assessments, among them David Icove. Icove was one of the first criminal profilers to specialize in serial bombers and arsonists. He had been attending a doctoral program in the evenings and working full-time as an arson investigator when the FBI first reached out to him. The bureau had added arsonist profiling to its behavioral science program based in Quantico, Virginia, and they wanted to recruit him for the unit. His arrival coincided with the ongoing UNABOM investigation, and during his nine years with the bureau, he traveled to a number of the UNABOM crime scenes to examine the devices and gather information to update the agency's profile. Based on the Unabomber's early targets, speculation was that the bomber was a disgruntled airline employee, or perhaps someone who had been fired from a university; he was likely a blue-collar worker and had little to no college education.

But now the perpetrator had turned in yet another direction, targeting a local computer rental company. The firm had no national presence, and there was little if anything that could tie it to the other companies that had previously been targeted. Was the Unabomber changing his MO, or was there some obscure connection between this disparate group of companies and institutions? If anything, the FBI task force's work seemed to have suddenly become even more complex than before.

CHAPTER 6

NO PERFECT CRIME

You've often heard it said that there is no perfect crime—that criminals always leave behind a clue. Thank goodness for that. But in the case of the Unabomber, for a while at least, the crimes were almost perfect. Why? Because he got away with them. Because he wasn't caught.

For more than a decade, he had been a virtual ghost, slipping in and out of college buildings, mailing his packages from public collection boxes, even delivering them to the homes and places of business of his intended targets without ever being seen. But that perfection started to crack just a bit with his first mistake, which he made while attempting to place a bomb in the parking lot of a computer store near the University of Utah on February 29, 1987.

For the first time, investigators had an eyewitness, a young woman named Tammy Fluehe who could provide details of the thinly bearded stranger she had seen in the parking lot through the blinds of a rear office window that afternoon. For a moment, the two had locked eyes. Tammy's identification proved absolutely key to the investigation and, later, to the prosecution.

At first, Tammy thought the man was being a prankster and letting air out of people's tires; then she observed him walking near her car. There had been a string of break-ins by vandals, mostly indigent and homeless people who tended to hang around the area, so she was concerned enough to alert her boss to the goings-on outside. She grew even more agitated as she observed the man lurking by the front of her vehicle.

"Can you come see what this guy is doing?" she yelled to her boss Gay Wright, who was the company's owner. The two women watched as the man knelt down, pulled something from a white canvas bag, and placed it on the ground next to Tammy's front left tire.

Seeing this made Tammy furious and she wanted to go outside to confront him, but Gay stopped her. "No, I'll send one of my sons to pick it up and throw it away," she told her, then coaxed Tammy back to work. There was a project that needed their attention.

Not long after, Gay's eldest son, Gary, who worked at the company, arrived back to the office. He had been at a sales call and pulled into the empty space next to Tammy's car. That's when he saw what he thought was a road hazard behind her left front tire and walked over to pick it up. It detonated the second he touched it, blowing two hundred pieces of shrapnel into his nose, his eyes, and his forehead, and permanently severing a nerve in his wrist.

Much like the device that had killed Hugh Scrutton, this one was also made of odd pieces of wood with protruding nails and was meant to look like nothing more than road debris. It had been deliberately placed in a trafficked area so some passerby would try to move it out of the way. Gary Wright had simply wandered by at the wrong moment—and he became a victim.

The device had two wooden "go plug" initiators rigged to detonate when they moved together. As with previous devices, examiners found the initials FC punched on the metal end cap of one of the pipes, a "signature" that lab technicians had found on all of the devices beginning with the fifth one.

When questioned, Tammy described seeing a Caucasian man between the ages of twenty-five and thirty, with curly, reddish-blond hair, a ruddy complexion with no pock marks or other deformities, and a thin mustache, who had been wearing aviator sunglasses and a light gray or white sweatshirt with cuffs gathered at the wrist; its hood was partially covering the man's head. She described the man she saw as approximately five foot ten to six feet tall and estimated his weight at about 165 pounds. Her account suggested the bomber was at least ten years younger than investigators had profiled him to be, prompting them to adjust their profile accordingly. Tammy's overall impression of the man was that he was healthy looking. She described his hands as being white and several shades lighter than his face. Both his hands and fingernails were clean. His fingers were long and thin, and she did not observe any hair or callouses on his hands.

Since the third bombing aboard the American Airlines flight, there had been agents from three federal agencies—the FBI, the US Postal Inspection Service, and ATF—actively investigating the case. Despite the massive effort, the suspect files remained disappointingly thin.

Tammy's eyewitness account marked the first time anyone had seen the elusive serial bomber since he'd begun his spree almost a decade earlier, and the description she provided resulted in the now-famous police sketch of the mustachioed man in aviators and a hoodie.

Authorities were ecstatic to finally have a drawing of the suspect and used it to generate publicity for the case. The sketch was widely distributed to the media and triggered nationwide print and television coverage, as well as lengthy articles in *Reader's Digest*, *Newsweek*, and even *Playboy*. It also rekindled interest from people at FBI headquarters who had grown increasingly frustrated with the lack of progress in the case. As promising as it seemed, the tips coming in didn't produce any fruitful information and the investigation continued to plod along.

———

In addition to UNABOM, Webb was working other bombing cases, including that of a man posing as a German count who persuaded his coke-ladled stepson to deliver a pipe bomb to his soon-to-be-ex-wife at her Bay Area office. The man had hidden the device in a basket of flowers, which his stepson agreed to deliver in costume to disguise his identity. The son's trial was just wrapping up when Webb learned he was being promoted to a supervisory role in domestic counterintelligence and would now assume administrative oversight of twenty-two federal agents and eleven support staffers. Though he had more responsibility and had been assured by senior officials that this truly was a promotion, Webb didn't feel that way. He routinely made staffers angry with his budgetary decisions and was no longer doing any investigative work. If there was a bombing, he would still get called to the scene—but he wasn't able to do any follow-up work; that was left to the men he supervised. He didn't actively work UNABOM once he assumed the new role, but he cooperated with the team and kept in touch.

Webb had been in the new supervisory position for three years when he got word that the head of the counterterrorism squad in San Francisco was leaving and he had been appointed agent in charge of the squad—his old team. He happily rejoined the group in January 1991, and once again, he was back on the UNABOM case; only this time he was responsible for overseeing the entire investigation.

The day before he assumed his new responsibilities in San Francisco, Webb was called to a top secret meeting in Washington, DC. There, he and other key FBI officials learned that the US would be launching Operation Desert Storm on January 16. The effort marked the start of the combat phase of the Gulf War and began with a massive US-led air offensive that lit up the skies over Baghdad. The FBI feared that the attack would trigger huge protests in San Francisco, and they wanted the office to be prepared. For a time, operations were moved to an undisclosed location to ensure the safety of agents and other FBI personnel.

With Webb at the helm, all Bay Area terrorism cases became his responsibility, and that included a handful of "old dog" cases the squad couldn't solve, among them UNABOM.

PART II

CHAPTER 7

ONLY A MATTER OF TIME

Every investigator interviewed for this book expressed having the very same fear during the UNABOM case: they knew it was only a matter of time until the Unabomber would strike again, and some innocent man, woman, or child would be harmed or killed. They also knew that senior officials and indeed the US populace would be looking to them for answers. They expressed guilt that despite their best efforts, they'd been unable to come up with solid leads or crack the case. Each one of them worried that somehow it would be their fault that they'd missed something. No one spoke of their secret fear to others in the unit.

By 1992, no one had heard from the Unabomber in five years, and there hadn't been any new leads in a while. Still, Webb and his squad were convinced that their suspect was out there somewhere and potentially using his time to perfect his bombing techniques. Though there was no way for them to know at the time, the agents had, in fact, been right in their hunch. After police had circulated their sketch of the UNABOM suspect, Theodore J. Kaczynski went deep underground, withdrawing from society and living like a hermit in the mountains of Montana.

In 1969, at the age of twenty-seven, Kaczynski had suddenly resigned from his job at the University of California at Berkeley—just two years after he'd signed on as an associate math professor, the youngest one ever hired by the institution. At Berkeley, Kaczynski was literally surrounded by technology and the math that underpinned many of man's latest advances. He'd grown to believe that technology was slowly destroying mankind, and he yearned to get away from it all, to retreat to some location where he could live a simpler life, closer to the land.

After resigning, Ted enlisted his younger brother, David, in building a primitive ten-foot-by-twelve-foot cabin with a simple pitched roof and no running water or electricity. For reasons that may never be known, Ted made a decision to leave his career behind, withdraw from society, and turn to a simple life as a mountain man in the woods—far from friends and family, a recluse.

In hopes of speaking with David Kaczynski for this book, I contacted him in the spring of 2018. He was prompt in his response, noting that over the years countless people had attempted to tell his brother's story, with many reaching out to him to ask questions. Hence, he'd decided to write his own book, *Every Last Tie*, published in 2016 by Duke University Press, as a way of sharing what he perceived to be parts of the story that hadn't been told and were most meaningful to him, mainly reflecting on his brother's childhood and their family. "Obviously, it's unlikely that I'll get to have the last word on any of this. But nevertheless, I've decided to say my piece, walk away, and move on with the rest of my life," he wrote in a brief but cordial e-mail, respectfully declining my request.

David's book, however, helped answer questions about the years he and Ted had shared together as boys, his elder brother's awkward teen years, including his acceptance to Harvard at the age of sixteen, and his increasing fear of technology and its impacts on mankind—a fear that ultimately prompted him to withdraw from society and retreat to the Montana forest.

David described a happy childhood filled with close friends and little league baseball, although growing up in the shadow of his older brother,

Ted—a certified genius with a 168 IQ, five points higher than Albert Einstein's—presented its challenges.

His mother, Teresa "Wanda" (née Dombek), was a stay-at-home mother. His father, Theodore Richard Kaczynski, fondly known as "Turk," was a blue-collar worker. The couple met at a Back of the Yards settlement house in Chicago, where local immigrants gathered to socialize and better educate themselves. Wanda and Turk were both first-generation Polish Americans, and they started what turned into a three-year courtship. Turk Kaczynski had never completed high school, but he was well-read. Wanda had attended two years of college. Both Turk and Wanda followed local politics and were civically involved. Their dates included countless walks around Chicago and some fiery political discussions too. Turk worked alongside his brothers, Stanley and Alex, in his uncle's factory, Kaczynski's Sausages, on the city's South Side.

After they wed, Wanda stayed at home and later tended to the couple's two children—first Ted, or "Teddy John," as his family called him, born on May 22, 1942, and then David.

Ted was six years old when his father's best friend, a child psychiatrist named Ralph Meister, decided to give him a Stanford-Binet IQ Test, an intelligence test comprised of four sections: short-term memory, quantitative reasoning, verbal reasoning, and abstract/visual reasoning. Little "Teddy John" scored somewhere between 160 and 170 (generally, an IQ of 100 is considered average), putting him in the .003 percent of the population (one in thirty thousand range) range and in the company of notables Albert Einstein and Stephen Hawking. Some years later, Meister would tell a reporter that Ted was the only child he knew to have read *Robert's Rules of Order*, a manual of parliamentary procedure in the United States.

In his book, David wrote of his brother's intellectual abilities. "I don't remember a time when I wasn't aware that my brother was 'special'—a tricky word that can mean either above average or completely off the scale," he wrote. "Ted, seven and a half years older, was special because he was so intelligent. In the Kaczynski family, intelligence carried high value."

As a result, "I wanted to be like Ted," David wrote. "As a young child beginning to gauge social perceptions, I thought of my brother as smart, independent and principled. I heard myself described by our neighbors, aunts and uncles as happy, charming, and affectionate—as if those were traits to be remarked on in a child. Even at a tender age, I sensed that adults contrasted me with my brother. Heck, anyone could be the way I was; it required no effort on my part. But not everyone could be smart, independent and principled like my big brother. Given a choice, I would gladly have embraced Ted's persona and relinquished my own."

David pursued sports as a way to distinguish himself from his brother, baseball in particular. An older boy in the neighborhood taught him how to catch and introduced him to baseball cards. "Who's your best player?" the child asked.

New to the hobby, David quickly glanced at the cards, choosing a name from the few that were visible to him. "Jim Rivera," he announced.

"Jungle Jim!" his new pal smiled. "I like him too."

That night David excitedly told his brother that Jungle Jim Rivera was his "best" player. Ted immediately corrected him: "Davy, you should say 'favorite' not 'best.'" He then asked his little brother his reason for choosing Jungle Jim, meeting David's response of "I don't know" with a disapproving nod of the head.

Years later, when Ted was living in Montana, he was approached by one of the townspeople who wanted to start a local newspaper and wanted Ted's opinion of the first edition. "I found 182 mistakes," Ted told him. The conversation went downhill from there.

Ted was ten and David three when the Kaczynski family moved from their duplex apartment on the city's South Side to a house in the working-class suburb of Evergreen Park. One of David's first memories was spending the summer playing in the big backyard. He recalled how even then, at age ten, his older brother, Ted, was both creative and skilled with mechanical things. At the time, David was too short to reach the knob on the screen door and often ended up stuck in the backyard waiting for a parent or his older brother to let him in.

One day he noticed his brother fiddling with a small wooden spool of thread, some nails, and a hammer. Ted took the thread off the spool, leaving only the wood portion behind. He threaded a nail through the spool and carefully banged it into the lower portion of the screen door— creating a small handle that David could use for himself. David never forgot his brother's kind and thoughtful gesture.

Growing up, Ted preferred to spend his time alone and would often retreat to the security of his bedroom. David wondered why his brother didn't have any friends, and concerned, he once asked his mother about it. No doubt it was a difficult question for a parent to face, and even more difficult to answer. But Wanda Kaczynski apparently responded with frank and honest conversation. She described a trauma that Ted had endured when he was just nine months old. An unexplained rash had appeared on his body, and he was hospitalized, with doctors believing he had some kind of allergic reaction. Back then, parents were not permitted to stay at the hospital with their children, so they had no choice but to leave and go home. Ted was only permitted to visit with his parents for a few hours every other day. His treatment also required countless blood tests and needle pricks, and his parents knew that he was "deathly afraid" of the procedures. The baby boy screamed in terror each time a nurse would take him from his parents at the end of a visit.

Wanda was convinced that her baby boy was forever changed by the experience. When Ted finally returned home from the hospital, his temperament had changed; emotionally at least, Ted was a different boy. For months afterward, she and her husband worked to soothe their son, embracing him often and speaking in reassuring tones. Over time Ted's memories of his time in the hospital faded into the past. Still, Wanda was convinced that Ted had developed a deep-set fear of abandonment that would stay with him for many years. Eventually, Ted seemed to recover emotionally. But Wanda insisted he never fully returned to the happy, smiling baby he had once been.

For David, the story was devastating. He fretted about what his brother had endured and promised his mother to never abandon him. Still, he wondered if that hospitalization fully explained Ted's lack of friendships and his tendency to be insensitive toward others. He suspected that there may have been something else that drove his brother's behavior. He recounted a family meal gone awry when his brother's prank nearly caused his mother bodily harm. David described how he, Ted, and their father were already seated at the kitchen table when his mother arrived with a pot of piping hot spaghetti sauce for their supper. She smiled when Ted jumped up to pull out her chair, never expecting him to jerk it away at the last second, causing her to fall to the floor with the pot of sauce in her hands. While she managed to avoid spilling it, saving herself from a potentially painful burn, the episode frightened her, and she lashed out.

"You could have hurt me!" she scolded.

Ted's failure to apologize infuriated his father, who ordered him to his room. The elder Kaczynski grew even more irate when his son began to laugh as he made his way from the table. His son's inability to feel what others were feeling was troubling, and he and his wife remained at a loss as to how to remedy it.

Wanda clung to the belief that it all stemmed from his early trauma at the hospital. But there appeared to be other factors at play. Their older son was off-the-charts intelligent; everyone in town knew of and spoke about Ted's brilliance. But people were unsure how to interact with him.

———

Music played an important role in the Kaczynski household. The radio was always on and tuned to a classical music station. Ted's father had taught himself how to play the piano, and Ted followed suit. As an adolescent, he would plop himself down at the bench where he remained for hours, often composing counterpoint in the style of the baroque masters. Like many brilliant mathematicians, Ted was gifted in music too.

On some nights, the whole family would play music together. Ted took lessons from a well-known trombone player. Sometimes he'd play accompaniment to his father on the piano, and David, when he was old enough, joined in on the trumpet. Wanda had a beautiful voice and sang along. Ted also liked to engage his brother in duets, with him on the trombone and David the trumpet; many of the pieces they performed were numbers Ted had written himself.

Camping was another activity the family enjoyed together. Ted's father was an outdoorsman and the more social of the two parents. He was friendly and gregarious and enjoyed strolling the campgrounds in the evenings chatting with the other families, while Wanda and her two sons preferred to remain close to the campsite. Wanda was more introverted, and Ted was a bit like her in that way. While the senior Kaczynski was an avid fisherman and had once enjoyed hunting, he had discontinued this activity after a rabbit hunt went awry on a farm in Indiana with his firstborn son.

At first, Ted had seemed eager to participate and excitedly trailed his shotgun-wielding father as they searched the tall grass for rabbits. When they finally spotted one, Turk trained his firearm at the small animal and shot it dead. Ted's expression changed as he stood over the lifeless creature before bursting into tears. "The poor bunny," he exclaimed. His visceral reaction struck a nerve in his father; years later, the elder Kaczynski would tell David that Ted's reaction forced him to "reflect on the pointless killing," and at that moment, he resolved to never hunt again.

Ted had a similar response when he returned home one day to find a baby rabbit his father had found in the family's backyard cowering in a wood cage with a screen top. The elder Kaczynski had put the bunny in a cage and was proudly showing it to some of the neighborhood kids when Ted arrived home that afternoon. Curious, Ted walked over and immediately grew agitated at the sight of the little brown creature tucked into one corner, looking scared.

"Let it go!" he pleaded.

Turk immediately responded to his son's distress, scooping up the cage and walking it to a wooded area where he set the animal free.

It's almost impossible to reconcile the young Ted Kaczynski who cared so deeply about a rabbit's welfare with that of the man who had retreated to the Montana wilderness to create dangerous improvised explosive devices designed to maim or kill. What had happened to Ted over the years to create the inner rage that sustained him year after year in the remote cabin?

It was an issue that Webb and other investigators also grappled with in the aftermath of Kaczynski's arrest. Webb described how Kaczynski would hunt for rabbits and other little game animals from the cabin, skinning them and even using rabbit pelts as a substitute for toilet paper. The agent also described how Kaczynski had strung wire between trees in the hopes of hurting or potentially decapitating snowmobilers who raced through the woods near his cabin during the winter. There simply is no way to explain Kaczynski's changed behavior over the years, and, indeed, that mystery may never be unraveled.

CHAPTER 8

TED

Ted was ten and in the fifth grade when he sat for a school-administered IQ test. His score prompted administrators at the Evergreen Park Central School to recommend he skip to the seventh grade, which greatly pleased his father. Turk had moved the family to Evergreen Park the previous year so his children could receive a better public school education. Ted's elevation to the seventh grade made him the youngest child in the grade, which presented certain social challenges but didn't appear to impede his progress. Ted's parents seemed to delight as their son continued to demonstrate his remarkable intellect. In a way, having such a talented son made them stand out in the community and afforded them a certain level of social status they both relished. They encouraged him to study even harder, and he was expected to achieve straight As in school. But Ted would later tell a court-appointed psychologist named Sally Johnson, who spent nearly twenty-two hours with Kaczynski following his arrest some thirty years later, that his parents' decision to skip him stunted development of his social skills.

When Ted was in the tenth grade, the administration at Evergreen Park Community High School, a two-hundred-student public high school, suggested he skip another grade—meaning that he would graduate from high school at the age of sixteen, a full two years ahead of his same-age peers. Some worried that it was too much of a leap and that the boy should be allowed to remain with his class. His high school band teacher unsuccessfully appealed to Ted's father not to allow him to skip a second year. But his son's educational achievements were too important to Turk, and he granted the school permission to advance the boy another year. The move took an emotional toll on Ted, who had an even harder time trying to fit in—and was regarded as a "freak" by many in the student body when he graduated.

"It isn't natural for an adolescent human being to spend the bulk of his time sitting at a desk absorbed in study," Kaczynski wrote of his parents' decision to skip him two grades. "A normal adolescent wants to spend his time in active contact with the real world."

Schoolmates at Evergreen Park Community High School remembered him as one of the "eggheads," the brightest kids in the grade, and Ted was considered the smartest among them, one of the "briefcase boys" who carried their textbooks in briefcases, not knapsacks like the rest of their classmates. Oddly, Ted's briefcase was made from alligator skin; he also had a pocket protector. The "eggheads" sat together in the cafeteria at lunchtime, stayed after school for math club, and occasionally experimented with explosives during chemistry lab.

Ted was twelve when he and some of his classmates began building their own explosive devices using batteries, copper wires, potassium nitrate, and other components they found and assembled. They'd sometimes go to a nearby field to set them off, covering themselves with a garbage can to avoid injury from the shrapnel created by their own devices. Mostly the devices would blow up a few weeds in the field at best; the excitement was in the noise from the explosions.

"We called them bombs, but they were really cardboard pipes with the ends closed up," one former classmate told the *Chicago Tribune* after Ted's arrest. "We were budding scientists. It was part of extended chemistry class."

Though Ted didn't have many friends and he preferred solitary pursuits, he still participated in a number of school activities. He was a member of the math club, biology club, chess club, and German club. He played trombone in the school's marching band as well. He was a bit short, at five feet, nine inches in height, and slender. More often than not, he'd leave his hair uncombed. But when he was groomed, his hair would be in a fifties-style pompadour.

Classmates remembered some odd moments with Ted during his high school years, including once when he handed a female schoolmate a "hand bomb," a piece of paper twisted in the middle and sealed at the ends. One end contained several drops of ammonia; the other had iodine. "Twist it open," he told his classmate, knowing that when the two chemicals ran together, it would explode in her hand. They both laughed when they heard the popping sound; it was a harmless prank, meant to surprise the young woman, not to hurt her.

"You're going to get suspended," she told him.

"No, I'm not," he grinned. "I'm too smart."

That same schoolmate remains convinced that it was Ted who put the skin of a cat the science class had just dissected in her locker as a prank, but she never learned for sure.

Lots of the boys at Evergreen Park Community High School took pleasure in playing jokes on others, and Ted was no different. His pranks were often viewed as childish or juvenile in nature, though perhaps that made sense given he was two years younger than everyone in his grade. "The thing that runs through my mind is how young he was," one classmate later told a reporter at the *Spokesman*. "At a social level, he was not traveling at the same rate as the rest of us."

Generally, none of Ted's horseplay was anything more than routine high school fare, and it seemed that he never meant to harm anyone. Some of the boys carried around firecrackers, and it was not unusual for someone to find a frog in his or her desk. A lot of the boys traded "bomb" recipes. But Ted may have taken things too far on at least one occasion. When a classmate in chemistry lab asked him how to build a more powerful bomb, Ted went ahead and showed him—constructing an improvised explosive device and then hitting it with a hammer to detonate it. The explosion blew out two of the classrooms' windows and caused permanent damage to a female student's hearing. Ted was punished as a result, but some of his classmates questioned whether administrators were just singling him out.

"It never entered Ted's mind that this was a dangerous thing," a schoolmate later recalled.

Ted also endured his share of teasing; being one of the "briefcase boys" made him a mark, but he seemed to be targeted more than others. In one instance, a group of boys stuffed him in a locker "just for grins"; years later, one of his tormentors remembered Ted being frightened by the incident.

In June 1958, he graduated at the top of his class and was named one of five National Merit Scholarship finalists. His acceptance to Harvard at the age of sixteen thrilled his hardworking parents, both of whom were first-generation Polish immigrants. Ohio's highly regarded Oberlin College also extended an invitation, but his parents chose Harvard for their intellectually gifted son. One family friend recalled pleading with Ted's father not to send his son away at such a young age. He argued the boy was not mature enough to attend Harvard, fearing the rigorous program and impersonal setting were not appropriate for a boy his age. After his arrest, members of the UNABOM task force obtained a copy of Ted's file from his time at Harvard. Included among the reports, transcripts, and records was a letter from Ted's mother, dated July 16, 1958, lamenting her son's impending departure for the school.

"Much of his time is spent at home reading and contriving numerous gadgets made up of wood, string, wire, tape, lenses, gears, wheels, etc.; that test out various principals in physics. His table and desk are always a mess of test tubes, chemicals, batteries, ground coal, etc. He will miss greatly, I think, this browsing and puttering in his messy makeshift lab."

Perhaps Wanda Kaczynski sensed that her son was not ready to make such a leap. Ted's acceptance to the Ivy League school provided his family, and in particular his father, an elevated status in the community, which was important to the Turk; in the end, he chose to ignore the warnings and send his boy off to Cambridge, Massachusetts.

As someone who attended Harvard Law School, I can attest to its allure. I was twenty-one when I began graduate school there, fully five years older than Ted when he entered as a freshman. I vividly remember how overwhelming and daunting the whole campus and experience was; halls were filled with portraits of old white men who had nothing in common with me, a young woman definitely not from an Ivy League pedigree. I can imagine being in Ted's shoes. Brilliant as he was, he was still so young that it must have been quite overwhelming for him. It's also pretty likely that he had some fear of failure. That certainly was the case for those like me who were outsiders in that Ivy League environment.

Debate continues to rage to this day over what impact, if any, Ted's time at Harvard may have had on him. His brother, David, was in the fourth grade when Ted left home for Cambridge, Massachusetts, to begin his freshman year in fall 1958. In his memoir, David included a photograph taken the day Ted left home. It captured the two boys posing outside the family's home in Evergreen Park, Illinois, both gripping the handle on Ted's single suitcase. "The picture illustrates how innocent and hopeful I was and how much I adored my older brother," David wrote. "Perhaps the moment was the beginning of the end for Ted. He might have been ready for the academic challenges of a place like Harvard, but he was not ready developmentally or psychologically.

"In retrospect, our parents' one serious mistake . . . was to send him away from home at such an early age. Mastery of learning—which Ted surely had—had little to do with mastery of life or self . . . But perhaps a genetic flaw, or predisposition to mental illness, would have taken Ted down eventually in any case."

———

Agent Webb told me that after Ted's arrest, agents interviewed his former roommates and others who may have known him while he was at the

Ivy League campus. "People who knew him there disliked him," Webb recalled. "He was standoffish and didn't make friends. Sixteen years old going to Harvard, where it's so intense, you can just see where he didn't fit in."

Ted was one of ten sixteen-year-old freshmen assigned to a university-owned house at 8 Prescott Street. The action was taken at the behest of Harvard's dean of freshmen who decided that this group of very bright and young incoming students should all be housed together in one building. His goal was to segregate them from other new students in what he hoped would be a more nurturing and comfortable environment than the much larger dormitories. But his effort backfired and created an even larger divide between the youngsters and others on the campus. The reality was that this group of sixteen-year-olds was already bookish and socially awkward, and many struggled to make friends. Putting them all together—and physically separating them from the other freshmen— just compounded the problem. Ted was one of six students given a private room, further isolating him from the group members, seven of whom were mathematical science majors and all but three of whom were from high schools outside of New England.

Ted was given a room on the top floor, and few of his housemates recall ever seeing him that first year. Those who do remember him recall a "shabby-looking" teen who alternated between two pairs of slacks and a few shirts. At Harvard, he went by the name "Theodore." While his tendency to isolate continued at Harvard, he was by no means a loner. His freshman year had him participating in sports, a requirement for all newcomers; he chose swimming and wrestling. He also continued with the trombone, playing for a short time with the Harvard band.

Ted also learned something about himself during that first year at Harvard that perhaps he hadn't anticipated: He was no longer the smartest and most capable kid in his class. There were others in Harvard's freshman class who were just as smart as he was.

Like all freshmen, Ted underwent a medical examination that also included a broad description of his personality and attitude. The doctor found the young man to be fairly normal, saying that he was "attractive, mature for [his] age, and relaxed." Kaczynski "likes people and gets on well with them. [He] may have many acquaintances but makes his friends carefully."

Additionally, he found Ted to be a "pleasant young man." "Apparently a good mathematician but seems to be gifted in this direction only," he wrote. "Plans not crystallized yet, but this is to be expected at his age."

Ted moved to the Eliot House, an upper-class residence with a dining hall, for his sophomore year. His room was one of the smallest and least expensive ones in the dormitory. Still, it was there that Ted spent his downtime with his door shut. He'd often opt to bring food in from the dining hall rather than eat with the others. One former dormmate recalled Ted's room smelling of spoiled milk and piled high with clothing, books, and trash.

That year Ted was one of twenty-two students chosen to participate in a controversial and disturbing experiment led by psychologist Henry A. Murray, head of the Henry A. Murray Research Center at Radcliffe Institute for Advanced Study. Murray is best known for his pioneering research in the area of personality tests and psychological assessments. In the lead-up to World War II, the US government asked him to prepare a psychological study on Adolph Hitler, and his work with the government continued throughout war, with Murray assisting the Office of Strategic Services, now the CIA, in assessing its agents. Murray's personality tests were later used by Harvard to screen applicants. At just seventeen years old when the experiment commenced, Ted was the youngest participant in the group.

The goal of Murray's research was to study the effects of severe stress on the human psyche by putting his subjects—Kaczynski and twenty-one of his classmates—under intensive interrogation, with attacks that were "vehement, sweeping, and personally abusive."

Students were asked to write an essay detailing their worldview and personal beliefs and philosophies. They were then sat in a chair before bright lights, wired to electrodes, and subjected to intensive interrogation, which included attacks by members of the research team aimed at the very ideals and principles the subjects had put forth in their essays. The purpose of the interrogations was to gauge and evaluate the effectiveness of interrogation techniques used by national security agents and members of law enforcement.

Critics of Murray's study have called the experiment inhuman, pointing out that subjects were not fully informed about what they would be expected to endure. Many were coerced or even tricked into participating and then deceived into continuing well past the agreed-upon time frame. In Kaczynski's case, what was supposed to be a one-year commitment stretched to encompass three years—basically the remainder of his time at Harvard. Equally troubling was that the aim of the experiment was to "break" enemy agents. Yet Murray and his researchers were using these procedures on young and vulnerable university students who lacked the wherewithal and the training to resist such grueling interrogations. Indeed, they were not enemy agents but Harvard students who were at the university to be educated, not psychologically broken. In order to preserve the anonymity of these unsuspecting human subjects, they had been given code names (ironically, Ted's was "Lawful").

In the years after his arrest, many have looked to Harvard, and more specifically, Ted's participation in the Murray study, as a possible trigger for his impending bombing spree. In 2003, Alston Chase, a Harvard alum who graduated from the Ivy League university the year before Kaczynski, published *Harvard and the Unabomber: The Education of an American Terrorist*, with W. W. Norton & Company. As part of his research, Chase secured permission from officials at Harvard to review some of the data Murray had collected from these experiments. By then, Ted's code name had been made public. In order to protect Ted's privacy, Chase was not permitted to review any data that pertained to "Lawful." Based on a review of the general materials, Chase suggested that Ted's social unease coupled with his unwitting participation in Dr. Murray's disturbing experiment may explain and perhaps even "justify" his crimes.

But Kaczynski himself would later dismiss that notion, claiming the experiment was not as harsh as some have characterized. After his arrest, Ted's court-appointed defense attorneys would ask him about the Murray experiment. They wanted to know why he kept going back given the brutal and unforgiving nature of the program. "I wanted to prove that I could take it, that I couldn't be broken," he told them.

He also boasted that his time at Harvard had served him well. Harvard was a "tremendous thing for me," he wrote in the second of two autobiographies he penned. The first took just three days to complete and was written at the request of Dr. Henry A. Murray as part of the psychological study at Harvard. The second, written twenty years later, was a 216-page autobiography of his life, portions of which he shared with Chase. In recounting his time at Harvard, Kaczynski told Chase he'd gotten "something that I had been needing all along without knowing it, namely, hard work requiring self-discipline and strenuous exercise of my abilities. I thrived on it. . . . Feeling the strength of my own will, I became enthusiastic about will power."

CHAPTER 9

FAILURE TO CONNECT

Ted Kaczynski left Harvard in 1962 having completed a bachelor of science in mathematics. His next stop was another respected institution, the University of Michigan in Ann Arbor, where he earned both a master's and doctorate in mathematics.

Today, the University of Michigan is home to the Ted Kaczynski Papers, part of the Special Collections Library's Joseph A. Labadie Collection, which "documents the history of social protest movements and marginalized political communities from the 19th century to present." The Ted Kaczynski Papers, which fill more than one hundred boxes, were given to the university by Kaczynski himself in 1998. The bulk of the collection includes letters written to and by Kaczynski since his arrest in 1996. There are also legal documents used during his trial, newspaper clippings, magazine articles, and audio-visual materials, as well as some of his other writings.

In 2012, the FBI files, which include photocopies of documents confiscated by agents during a raid on Kaczynski's Montana cabin in 1996, were sent to the university by Ted's defense attorneys to be made part of the archive.

Most of the photocopies are from Ted's journals, which are written in English, Spanish, and in a "code" that agents were able to decipher using a "key" they found during their search of his cabin. There are also maps, identification papers, mathematical problems, correspondence with family members, and dozens of letters from media outlets such as *20/20*, the *New Yorker*, *The Roseanne Show*, and *The Today Show*, all of which Ted declined to appear on. A list of books from his personal collection can also be found in the archives; it includes such titles as Leo Tolstoy's *The Cossacks and the Raid* and *The Elements of Style* by Strunk and White.

Ted had been just twenty years old when he arrived at the University of Michigan campus in Ann Arbor, where he is listed as a "notable" alum. His conservative attire—white shirt, coat, and tie—made him stand out amid the sea of denim-wearing students. University of Michigan had not been his first choice. He had also applied—and been accepted to— the University of California at Berkeley and the University of Chicago. Kaczynski had expected that at least one of the three schools would offer him financial aid and/or a paid teaching position. But no offers were forthcoming. Perhaps it was because of his less than stellar performance at Harvard, where he graduated with a 3.12 GPA—a commendable finish, but not what many had expected from a child prodigy with a 168 IQ. In the end, the University of Michigan offered Ted a fellowship that came with a small grant to work as a student teacher for three of his five years at the college, and he accepted the offer.

Ted described his time in Ann Arbor as "unpleasant." "These were the most miserable years of my life (except for the first year and the last year)," he wrote in his unpublished autobiography.

His teaching duties put heavy demands on his time, so he chose to restrict his coursework to just two classes per semester. While his academic performance at UM far exceeded his showing at Harvard, his teaching skills were lackluster. An evaluator who observed one of Ted's classes in fall 1962 found his subject knowledge "good," but scored his ability to engage his students as "average." Still, he continued to dazzle members of the math department with his uncanny ability to solve challenging problems, and he had his works published in esteemed academic journals. Evaluations by faculty were nearly unanimous in their praise of Ted's mathematical prowess, although one professor noted he seemed "a little too sure of himself."

In 1964, Ted completed his master of science in mathematics. President John F. Kennedy had been scheduled to give the commencement address that spring, but after his assassination in 1963, the university's president Harlan Hatcher invited the new president, Lyndon B. Johnson, to fill the role. It would be the university's first commencement delivered by a sitting president, which he delivered at Michigan Stadium to an estimated seventy thousand attendees. That same year, Ted learned that his father had sold the Kaczynskis' home in Evergreen Park and was moving the family to a small town in Iowa, where he had been relocated for work. After leaving his uncle's sausage business, Ted's father had obtained employment with a food-products company and later with a foam-cutting company in the Chicago area; it was with this company that he was being transferred to Iowa.

The plan was for David and his father to set off first in one car. Ted and his mother would finalize arrangements with the movers and then travel together in a second car later in the day. In his book, David recalled that his brother was oddly quiet when Ted and their mother arrived in Iowa that night. The following morning, Wanda cornered him and worriedly explained that Ted had not been himself when they were dealing with the moving men back at the house. The entire time she was trying to speak with them, he stood nearby, shouting, "Make them go away! Make them go away!" She didn't know what to make of it and tried to get her son to open up and tell her what was going on during the four-hour trip to their new home. But Ted had no response and the ride continued without a word between the two.

David was unable to explain what was bothering Ted. He hadn't seemed opposed to the move. "In the back of my mind, I wondered if Ted was upset to see his house of memories dismantled, perhaps signifying the loss of the only safe emotional refuge he'd ever known," David wrote in his memoir. "Didn't he know that all things change and that the loss of our material house (as poignant as that might feel) in no way endangered the sense of home Mom and Dad had always maintained for us?"

In Iowa, Ted's mother returned to college to complete her degree in teaching and found work in a local school. Meanwhile, Ted remained at the University of Michigan, graduating in a commencement service in August 1967 where he was awarded his doctorate in mathematics. His eighty-page doctoral dissertation, *Boundary Functions*, published in 1968, earned him the university's coveted Sumner Myers prize for best mathematical thesis, one hundred dollars in cash, and an honorary plaque that is still boldly displayed near the entrance to the school's East Quadrangle residence hall, Prescott House, where Kaczynski lived during his first two years at the college. "This thesis is the best I have ever directed," one member of Ted's dissertation committee wrote in an evaluation of the paper.

"It is by far the most important application in physics and engineering," said another. "It is a complex analysis that involved complex equations using imaginary numbers."

Outside of Ted's professors in the mathematics department, few remember him from his time in Ann Arbor. Ted was an introvert, someone with a kind of laser focus on his studies, a shy, albeit polite young man with his head in the books. But a detailed psychological profile, performed in 1998 by court-appointed psychiatrist Sally Johnson at the behest of the federal judge presiding over Kaczynski's trial, divulged that beginning in the summer of 1966, Ted experienced what he described as a gender-identity crisis that prompted him to consider a sex-change operation. He claimed that beginning that summer, he was plagued by "intense and persistent sexual excitement involving fantasies of being a female" and became convinced he should undergo a sex-change operation.

Kaczynski told Johnson he was aware that gaining authorization would require a psychiatric referral. That fall he went to see a psychiatrist at the University Health Service to begin the process. But while in the waiting room, he lost his nerve. The idea of revealing his desire to the doctor filled him with anxiety and humiliation. He managed to meet with the psychiatrist, but he failed to disclose the true purpose of the meeting, claiming instead that he feared he could be drafted into the military should his "deferment status" be dropped. The Vietnam War was raging, and young, college-age men were being drafted to serve. Kaczynski, however, had been able to defer his service because of his student, then teacher status. The psychiatrist reportedly told Kaczynski his anxiety and depression over the issue were not uncommon. Ted admitted that his failure to impart his true intentions left him feeling anxious, humiliated, angry, and ashamed, and he flagged this day as a turning point in his life.

"As I walked away from the building afterwards, I felt disgusted about what my uncontrolled sexual cravings had almost led me to do and I felt—humiliated, and I violently hated the psychiatrist," he wrote in one of his journals. "Just then came a major turning point in my life. Like a Phoenix, I burst from the ashes of my despair to a glorious new hope. I thought I wanted to kill that psychiatrist because the future looked utterly empty to me. I felt I wouldn't care if I died. And so, I said to myself, why not really kill the psychiatrist and anyone else whom I hate? What is important is not the words that ran through my mind but the way I felt about them. What was entirely new was the fact that I really felt I could kill someone. My very hopelessness had liberated me because I no longer cared about death. I no longer cared about consequences and I said to myself that I really could break out of my rut in life and do things that were daring, irresponsible, criminal."

———

In fall 1967, Ted became the youngest assistant professor of mathematics in the history of the University of California, Berkeley. There, he taught undergraduate courses in calculus and geometry in the Department of

Mathematics located in Campbell Hall. He rented a tiny cottage—not much more than a shack—behind a house in the community of Albany, just north of Berkeley. He didn't own a car and instead biked to campus. While there, Ted spent time in the woods of Northern California, taking up deer hunting and purchasing a rifle.

After Kaczynski's arrest in 1996, Webb and members of the UNABOM task force went to the campus and interviewed his landlord and every student he'd worked with. "The landlord just took him as another odd bird," Webb recalled. "This was Berkeley, after all, and he was a Berkeley professor."

Webb reported that Kaczynski was uniformly disliked—even hated—by his undergraduates. They expressed dismay that he refused to respond to questions in the classroom and were frustrated that he would never, ever show up for his promised weekly office hours. When students were asked to rate Kaczynski as a teacher, he scored very poorly.

"To a person, all of his students gave him a D," Webb recalled.

After two years at Berkeley, on June 20, 1969, Ted abruptly resigned from his post at the university, providing no explanation. Based on the interviews members of the task force had conducted, Webb believed that Kaczynski had hoped to be tenured but that he resigned rather than face termination because of bad reviews from students and other faculty members. But not everyone agrees on that point. In interviews after Ted's arrest, some administrators claimed that Ted had abruptly handed in his resignation for unknown reasons. This seems to support Ted's explanation of his departure. He told people that it had always been his intention to work just long enough to put together a little nest egg and buy himself a piece of property, where he could live isolated from society. The year of Ted's arrest, Calvin C. Moore, vice chairman at UC Berkeley, told the *Buffalo News* Kaczynski "could have advanced up the ranks and been a senior member of faculty today."

David recalled that around this time, Ted had become enamored with a book written by Jacques Ellul, *The Technological Society*, which was first published in French in 1954 and later translated into English and several other languages. The subject matter so moved him that he began a correspondence with Ellul, telling the author he had read his work multiple times. Later, Ted drafted an essay in which he argued that the never-ending push for scientific and technological progress was wrong and would bring about the end of individual liberties. In Ted's view, society's power to control individuals was quickly expanding and would ultimately make it impossible for men and women to follow their own paths. He wrote about propaganda, educational guiding of children's emotional development, operant conditioning, and "direct physical control of emotions via electrodes and "cheminrodes" (sic). Ted proposed founding an organization dedicated to stopping federal aid to scientific research, thereby preventing the "ceaseless extension of society's powers."

In a separate journal entry in the early 1970s, he wrote:

> True, I would not fit into the present society . . . but that is not an intolerable situation. What makes a situation intolerable is . . . that in all probability, the values that I detest will soon be achieved through science . . . with a total extrication of everything I value. Through super human computers and mind control there simply will be no place for a rebellious person to hide and my kind of people will vanish forever from the earth . . .

Ted spent the summer of 1969 traveling through western Canada with his brother, David, in search of a plot of land to homestead. At the time, David was enrolled in Columbia University and was home on summer break. Ted identified some land in British Columbia near Prince George. But his efforts to acquire the property were thwarted when Canadian officials denied his application for a homesteading permit, and he ended up moving back in with his parents, who were now living in the suburbs of Chicago. Members of the Kaczynski family noticed a change in Ted's mood. He became increasingly withdrawn, holing up in his room reading for hours at a time.

Upon graduating from Columbia, David moved to Great Falls, Montana, where he secured a blue-collar job working in a zinc smelting factory. Ted, meanwhile, refocused his land search to the Alaskan wilderness.

In his memoir, David recalled a frantic phone call from his parents, asking if he had been in contact with his brother. Ted had been employed for a short time at Abbott Consultants in nearby Elmhurst, Illinois. David's parents explained that Ted had suddenly packed up and left their home, leaving a worrisome letter behind that sounded a bit like a "final" goodbye. "No one could want better parents," he wrote, adding that he was sorry if he disappointed them.

Theodore Sr. asked David if Ted had been in touch or if he had any idea where his brother might be headed. David had reason to be worried; his dad wasn't the kind of guy who would carelessly sound an alarm. But there wasn't much that David could say to reassure his parents. Ted's father was particularly alarmed by the tone of the correspondence and expressed concern that his elder son intended to take his own life. Ted had written that he was sorry that he had failed his parents and assured them that they shouldn't have any regrets because they had been "good parents." "Dave," the senior Kaczynski told his son, "I have this uneasy feeling that your brother left in a very bad state of mind. His goodbye sounded so final—almost like a suicide note."

The following morning, Ted turned up in Great Falls and announced that he had a proposal for his brother. He suggested that they pool their funds to buy a piece of land to live on. David asked Ted what had happened between him and his parents.

"I just couldn't stay there anymore," he replied.

David was surprised, but happy that Ted had a plan for the future and that the plan included him. They eventually identified a modest plot six miles outside of Lincoln, a sleepy town of about a thousand residents located just west of the Continental Divide, between Great Falls and Missoula.

Webb described to me how Ted had arranged to purchase the piece of property from the father of a local businessman, Butch Gehring. Butch ran a sawmill in Lincoln and did business as Gearing Lumber Company. His father was retired and elderly. The Gehrings had extensive holdings around Lincoln, including the tract where the sawmill was located and surrounding wooded property. Kaczynski learned that Butch's elderly dad owned a small 1.4-acre parcel off a logging road that ran through the tract. Ted appealed to the father to sell him the property, assuring the man that he just wanted to build himself a little cabin and wouldn't be any trouble to anybody. Butch's dad apparently acquiesced and agreed to sell Ted the parcel along Stemple Pass Road for $2,100. Each of the brothers put up $1,050 for the property. But before the sale could be consummated, the elderly Gehring passed away, and it was Butch who actually completed the transaction.

"He'd see Kaczynski go by some days," Webb recalled. "Butch was a good guy; he is a businessman, a smart guy, and he has a big log cabin office and it looks over the yard and the mill and the equipment. One day he sees Kaczynski walk by on one of the hottest days of the summer. It must have been around ninety degrees outside. So Butch does the neighborly thing and invites Ted in to have a cold beer. Ted accepts the invite and saunters into the office. He sits down, pops open the beer, and has one sip. Then he stands up, says 'thank you,' and walks out." Butch didn't know quite what to make of the meeting, but the two of them didn't have a lot of contact after that, Webb told me.

Kaczynski's interaction with Butch Gehring was illustrative of the manner in which he interacted with folks in Lincoln. He was quiet, tended to keep to himself, and just seemed a bit odd. But Ted wasn't the only one who had moved to Lincoln to get off the grid. There were plenty of others who were also recluses, so the locals didn't pay him much mind.

Ted purchased lumber and supplies and on his own and with David's help built a simple ten-by-twelve-foot cabin on the property, tucked inconspicuously between ponderosa pines and aspens. The small, A-frame structure had one room with a tiny loft reached by a ladder. There was no running water or electricity, just a woodburning stove to warm the small quarters. David wound up staying in Great Falls, where he continued to work at the smelter, eventually returning to the Chicago area. He thought that someday he might be able to build a cabin next to his brother's. But something Ted said upon David's departure from Lincoln that summer troubled him. SSA Webb recalled a conversation David recounted for investigators after his brother's capture.

"Well, I might never see you again," Ted reportedly told him the day he left Lincoln for Great Falls.

"Well, I'll correspond with you," David had replied. The two had been corresponding to this point, mostly by letter. But it appeared Ted was looking to cut ties.

"If you ever need to get ahold of me urgently, send me a letter and put a red circle around the return address and I'll know it's important."

David was perplexed, but he agreed to his brother's terms.

For the next six years, Ted moved between Lincoln, Chicago, and Salt Lake City, Utah—the site of his October 1981 bombing—picking up odd jobs to fund his modest existence. He favored very simple, blue-collar jobs that didn't pay very much, and there didn't seem to be any pattern in the ones he selected. In September 1974, Ted worked at a gas station in Montana for three weeks, earning several hundred dollars before abruptly quitting. That winter he sent a letter to his family in Illinois, advising them that he would be away camping for a while and they shouldn't be alarmed if they didn't hear from him. In January 1975, he visited Oakland, California, where he stayed until March, although it's unclear what he was doing there.

In the summer of 1978, he returned to the Chicago area and temporarily moved back home with his family in Lombard. That June he was hired as a crew member at Foam Cutting Engineers, a foam-making plant outside Chicago, where his brother, David, was a foreman and his father served as plant manager. But just a short time into his employment he was asked to leave because he wasn't able to get along with the other people at the company.

During his brief tenure, he met a woman, a supervisor, who accepted his invitation for a dinner date. The evening out was anything but ordinary, according to FBI Special Agent Kathy Puckett.

Puckett, who served on the UNABOM task force from 1994 to 1998 and played an instrumental role in Kaczynski's capture, is one of the few people to have read all of Ted's writings, including his notes on the outing and extensive other activities. Hers was one of the first names SSA Webb provided me when I asked about others I should speak to for this book. When I reached her at her home in California in the summer of 2018, she was happy to discuss her involvement in the case. During several lengthy face-to-face interviews, she provided a startling peek behind the scenes of the investigation. Puckett spent twenty-three years as an FBI special agent, where she was primarily involved in the investigation and analysis of cases involving foreign counterintelligence and domestic and international terrorism.

Before joining the bureau, she was an officer in the Air Force Office of Special Investigations, where she was involved in investigations of Soviet and Eastern Bloc espionage. Upon leaving the Air Force, she was heavily recruited by both the FBI and CIA. By the mid-eighties, she had learned Russian and was working against Soviet intelligence in the San Francisco Division of the FBI. In 1994, she was asked to join the UNABOM task force.

She told me about a journal entry that strongly suggests the evening out was one of Ted's few, if only, interactions with a woman. He seemed both detached and confused by the encounter and had no clue how to react when she tried to French kiss him.

"He writes about how she kissed him," Puckett recalled. "And he describes it like a Martian meeting an earthling. He said she was doing something with her tongue that he couldn't quite understand. He had never kissed another woman in his life, because if he had, he would have written it down," she explained, noting the incident appeared to perplex him. It was almost as if he was a third-party observer watching the two kiss on a movie set rather than something he was doing in real life.

The two reportedly went out a few times, but the woman's lack of interest in pursuing a romantic relationship angered Kaczynski. Her brother would later tell the *New York Times* that while Ted may have fantasized their relationship into something more, it had been strictly platonic in nature.

According to people at the foam-making company, Ted wrote an insulting limerick about the woman shortly after their outing, made copies of it, and pasted them on the walls of the factory for all to see. Although he hadn't signed the verse, another supervisor quickly figured out that Ted was the culprit and admonished him to take the offending poetry down. Instead, he wrote another limerick and taped it to the wall by the second supervisor's work station. Not long after, Ted was let go.

Amazingly, it was during this time that Ted planted his first bomb in the parking lot of the University of Illinois Chicago Circle campus (less than thirty minutes from the family's Lombard home) and then remained in the Chicago area, working at the foam factory until his dismissal in early August.

Puckett noted several other failed interactions Ted had journaled about, "long agonizing passages that we took from the cabin about how he had a crush on a girl who worked at a gas station in Montana, and he bought a new pair of jeans in an effort to walk up to her, and he ended up sobbing in front of his campfire, because he couldn't bring up the nerve to talk to her." In another instance, Ted traveled back to Berkeley where he tried to join the Sierra Club's singles group. "He goes on a hike and is trying to talk to people, and he writes about this beautiful woman, but he couldn't talk to her. He couldn't make the connection."

Remarkably, even after losing his job at the foam-making plant, Ted didn't leave the city, opting instead to secure a job at another local factory that assembled restaurant machinery. By late fall, however, he was back in Montana, with no one having a clue that in Chicago he had commenced what would turn out to be a seventeen-year bombing spree.

CHAPTER 10

BECOMING THE UNABOMBER

Despite investigators' best efforts, Ted Kaczynski's bombing attacks continued unchecked for more than a decade. While agents pored over the remains of his IEDs and scoured the countryside for clues to his identity, Kaczynski continued to live in his tiny cabin, perfecting his lethal craft and taking copious notes about his activities in a series of journals. Later, those detailed writings provided a treasure trove of materials for investigators and FBI behavioral analysts to comb through and create theories to explain how a genius mathematician had turned into a recluse and domestic terrorist who sought to tear away at the fabric that holds society together.

The entries are at once disturbing and depressing. They paint an image of a man who has withdrawn from society, who has no real friends, and certainly no companionship (or love) from the opposite sex. Ted knew how to integrate himself into society, but he chose not to. Indeed, he had no interest in building a career, and he had no idea how to start a relationship with another adult—or start a family. He built walls between himself and others and kept himself an outcast. He cultivated anger and disgust toward the people around him and spent countless hours plotting to maim and kill. There is little in Ted Kaczynski to like or empathize with. Perhaps that is why some have spent so much time contemplating what impact the Harvard psychology project had on his psyche.

Ted's desire to take a life surfaced with some regularity in his writings of the early 1970s, although vague references to homicide dated back to as early as 1966.

"My first thought was to kill somebody I hated and then kill myself before the cops could get me," Kaczynski wrote in one undated passage. "(I've always considered death preferable to long imprisonment.) But since I now had new hope, I was not ready to relinquish life so easily. So, I thought, I will kill but I will make at least some effort to avoid detection, so that I can kill again . . ."

On May 9, 1979, exactly one year after his first bomb attack, a second device exploded at Northwestern University in Evanston, just forty-five minutes from his family's modest five-room home in Lombard. This device was hand delivered and was found with no address and no postmark. Kaczynski detailed his bombings in his journals and even explained his rationale for sending explosives to unsuspecting and innocent individuals across the nation. "I intend to start killing people," Ted wrote in one entry that was later submitted to the court by a government psychiatrist as proof that Kaczynski was not mentally ill and was fit to stand trial.

> If I am successful at this, it is possible that, when I am caught [not alive, I fervently hope!] there will be some speculation in the news media as to my motives for killing people (as in the case of Charles Whitman, who killed 13 people in Texas in the 60's). If such speculation occurs, they are bound to make me out to be a sickie, and to ascribe to me motives of a sordid or "sick" type.

Kaczynski went on to explain that it was for this reason that he was keeping a journal, "an account of my own personality and its development that will be as accurate as possible," as a way to ensure that his motives—and more importantly the psychology behind them—would not be "misrepresented" if and when he was caught.

He admitted that putting his thoughts down on paper provided him an outlet for his hatred, sparked in part by the social rejection he had experienced throughout his life, as well as the sexual frustration he endured. "Organized society frustrates my very powerful urge for physical freedom and personal autonomy," he penned shortly after his second attack, which occurred on the campus of Northwestern University in May 1979.

Not surprisingly, Kaczynski's criminal behavior was not limited to his bombing attacks. After his arrest in 1996, task force members discovered that he had been quietly terrorizing both residents of and visitors to Lincoln, Montana. Ted took pleasure in sabotaging equipment of others who were working in the woods. Even more disturbing was his practice of laying dangerous traps for snowmobilers and motorcyclists who dared to venture up Stemple Pass Road, stringing wire between trees along trails with the hope of decapitating his victims.

Two pairs of shoes of different sizes were collected during the execution of a search warrant on his cabin, and investigators were able to confirm that Ted's vandalization of the homes and properties of others in town had been performed while wearing a special set of shoes designed to throw off anyone who might be trying to track him through the woods. Tinkering away in his cabin, Ted had found a way to attach a second—and much smaller—pair of soles to the bottoms of his own. As he walked, Ted left shoe prints that were smaller than his. Investigators said that police could reasonably be misled into thinking that they were tracking someone smaller than Ted, who stood five foot, nine inches tall and weighed 150 pounds.

After his first two explosive devices failed to produce the desired outcome—death or severe injury—he doubled down on his research and began experimenting with various types of improvised explosive devices in the woods near his cabin. Ted's goal was to create a lethal explosive device. He also continued experimenting with various ways to avoid leaving fingerprints or other evidence behind for bomb technicians. For example, he described in his journal a technique for treating stamps with soybean oil and salt water to avoid leaving any fingerprints on his IEDs.

A number of his entries about the bombings were written in a code that Kaczynski himself devised and FBI agents later deciphered. Of the June 1980 attack on United Airlines president Percy Wood, he wrote:

> According to newspapers he [Percy Woods] was hospitalized with cuts and burns and had surgery for removal of fragments. . . . FBI said bomb had enuf [sic] powder to kill, but "faulty craftmanship weakened it cause culprit "left something loose." This false, tho [sic] my design may have been poor due to ignorance of the technology. . . . I know for certain there was nothing 'loose' in the explosive unit itself, cause the ends of the pipe were stopped with pooddn [sic] plugs fastened with epoxy and for each plug two nails passing thru plug and both sides of pipe . . . After complicated preparations I succeeded in injuring the pres of United A.L.

Other decoded entries relate to his fifth attack at the University of Utah in Salt Lake City, as well as the sixth device he sent to computer science professor Patrick Fischer who, unbeknownst to him, had left Penn State for Vanderbilt University, where the package was eventually forwarded.

Of the device found at the University of Utah Business School, a device that he deemed a "failure," he wrote:

> My projects for revenge on the technological society are expensive and I need money to carry them out. For instance, last fall I attempted a bombing and spent nearly three hundred bucks just for travel expenses, motel, clothing for disguise, etc. aside from cost of materials for bomb. And then the thing failed to explode. Damn.

Upon failing to get his bomb to its intended target with regard to the device he mailed to computer expert Patrick Fischer in May of 1982, he lamented:

His secretary opened it. One newspaper said she was in hospital? in good condition? With arm and chest cuts. Other newspaper said bomb drove fragments of wood into her flesh. But no indication that she was permanently disabled. Frustrating that I can't seem to make lethal bomb . . . Revenge attempts have been gobbling much time . . . But I must succeed, must get revenge.

Perhaps the most disturbing passage in Kaczynski's journal was his admission that "committing these crimes" helped him to "feel better."

I am still plenty angry, you understand, but the difference is that I am now able to strike back, to a degree.

Of his first attack on the University of California, Berkeley, in July 1982 that injured Professor Angelakos (Bomb Number Seven), he wrote:

I placed in Computer Science Building a bomb consisting of a pipe bomb in a gallon can of gasoline. According to newspaper, vice chairman of computer sci. dept. picked it up. He was considered to be 'out of danger of losing any fingers but would need further surgery for bone and tendon damage in hand. Apparently pipe bomb went off but did not ignite gasoline. I don't understand it. Frustrated. Traveling expenses for raids such as the foregoing are very hard on my slender financial resources.

The Unabomber was equally callous when describing the second Berkeley attack three years later in May 1985 (Bomb Number Eight) that permanently maimed pilot and aspiring astronaut John Hauser:

I am no longer bothered by having crippled this guy. I laughed at the idea of having any compunction about crippling an airplane pilot.

The two Berkeley bombings were followed by attacks on the Boeing aircraft warehouse in Sacramento and the University of Michigan in Ann

Arbor, where Ted had spent five years doing his graduate work. While he had little in the way of criticism for those at Harvard, his writings were filled with disdain for the faculty at the University of Michigan, railing about their audacity in showing up unprepared to teach their courses and incapable of solving the mathematical proofs assigned to their students:

> The fact that I not only passed my courses (except on physics course) but got quite a few A's, shows how wretchedly low the standards were at Michigan . . . most instructors and most students did only what they had to do . . . their sloppy, careless, poorly organized teaching can destroy the morale of many students.

Despite Kaczynski's "best efforts" at fabricating bombs, he wasn't able to succeed in his goal of killing someone until his bombing of the RenTech Company on December 11, 1985 (Bomb Number Eleven). He celebrated the moment by writing in his journal:

> Experiment 97. Dec. 11, 1985 I planted bomb disguised to look like scrap of lumber behind Rentech Computer Store in Sacramento. According to San Francisco Examiner . . . the 'operator' (owner? manager?) . . . was killed, 'blown to bits' . . . Excellent. Humane way to eliminate somebody. He probably never felt a thing. 25000 dollar reward offered. Rather flattering.

He didn't stop there. Fourteen months later, on February 20, 1987, he left an explosive device (Bomb Number Twelve) in the parking lot of CAAMs Inc., the computer store in Salt Lake City. Despite all his preparation and efforts, he made a mistake and was seen by Tammy Fluehe, resulting in the famous Unabomber sketch of the man in the hoodie and the aviator sunglasses seen by Americans from coast to coast. Soon after, Ted Kaczynski went underground.

Ted Kaczynski's targets were a puzzle. He left the first two bombs on college campuses in Chicago and Evanston, Illinois. He then took aim at the University of California, Berkeley, placing two bombs there. He next mailed a bomb to Dr. James McConnell at the University of Michigan. In all, he targeted two universities in his hometown and each of the other institutions he attended or worked at, with one exception—Harvard. Why didn't he target Harvard, where he had supposedly been subjected to emotional torture in an experiment? That would be the one place people would have expected him to put at the top of his list. He would later tell his court-appointed defense attorneys that he refused to leave the experiment because he wanted to prove that he couldn't be broken. Maybe he avoided Harvard specifically because of that experiment. If he'd attacked the institution, people would have accused him of seeking vengeance against those who broke him. If he left Harvard off his list of targets, analysts would have no choice but to look deeper for a motive. He couldn't just be dismissed as a "sicko" who attacked the people who tried to break him.

PART III

CHAPTER 11

THE ELUSIVE MOTIVE

By 1992, the UNABOM investigation seemed to have once again lost momentum. Six years had passed since the bomber's last attack, and people back at FBI headquarters in DC were becoming convinced that the release of the eyewitness sketch had likely driven him underground for good. In San Francisco, Agent Webb still had one case agent working on the investigation full-time—John Conway.

Conway had taken over for Don Ulrich and was dutifully plugging away on the case. Still, it was difficult to point to any real progress, and that was tough for everyone involved. Conway was universally liked by his colleagues—and that included Webb, who called him a "really great guy." He had a great sense of humor, which helped him grind away day after day. He had some odd talents for an FBI agent too. If he wasn't a federal agent, he likely would have been an actor. He had an ear for accents, and he could do voice changes. At heart he was a thespian, and he often performed in community theater productions.

It's easy to understand why agents were having an extraordinarily difficult time with the UNABOM case. More often than not investigators can determine some kind of motive for criminal activity. But in this case the suspect had never given law enforcement any idea of what was motivating him, or what his ultimate goal might be. There was no apparent rhyme or reason to the bombings; there was no clear connection between the airlines, university campuses, and a small no-name computer shop.

To make things even more difficult, they were dealing with someone who was very astute at covering his trail. The Unabomber took great pains to ensure that the investigators couldn't track his various bomb components back to him.

I've seen many white-collar criminal cases or fraud cases that have gone on for years with very few leads and paper trails that often lead to dead ends. But this was a criminal case, and still nothing existed to give investigators traction. "Follow the money" is the mantra for many investigations, but in the UNABOM case there was no money to follow. There was no effort at extortion, no manifesto that would help define motive. The investigators were trying to track down a ghost, and thousands of pages of documents proved of little or any value.

The lack of a clear motive was the most perplexing question. Why was he sending these bombs? The fact that the case was multijurisdictional was presumed. That's why it became a federal case, after all. But the lack of a consistent target or theme behind the targets was an enormous frustration.

Investigators can't analyze or look for clues in a vacuum. They have to analyze them against the backdrop of a potential motive, to think of why a person or persons would act the way they do in order to predict why they will act a certain way in the future.

In the bank robbery cases I prosecuted, I would look at a bank robber and see what he had done, his pattern and behavior over time; and more than once I had been able to anticipate and catch him at his next job. In those instances, the motive was obvious: money. I just had to analyze pattern and behavior. With the Unabomber, there was seemingly no way to analyze pattern or behavior to ascertain motive, and no motive emerged no matter how long and hard investigators analyzed the case.

With the Unabomber, investigators were dealing with someone who was very intelligent, but the usual motives—money, revenge, sex—did not seem to apply. So what was it that had him targeting professors and grad students and researchers and computer store owners and airline executives? And, more important, why had he suddenly stopped?

This brought the FBI to the pivotal point where, because of the lack of any real progress in the case, some at headquarters questioned whether the bureau should continue to support the investigation. There was speculation that the Unabomber might never resurface either because he was no longer alive, or because he had been arrested and was incarcerated for some other crime.

In early December, Webb received the call from headquarters directing him to stage what would prove to be the pivotal UNABOM conference in San Francisco, where Webb and the others working the case would learn that headquarters intended to close down the investigation. It had been nearly six years since the drawing of the suspect had been released to the public, and despite countless tips and innumerable man-hours from investigators, the team still had no solid leads and was no closer to arresting someone than they had been six years earlier. It was there at the Holiday Inn at Union Square that Bob Pocica from the Criminal Investigation Division revealed the bureau's waning interest in pursuing the Unabomber. It is anyone's guess how things would have shaken out if Agents Webb and Conway hadn't taken it upon themselves to convince Lab Chief Chris Ronay to fight to keep the task force running for another year.

CHAPTER 12

GREEN LIGHT

With a green light from headquarters to continue the investigation, Webb and members of his squad began brainstorming new avenues of inquiry and revisiting old case files looking for clues they may have missed. Six and a half years had passed since the Salt Lake City bombing outside Gary Wright's computer store, and while some at the bureau remained convinced they'd heard the last of the Unabomber, Webb and his case agent, John Conway, were confident he'd resurface, eventually, and they were determined to make headway.

The squad's reinvigorated efforts had them implementing tried-and-true investigative techniques that had proved successful in prior bombing investigations. One, the "dog walker," had agents surveilling locations the Unabomber may have visited while in the Bay Area. They knew he had mailed one of his packages from a public mailbox in Sacramento and that he had scouted a neighborhood of Oakland to conjure up a plausible return address for the "Weinberg Tool and Supply Company" to use on the Boeing package. He had also visited Cory Hall at the UC Berkeley campus at least two times to deliver his homemade bombs. Agents were to visit these locations, performing tasks such as walking a dog, watching for any suspicious activity, and questioning regulars during the times the Unabomber may have been there on the off chance someone remembered seeing a person who had looked out of place—someone who hadn't appeared to belong.

Just six months after the major case conference at the Holiday Inn, Webb got word of the bombing at the home of geneticist Charles Epstein. His ability to recall even the small details surrounding that event after nearly three decades was noteworthy. He was crossing the Golden Gate Bridge en route to his home in Marin County, having just picked up his wife at the airport, when his portable phone rang. Back then, commercial cell phones were still a novelty and had only been made available to the public two years earlier. Although they were technically considered hand-held devices, they were bulky, cumbersome, and heavy, weighing close to two pounds and by no means portable. Webb recalled it was one of those big old handset phones—a box phone. "It was like five watts; you could call Mars with the damn thing!" Most were installed as car phones, being too big to fit into a jacket pocket, and they operated on a 3G network, which meant spotty service and lots of dropped calls. Webb found a safe place to pull over to take the call.

It was Denise Monde, his colleague in the San Francisco field office. "There's been a bombing in Tiburon," she told him. "I think you should go."

Webb hadn't seen his wife in weeks, and this was one of the rare occasions he'd actually been free to pick her up after a trip east to visit family. Still, being the wife of an FBI agent, Florence was accustomed to spur-of-the-moment changes. She knew time was of the essence and arranged for her elder daughter, Sarah, to fetch her at the Safeway in nearby Mill Valley so her husband could be on his way.

———

Tiburon is an incorporated town on the southwest corner of the Tiburon Peninsula that can be reached by ferry from San Francisco. The wealthy enclave is isolated from the rest of the Bay Area, with a quaint downtown district and just two roads in and out of the community. Webb was about fifteen minutes away on Highway 101 when he got the call that afternoon; he knew he was getting close when he saw an ambulance with flashing lights pass him in the opposite lane, no doubt carrying the victim to the hospital. A sergeant from the Mill Valley Police Department looking absolutely baffled was posted outside the residence when Webb pulled up to the scene that afternoon. The sergeant had never been to a bombing crime scene, and he'd never seen anything like what had just confronted him inside the residence. His superior had advised him to wait for the FBI, and he looked relieved when he saw Webb step out of his car. All he knew was that the victim had been taken away in an ambulance and that the man's dining room was all torn up as a result of the explosion. This would be the Unabomber's thirteenth attack, and the third one attended by Webb.

Webb's arrival on the scene coincided with that of the chief of the Mill Valley Police Department. "We'll handle it from here," Webb advised him.

Before entering the residence, Webb made sure to alert ATF and the Postal Inspection Service, then joined members of his team in the kitchen where the bomb had detonated. The room had expansive windows boasting a view of the San Francisco Bay and the army barracks across the way.

A review of the evidence determined that Dr. Epstein had been sitting at the kitchen table when the device detonated. Alone and gravely injured, he tried to call for help. But he was unable to dial the telephone because his fingers had been ripped from his hand in the explosion. As a result, he would never play the cello again.

Over the next several hours, more than a dozen agents flooded the area, with some going through the house in search of evidence and others talking to neighbors who might have witnessed something. Bomb tech Don Sachtleben was dispatched to the hospital to interview Dr. Epstein and called Webb at the crime scene to report his findings. According to Sachtleben, the only thing the victim remembered was zipping open the padded envelope before it exploded. Webb's initial examination of the components at the scene had him uneasy. There was something about the device's construction that bothered him; it was certainly unconventional in the way it was built, incorporating batteries and a spring trigger. It had arrived in a Jiffy envelope no bigger than a VHS tape, which meant it had been small in nature, and had a return address listed as "James Hill, Chemistry Department, California State University, Sacramento, California." Agents located Professor Hill, who, like the others, had no knowledge of the package.

"Let's go to the office tomorrow morning and lay it all out," Webb told his squad members. He didn't want to jump to an early conclusion, but his gut was telling him that the Unabomber was back.

During the car ride home, Webb called the office and asked Alexandria Jacobson, an analyst on the squad, to pull the UNABOM slide set, which contained photographs of all of his previous devices. He wanted to compare them to the components the team had collected from the Epstein bombing scene to see if they matched.

The following morning, Webb and about a dozen others from the San Francisco Division spent several hours poring over the slide set, examining the various components: the springs, the batteries, the metal end plugs, the insulated wire, the improvised flip switch, the handmade wooden boxes.

"Hey, the end piece on that pipe is identical to the Epstein device," one person remarked.

By noontime, everyone agreed: the Unabomber was out of hiding. Webb got on the phone to headquarters to alert the guys in the explosives unit and before long, everyone at headquarters knew.

The next morning, Webb was driving along the marina on his way to the office when he got a call from someone at headquarters. "Pull over!" the supervisor instructed. "Are you parked safely?"

"Yeah, what's going on?" Webb quizzed.

"There's been a bombing at Yale University. We think it's UNABOM."

Webb learned that the victim was a computer science professor named David Gelernter, and he had been critically injured in the explosion. Apparently Gelernter had been away in Israel. Upon his return to campus, he found the envelope on his desk, which was located in a fifth-floor office of Arthur K. Watson Hall in the university's Computer Science Department. According to FBI agents on the scene, the mailing label and padded envelope appeared identical to the one received by Dr. Epstein, right down to the typewritten mailing label. It was postmarked from Sacramento, California, indicating it had gone through the US mail system.

The enclosed IED utilized a passive booby-trap designed to explode if handled by someone—in this case Dr. Gelernter, who lost several fingers in the ensuing explosion. After the bomb went off, he managed to stagger down five flights of stairs and get himself to a nearby hospital where he received treatment. His right hand and eye were permanently damaged.

A forensic examination of the two devices indicated the Unabomber had used his time in hiding to further perfect his bomb-making skills. His latest devices were smaller than his previous bombs and had been meticulously constructed to withstand being tossed around without the risk of detonating. This meant he could easily send his devices through the US mail system, ensuring that he didn't have to make any deliveries and risk exposing himself as he'd done in the computer store case.

Within hours of the Gelernter attack, a man called the Veterans Affairs Medical Center in nearby West Haven and told the switchboard operator, "You're next." Authorities were unsure if the call was related to the Yale attack and commenced an investigation.

That same afternoon, Warren Hoge, the assistant managing editor of the *New York Times*, received a typewritten letter, postmarked June 21, 1993, from Sacramento, California, that was purportedly from an anarchist group calling itself "FC," or Freedom Club—the very same initials lab examiners had found scratched into many of the Unabomber's devices.

"We are an anarchist group calling ourselves FC," the letter began. "Notice that the postmark on this envelope precedes a newsworthy event that will happen about the time you receive this letter, **if [crossed out] nothing goes wrong.** This will prove that we knew about the event in advance, so our claim of responsibility is truthful."

The author claimed the purpose of the written communication was twofold—to establish the group's identity and to supply the newspaper with an identifying number, a secret code, if you will, provided in the format of a social security number, that it would use in all future correspondence to ensure that others could not take credit for attacks carried out in its name. This correspondence marked the first time the Unabomber communicated directly with the public, and his veiled threat of future violence evoked concern.

Hoge immediately reached out to the FBI, both to report the arrival of the letter and to elicit comment for publication. Word of the correspondence and the *Times'* inquiry promptly reached FBI director William Sessions' office, and he was immediately informed of the development. Sessions, who had flown out of DC that morning and happened to be on his way to San Francisco to appear at an event unrelated to the UNABOM investigation, quickly amended his schedule to include a stop at FBI headquarters to address staff and hold a press conference. At the time, Sessions was under fire for his mishandling of expense money and improper use of a Gulfstream V jet. Some suspected he'd planned the trip to California in order to escape DC for a bit. Now, however, he had no way to escape additional scrutiny.

As head of the UNABOM task force, Webb elected to meet Sessions at the airport and accompany him back to the office. During the drive, he began to update Sessions with the latest developments in the case, but their conversation was interrupted by a call from the White House. Webster Hubbell, President Clinton's assistant, was phoning to say that Clinton was prepared to fire Sessions immediately and that he should return to Washington as soon as his obligations in San Francisco were finished. Hubbell had a booming Southern voice, and Webb and the others in the vehicle could hear every word he said.

An awkward silence took over in the car, and for the rest of the ride, no one spoke. When they arrived at the federal building on Golden Gate Avenue, Sessions gave five minutes' worth of tepid remarks to the staff, followed by a clumsy press conference. Sessions advised the media that the FBI had sent a message by computer network to most universities, and to professors in particular, alerting them to be wary of suspicious packages, particularly those with excessive postage, misspelled words, incorrect titles, or no return address. Following the press, Sessions went off to give his scheduled speech, then returned to the airport for a flight back to DC.

Examiners at the FBI lab in DC ultimately determined that the letter to the *Times* had been typed using an LC Smith Corona with 2.54 spacing, the same typewriter used in many of the earlier UNABOM attacks, further confirming what many at the agency already suspected. The Unabomber was back, sparking renewed focus on the investigation and incited concern with those at the highest levels of law enforcement. The lab technicians also made another startling discovery. When viewing the letter under ultraviolet light, they observed indented writing. They were able to decipher the words: *CALL NATHAN R. WED 7 PM.* Finally, a clue, but what did it mean?

Perhaps the letter writer had mistakenly written the words on a second piece of paper that he'd placed over the one he sent to the *New York Times*, not realizing they would imprint onto the page beneath it. If so, then who was Nathan R? An accomplice, perhaps? More plausible was the possibility that the editor or someone else at the newspaper had scribbled a note to himself that had accidentally transposed onto the letter from FC. There was no way to know for sure. Still, it was a clue to be followed.

Up to this point, the UNABOM investigation had been left to Webb and his small squad. Now it would become far bigger as federal agencies dramatically increased their involvement. The following week, Agent Webb and his case agent, John Conway, were on their way to DC for a meeting at FBI headquarters to discuss the latest developments and learn of next steps.

CHAPTER 13

UNABOM TASK FORCE

Weather in the nation's capital was surprisingly mild for mid-February, with temperatures hovering in the mid-fifties, although the cloudy, gray skies made it seem colder. After a quick breakfast at the J. W. Marriott, Webb and Conway walked the half block to the J. Edgar Hoover FBI Building, a sprawling complex that was opened in 1974 and is bounded by Pennsylvania Avenue and E Street and Ninth and Tenth Streets, Northwest.

Janet Reno had just taken over as United States attorney general and had called for a conference to discuss the creation of an FBI-led UNABOM task force. Her appointment by President Bill Clinton made her the first woman to serve as head of the US Justice Department, and people at the bureau were eager to work with her.

Webb and Conway strode into the FBI headquarters that morning as they had many times before and made their way across the expansive lobby to a bank of elevators. The meeting was being held in an upper-floor conference room. Webb was surprised at the number of folks who had been invited to attend. More than thirty people, mostly younger agents in dark suits and starched collared shirts, were standing around chatting quietly in small groups. They hardly acknowledged the two as they made their way to the front of the room.

Within minutes, a staffer appeared and began circulating through the room, handing out copies of an agenda. Webb gave it a quick glance and raised an eyebrow after seeing his own name on the document; he was listed as the first speaker.

Webb had gotten a call the day before notifying him that Janet Reno had called for the creation of an FBI-led UNABOM task force that would include more than 150 full-time investigators, analysts, and others from the FBI, US Postal Inspection Service, and Bureau of Alcohol, Tobacco and Firearms. And Webb's former supervisor, George Clow, had been named inspector in charge. Clow had been the ASAC in San Francisco for three years before accepting a transfer to headquarters as a roving inspector. Webb knew him to be a *very* intense man, high-strung and even overbearing at times. But this was going to be a joint task force incorporating agents from ATF; it needed someone who knew how to work with them, and Clow was that guy.

Webb and Conway greeted their old boss before making the rounds, chatting up old colleagues as they waited for the meeting to get under-way. It was supposed to kick off at 10:00 a.m. and people were anxious to get rolling, but it was standard procedure in the FBI to wait until the senior-most official showed up. Basically, everyone was waiting for Larry Potts, "Potsy," as Webb referred him. Potts was the executive director of the bureau and the number two guy in the agency. Word was that he was held up in a meeting at the Justice Department and would be along shortly. When he finally blew in, he made a beeline right for Webb, and as dozens of nattily dressed agents quietly observed, threw him into a big bear hug.

"Hey, thanks for doing this," he whispered. "Thanks for identify-ing that it's Unabomber. We are back in the game, so let's do the right thing."

It was a moment Webb deeply appreciated—though he tried not to show that in his body language or facial expression. He and Potts had been in the training class at headquarters in 1974 and had known each other for almost twenty years. But the moment carried even more significance for the many younger agents in the room who yearned for that kind of appreciation and recognition from such a senior FBI official.

Webb laughed, recalling how suddenly the young agents were looking at that old dog Webb in a different light; maybe there was reason to get close to this guy and earn his respect after all. "If I was just a mouse turd, at that moment I became a king," Webb chuckled.

Potts knew that Webb had been leading the investigation for the past few years and wanted his assessment. "Can we get this done?" he asked, referring to the UNABOM investigation and the possibility of bringing in a suspect. They continued to talk about the case for another five minutes before Potts broke it off, walked to the front of the conference room, and kicked off the meeting, immediately tossing Webb the floor. "Okay, let's have Pat Webb tell us where the case stands."

Webb's remarks were followed by those of an agent from the New Haven field office who provided a rundown on the Yale bombing. Chris Ronay, head of the FBI lab, was also on the speaker's agenda. Ronay reviewed the highlights of what he'd found out about the bombs in his laboratory analysis. People from ATF and the US Postal Inspection Service shared information they'd gleaned from their investigations too. Potts kept his remarks brief, trying to rally support for the investigation from those in the room. Because now the agency was under pressure. Janet Reno had been attorney general for about a week, and she'd already called Potts and Clow over to her office. She was a very forceful person, and she said to Clow, "I want you to solve this case," poking fingers on his chest. So he took it like an order from the pope.

Since the case was currently being run out of the San Francisco Division, it was decided that the task force would be based there, although it would operate autonomously, with members reporting directly to headquarters. The remainder of the day had Webb and some of the higher-ups at the FBI, ATF, and Postal Inspection Service coming up with a game plan. Denny Hagberg, the postal inspector in charge of the San Francisco Division, was there and offered to provide whatever assistance was needed. "We've got a guy, and he is the assistant inspector in charge in San Francisco, Don Davis, and we will give you Don," he said.

Webb explained that Postal was hanging out on this case as much as the FBI was; the packages were coming through the mail, so Postal was under just as much pressure to solve the case. Getting ATF to cooperate wasn't quite as easy. They, too, had to sacrifice agents to the task force, and not just agents—they had to send a supervisor with them, so that meant they had to send a group supervisor and a group of special agents to San Francisco, which meant pulling them from other assignments. ATF was already on the hot seat for all kinds of things and the bureau had to bail them out. They also didn't have the staffing numbers of the bureau, so sacrificing agents and supervisors was a hardship. Still, they agreed to cooperate as best they could.

By day's end, the three agencies had worked out a set of ground rules and agreed on how many investigators each agency would assign. The San Francisco Division would have to allot agents, so Webb called the acting SAC, Bud Covert, to give him the heads-up. Meanwhile, Inspector Clow called Webb's boss to advise him that he needed Webb and Conway on the team. That meant Webb had to turn over his squad to his number one guy, Donald Sachtleben. Although the task force would be operating from San Francisco headquarters, it would be autonomous and report only to higher-ups in DC. Members of the task force would still ask for and expect assistance from San Francisco, but basically those assigned to it would be viewed more as "rent-a-goons" occupying the space.

As the meeting wound down, Webb asked Clow when he wanted to start working. "I will drive my truck out to San Francisco, and we will start Monday morning!"

Fortunately for Clow, his transfer to DC had been recent enough that he hadn't yet sold his house in California or moved his wife and kids to the East Coast, opting to let the children finish the school year in

California rather than uproot them mid-term. No one was all that surprised that he expected the task force to be up and running in three days' time. That Friday he packed up his few belongings, tossed them into the back of his Chevy S-10 pickup, and headed west, completing the grueling cross-country drive in under sixty hours.

PART IV

CHAPTER 14

THE BIG PICTURE

When I first visited Agent Webb at his home in New Hampshire, he told me something that surprised me. "Things didn't get interesting until the UNABOM task force was created," he said with a grin. He paused for a moment before continuing. At the time, I didn't understand why he felt that way. But after learning of the inevitable—and wildly frustrating—lack of coordination between the various law enforcement agencies early in the investigation, I appreciated what he meant.

"Despite its best efforts, I don't think the FBI was able to see the big picture," Webb explained. Prior to the task force's creation, there was no framework for interagency coordination. The personnel in the explosives units at the three agencies talked to each other all the time, but their counterparts in the investigative units didn't. That meant there were gaps between the agencies, and all of them were working with only select pieces of the puzzle. The task force created a framework for coordination that was desperately needed to make progress. Suddenly, and for the first time, there was a system in place for sharing information, tips, and an investigative strategy. Now everyone was able to work together as a team.

"Now all the horses were going in the same direction," Webb told me.

To illustrate his point, Webb provided an example. Months before the task force was created, he got a call from the FBI guys in Seattle, Washington (where I would one day be a federal prosecutor). "I've got a UNABOM lead," the agent told Webb. "But you guys have to follow it up." Agents in Seattle were in the middle of the Tylenol investigation; since 1982, someone had been tampering with Tylenol bottles in the Chicago-metro area, lacing the capsules with potassium cyanide. Seven people had died as a result, sparking a string of copycat crimes across the nation. The FBI office in Seattle was investigating one such case in which someone had tampered with Excedrin capsules, resulting in the deaths of two people. (Ironically, police would ultimately look at Ted Kaczynski as a possible suspect in the original seven Tylenol deaths in the Chicago area, as his first four bombings all occurred in Chicago and its suburbs. In May 2011, the FBI requested samples of Ted's DNA. He denied ever possessing potassium cyanide, and no link to his DNA was ever found.)

But the drug tampering was not the reason Webb was being asked to travel to Seattle. A local news reporter had been contacted by someone claiming to know a lot about the Unabomber. The tipster had engaged the reporter in a handful of cryptic telephone conversations and was now insisting that the two meet face-to-face. After agonizing over what to do, the reporter contacted an attorney, who reached out to the FBI. Webb called the attorney, who explained that the reporter was willing to meet with the source but he didn't want to do it alone.

Arrangements were made for Webb and his case agent, John Conway, the main agent on the UNABOM case, to fly to Seattle. Green-lighting the operation was an operation in itself. Webb and Conway couldn't just arrange a meeting with the reporter. First they had to go through the Department of Justice and sign waivers and warnings (a process that took two full days); they also had to meet with the FBI's legal counsel and get a local attorney to sign off on the mission because they would be operating in a different district, the Western District of Washington.

Webb had grown up in Seattle, so he knew the city well. He chose the

Elliott Bay Book Company, a Seattle landmark near Pioneer Square, for the encounter, then obtained permission from the office in Seattle to wire the reporter up. Webb and Conway spent the better part of the morning studying the UNABOM case, familiarizing themselves with information only the Unabomber would know: return addresses on some of the packages, the types of explosives he used, and more. In a way, the factoids could be thought of as the ultimate trivia questions—questions that no one but the perpetrator could answer. The agents then prepared a list of ten questions for the reporter, instructing him to slip at least five of them into the conversation.

The reporter was visibly nervous, but he calmed down once he realized that Webb and Conway were skilled professionals who could be relied on. They would be right there with him at a nearby table with listening devices, ready to spring into action should things start to go awry. Webb recalled that everyone was in place and waiting when the man walked into the bookstore that afternoon. "He was not a homeless guy, but he was not dressed in a tux," Webb recalled.

The two men introduced themselves and launched into some idle chatter for a bit. About ten minutes in, the reporter started slipping in the questions Webb and Conway had prepared for him.

"What about Sacramento?" the reporter asked, referring to the device at the Boeing warehouse.

"Oh, that one didn't go off," the man replied.

About thirty minutes in, Conway gave Webb a disgusted look. The tipster was clearly struggling to provide the correct answers; he seemed to know some details about the crimes, but for the most part, he was missing the mark.

"Let's pull the plug on this," Conway said in a low voice.

Rising from his chair, he walked past the reporter and motioned for him to cut the guy off. It turned out that the tipster was just a homeless person who had spent a lot of time at the library. The man eventually admitted to reading the *Reader's Digest* article about the Unabomber, and that was how he knew details about the case.

By late afternoon, Webb and Conway were on a flight back to San Francisco. But not before the obligatory call to San Francisco to alert the office that the guy was not their man. During the investigation, there had been hundreds of tips like this one, followed up by FBI agents in the various field offices, as well as by investigators from ATF and the Postal Inspection Service. The problem was, no one was sharing these leads, which meant that Webb and Conway's trip to Seattle was known only to those in the San Francisco Division and was never shared with ATF or Postal.

Now, with the creation of the UNABOM task force, all leads, no matter how small, would be known to people at all three agencies, making it easier to coordinate and also to avoid duplicate investigations.

——

Getting the UNABOM task force up and running was no small task. Because of his role in the FBI's San Francisco office, much of the early coordination fell to SSA Webb. Within hours of the UNABOM conference in DC that authorized the task force, he was on a plane and headed back to the West Coast to ready the office for the team's arrival. His first task was creating a work space where all task force members—agents, support staff, and all their equipment—could gather and work effectively as a team.

During Webb's tenure as the office's administrative supervisor, the FBI had occupied the entire sixth floor and half of the seventh floor of the Phillip Burton Federal Building at 450 Golden Gate Avenue. Now the division would operate from a much larger eighty-five-thousand-square-foot space encompassing both the twelfth and thirteenth floors of the building. Plans included the addition of a "swing" space, a separate area on the twelfth floor that could be cordoned off and that could accommodate a drug or gang task force, or a big special case such as UNABOM that would require bringing in a team of investigators on a temporary basis.

Webb's redesign included a corner office for the person in charge, a secretarial space, and two large, open work areas that could accommodate up to twenty people. Upon returning to San Francisco, he wasted no time getting the "swing" space in working order before Inspector George Clow's impending arrival. This meant running extra phones lines, adding additional desks, and identifying support staff available to assist the incoming team.

To no one's surprise, Inspector Clow was among the first to arrive that Monday morning. He had completed his drive from Washington, DC, to the East Bay in under three days; and despite the grueling cross-country journey, he was wide-eyed, caffeinated, and ready to dig in. Short in stature, with a three-pack-a-day cigarette habit, Clow had a reputation as a very intense and driven professional. Most of the agents in San Francisco knew what to expect, having worked with him at some point over the years. He could be uncompromising at times, but he was well organized, and in the coming days he would pick good people from all over the FBI to work the task force. He made it clear that nothing was going to stand in the way of solving UNABOM. He was always the first one to appear in the morning and the last to leave in the evening. Headquarters had given him free rein over the investigation; whatever he needed—manpower, equipment, personnel—he was to get in the San Francisco Division.

Much of the first week was spent getting the task force staffed with people from the three participating agencies. SSA Webb, John Conway, and one or two of the postal inspectors were the only leftovers from the previous team of investigators. Everyone else was coming to the investigation fresh. The people at the top had decided they wanted fresh eyes and fresh views on all the investigative materials. It's always possible for an investigator to miss some small detail; the influx of new blood would help improve the odds of apprehending the individual or individuals behind the random bombings. Webb would now be the longest-serving member of the group, and Conway was right behind.

It had been agreed that each of the participating federal agencies would provide a supervisor and a certain number of investigators and computer specialists. The FBI needed fifteen agents in San Francisco. Headquarters sent five supervisors to the Bay Area as part of its rapid response team. The team's goal was to create the framework and infrastructure for the task force and then turn the operation over to local team members for its continued oversight.

The rapid response team's work was designed to be short term in nature; the five team members were in and out in a matter of months. Among them were John Loudon, Wylie "Bucky" Cox, Bill McGarry, and Bob Pocica, the CID desk supervisor who, months earlier, had been tasked with closing the UNABOM investigation down. Agent Webb was asked to give up his counterterrorism squad and serve as a supervisor, with Conway working alongside him.

Inspector Bruce Gebhardt was also transferred to San Francisco to work as Clow's chief assistant and the task force's second in command. Gebhardt was a longtime friend of Webb's. The two had met at the FBI Academy in 1974, with Gebhardt graduating one class behind Webb. The son of an FBI agent, Gebhardt had a strong reputation at the bureau. During his career he had served in FBI field offices in Denver, Los Angeles, Newark, Phoenix, and now San Francisco. In 1976, he was awarded the FBI Medal of Valor, the agency's highest honor for heroism, for his role as a special agent during a plane hijacking at the Denver Airport. Gebhardt was calm and even-tempered, and as the number two guy on the task force, he proved a perfect foil to Clow's unpredictable and easily excitable nature.

Having worked with a number of the agents in the Bay Area during his time in San Francisco, Clow knew their capabilities and had a good sense of who he would tap to join the team. He told Webb he was eager to staff the task force with hard-chargers. So Webb suggested he draft Agent Donald "Max" Noel from the Oakland Resident Agency. The two had just completed an internal investigation together. Clow was looking for hard-chargers, and Max was as qualified as they come.

"He'd been in San Francisco longer than I had," Webb recalled. "He got there in 1973; I got there in 1974. He was a firearms instructor, so he taught us to shoot and did a refresher for us every quarter. He was on the SWAT team. When I was an agent only three years in, we had a guerilla group under investigation called the Emiliano Zapata Unit. They blew up eleven Safeway supermarkets, and we identified them because they tried to do a big marijuana robbery in Marin County to finance themselves. And there was a guy who was kind of their leader and they all got arrested. We got nine convictions out of that investigation. At one point, we identified this house in Richmond where these nine people were hiding out. Max and I were among those who responded. One kid drew a .38 pistol on Max, and Max didn't shoot him. Instead, he stood his ground and calmly said to the kid three times, 'Drop the gun.' The kid dropped the gun, and Max arrested him."

"Pack your bags and come to the city," Webb told his old pal Max when he reached him by phone that afternoon. "You are now a member of the newly created UNABOM task force."

Webb's invitation was met with a lengthy silence.

No one in the bureau wanted to work UNABOM, least of all Max Noel, who was "posting and coasting," as they say in the FBI—resting on his laurels and getting ready to go into retirement. Since joining the bureau in 1968, Noel had spent the bulk of his career in the Bay Area, beginning with a six-month stint in the Sacramento field office, then Modesto, and finally San Francisco, where he would be for the balance of his thirty-plus years. His first assignment in San Francisco was to locate deserters; it was 1969, and the Selective Service System conducted the first draft lottery to determine the order of call to military service for the Vietnam War. San Francisco was a magnet for draft dodgers, and Agent Noel arrested 129 evaders that year. Like Webb, Noel had also worked cases involving anarchist groups like the Weather Underground and the Symbionese Liberation Army, whose members are most remembered for kidnapping heiress Patty Hearst. In the late seventies, Noel was assigned to the newly formed labor racketeering squad and tasked with looking into the disappearance and likely murder of union leader Jimmy Hoffa.

Agent Noel had just been assigned to the field office in Oakland when Clow tapped him to join UNABOM. Like most of the agents being drafted onto the task force, he did not come willingly. He was happy in his new digs, and the last thing he wanted was to commute an hour and a half over the Golden Gate Bridge to the city each day. Like most people at the bureau, he viewed UNABOM as a loser of a case that could only do harm to an agent's career. For all intents and purposes, the bomber was a lone-wolf terrorist, and he was not communicating with anyone.

Investigators had not heard from him since his attacks on Drs. Gelernter and Epstein, and his correspondence with the *New York Times*, which had seemed promising, appeared to have been a one-off, not the opening to a dialogue the FBI had hoped for. Additionally, Noel had just completed work on a high-profile case involving a sitting federal district judge and a major former Teamster official named Abe Chapman, who was reputedly the last surviving member of Murder, Incorporated. The last thing Max wanted was to be involved in another high-profile case, especially one that he and others viewed as an "old dog" that was never going to be solved.

Still, there was no negotiating with Inspector Clow; if he wanted you, that was that. Clow did, however, promise Noel he could return to Oakland after serving one year on the task force, which seemed to appease the bomb tech and make the transfer more palatable. Webb never told Noel that it had been his idea to put Noel on the task force.

Agents from the FBI weren't the only ones reluctant to sign onto the UNABOM case. Investigators from both the US Postal Inspection Service and the Bureau of Alcohol, Tobacco and Firearms were equally unenthusiastic.

The Postal Inspection Service, whose detailed knowledge of the nation's postal delivery system made it critical to the investigative process, sent five inspectors, starting with a postal police sergeant and inspector, Don Davis, who was the assistant inspector in charge. The Postal Inspection Service added more investigators to the task force over the next few months. That was a big commitment for the organization based on the total number of inspectors in the division.

The Bureau of Alcohol, Tobacco and Firearms also sent a team to the West Coast, led by Supervisory Special Agent Charlie Barnett. The men from ATF were still recovering from the brutal Waco massacre, which started on February 28, 1993, and included a fifty-one-day standoff between federal agents and members of the Branch Davidian religious cult run by David Koresh. The standoff culminated in a massive fire in the compound and the tragic deaths of seventy-six of its members, including men, women, and children. The horrific end to the event, and the deaths of so many people, was incredibly difficult for even the highly trained agents to comprehend and react to. The incident was made worse by the loss of four of ATF's own agents. Like any law enforcement unit, ATF is a bit like a family, and many of the agents had bonded over their long time and difficult experiences on the job. The agents who were freshly off that assignment were dispirited and embarrassed at the outcome.

———

Task force members were expected to attend a morning meeting that began promptly at 7:30 a.m. Webb, who commuted into the city from his home in Marin County, sweated his daily drive. Traffic across the Golden Gate Bridge was always an unknown, and he never knew when or if he was going to hit a snarl as his watch ticked off the seconds toward that 7:30 start time. It wasn't unusual for his stomach to start acting up first thing in the morning as he began stressing out about the day ahead and wondering which of his case files was going to be dissected and critiqued. Every single day was a grind, and Webb had no reason to be upbeat.

He quickly became a target for Clow and others as the team pored through the case files and picked apart each and every step of the UNABOM investigation. Webb was constantly fielding questions: *Why didn't you do this? Why did this take two months? Who was in charge of this?* His case agent, John Conway, was also in the crosshairs.

Everyone knew the pressure was on from the top, from Attorney General Janet Reno herself. During one of his first meetings with the team, Clow made a point of recounting how Reno had called him into her office and made it clear that she expected him to find a way to solve the case. There was no margin for error, and time was critical. Still, the constant Monday-morning quarterbacking proved hard on Webb, and he began to dread coming to work.

The situation was even more challenging than normal because the team was waiting for the new special agent in charge, James Freeman, to arrive from Honolulu, where he had been running the FBI's field office. When Freeman finally did touch down in San Francisco, he was immediately pulled into the Polly Klaas kidnapping case. On October 1, 1993, the twelve-year-old Petaluma girl was snatched at knifepoint from her bedroom during a slumber party with friends. An unknown male intruder entered her bedroom just after 11:00 p.m. that night, put pillowcases over the girls' heads, and tied their hands and feet before making off with Polly. One of the remaining children managed to free herself and alert Polly's mother to the abduction.

The Klaas case was the first in the nation to use the Internet to assist in the investigation. The day after Polly's abduction, two local residents approached police with a helpful, and technical, tip: Polly's "missing child poster" could be digitized to enhance the quality of the image and potentially make the child more recognizable to anyone who might see her. With the help of a local syndicated newspaper columnist, the poster was shared on several sites on the World Wide Web, with more than two million people viewing the image. It was a remarkable breakthrough, and one that helped shine a light on how the Internet could be used in police investigations.

Two months into the massive manhunt, police stumbled upon some children's clothing in a wooded area off a highway in Northern California. They also discovered an abandoned car several yards away and traced the vehicle to a homeless grifter named Richard Allen Davis, a recent parolee and twice-convicted kidnapper with a lengthy criminal history. Once in custody, Davis admitted to killing the child and led detectives to her body, which he had hidden beneath some brush off Highway 101, just south of Cloverdale. Californians were outraged to learn that this career criminal was back on the streets, and the state's justice system came under heavy scrutiny for his release.

SAC Freeman's attention remained focused on the Klaas case for a number of months, but even without his immediate participation and oversight, there was a sense that the UNABOM investigation was picking up speed—though the group was still a long, long way from apprehending a suspect. Morning meetings with the supervisors took on a more positive tone. Agents would toss out ideas for consideration, knowing that nothing was too far-fetched to be considered. Some suggestions were pursued, while others were set aside to be considered at a later date. At last some of the anger and tension dissipated and more work got done. There were only two rules: "everything was possible," and "no psychics" (the latter because they were viewed as a distraction and a time suck).

The way the swing space was configured, Clow was in one office and Bruce Gebhardt, his number two guy, in another. Assistant Inspector in Charge Don Davis, FBI Supervisory Special Agent Pat Webb, and ATF's supervisor, Charlie Barnett, shared a third. Everyone else was assigned desks in the bullpen, a big room with windows along one wall and desks with cubicles.

Davis and Barnett would prove important and dedicated members of the UNABOM task force, or UTF as it became known. Task force members were particularly impressed by Davis's uncanny ability to remember even the minutest details and became convinced he had a photographic memory.

Clow put numerous strategies into place to help keep team members focused and on target. He was also willing to listen and was open to almost any idea. Still, he kept a lot of folks on edge. He was a taskmaster and could bark orders, issue commands, and make a person's life miserable.

During this first iteration of the task force, the team was broken up into five different squads, populated by a mix of investigators from the three participating agencies. This was done purposefully so that members of one agency, whether it be the FBI, ATF, or Postal, could not claim it was being left out or that information was not being shared. Webb and the other four supervisors were each put in charge of a squad, and members were expected to report their findings to whomever was heading up his or her team. Each squad was given a different assignment.

One was tasked with looking back at prior attacks to find any leads or avenues of inquiry that may have been missed; the second was assigned to revisit old suspects; and the third was to track down new suspects. A fourth group, the victimology team, fell to the behavioral unit of the FBI, which was charged with revisiting the files with an eye to uncovering possible links between the Unabomber's many victims.

Every day there was more work to be done. Old suspects got a second look, and new leads kept coming in. If anyone had an idea that might advance the investigation, all he or she had to do was bring it to a supervisor—unless, of course, it involved a psychic.

CHAPTER 15

SETTING PRECEDENTS

U nder Inspector Clow's direction, the UNABOM task force imple-
mented a number of precedent-setting procedures that are still
used today. The first was the creation of a single, digitized, and searchable UNABOM case file for task force members. In these times when
computer use and the Internet are so integral in daily life, it is hard to
fathom the circumstances under which the task force was operating.

A fifth squad, the "computer capture group," was charged with creating the UNABOM database, which entailed the scanning of millions of
documents to create a central fact set. This was the first time ever that
the bureau was creating one centralized database for a case, and its creation was top priority for Clow.

Until then, hard-copy files pertaining to the UNABOM investigation were held in various FBI field offices across the United States.
The US Postal Inspection Service and the Bureau of Alcohol, Tobacco
and Firearms also had case files based on investigations they had
undertaken during the Unabomber's ongoing reign of terror. Despite
involvement from the various agencies, there had been no real coor-
dinated effort. But that ended with Clow, who authorized that all

files from the three agencies pertaining to UNABOM be sent to San Francisco.

The FBI acquired a massive parallel computer processing system from the US Army for $1 million and contracted with computer expert Casey Henderson, whom they nicknamed "Agent Futurist," to digitize thousands of pages of documents, and transfer everything from verbatim transcripts of interviews to lab analyses and subpoenas to crime-scene diagrams. It was basically every piece of data that had been collected in the case over the past sixteen years, and it was truly a gargantuan task. It was something that the FBI had never even attempted before. But their hope was that the computer's power could help the team identify some fact pattern or connection that the agents may have missed. The volume of material was so great that it was unreasonable to expect any single person to even attempt to assimilate it.

Agent Noel was assigned to the computer capture team and spent the early weeks combing through the files and tagging anything of investigative note for inclusion into the computer system. All told, the team loaded 11.8 million pages of hard text into the system. Once all the information was inputted, the team downloaded the pertinent investigation documents to a complete text-retrieval program called ZyIndex, a powerful indexing tool that makes text searching possible.

Every agent on the task force had a computer at his or her desk in anticipation of the database's completion, as this case was well beyond the card index file type of investigation. Members needed to familiarize themselves with the material, and they also needed to double-check everything that had been done in the past, looking for something that may have been overlooked. The four teams did extensive work and dug deep trying to find a common thread between all the previous attacks.

Eager to bring in new lines of inquiry, Inspector Clow proposed a toll-free 800 tip line (1-800-710-BOMB), which required a T1 fiber optic cable, or circuit, to carry the anticipated volume of calls into the building.

Opening up a tip line meant setting up a call center on the thirteenth floor and bringing in people to staff the phone lines, a job that fell to SSA

Webb. The division had a tech room with a raised floor just down the hall from the swing space where the task force was operating, so Webb arranged a meeting with the people from the phone company to explain what they needed.

"You can hire a service for this," the technician told him.

"Screw that," Webb replied, knowing full well that there was no way the agency would trust outside contractors to run an element of the biggest and most important investigation in the nation and risk something going wrong. "We don't want somebody in prison in Alabama answering our 800 line."

"TWA does it," the technician retorted, referring to the now-defunct Trans World Airlines, to which Webb shot him an incredulous look. There was no point in any further discussion with the agent. Webb already knew what he had to do.

Clow became incensed when the phone company advised the team that they could only give the task force one hundred megabytes per second. "This is the most important case in the bureau!" he bellowed. "We need a thousand megabytes yesterday!"

The new call center had more than a dozen phones. There weren't enough available people in San Francisco to staff the lines, so Webb brought in folks from other field offices around the Bay Area and trained them on how to log and track the calls. "The idea was, if they got a good lead, someone from the task force would take over the call and follow up the lead."

At the start, the lines were manned twenty-four hours a day, seven days a week. The round-the-clock operation required a sizeable staff—and carried a heavy cost. But the FBI's bean counters knew better than to interfere on this case.

The launch of the 800 tip line coincided with the arrival of a new director at the FBI. That September, William Sessions was officially out and Louis Freeh, an attorney and former judge, stepped into the role, making him the FBI's fifth director and new task force leader. Freeh began his career as a special agent with the bureau before becoming an assistant United States attorney and later United States District Judge of the United States District Court of the Southern District of New York (SDNY). He was appointed as FBI director by President William Jefferson Clinton. Agents found him likable and easy to talk to; he wasn't all about the chain of command. He preferred to speak directly to the guys on the ground, not just their supervisors.

That October, one month into his tenure, Freeh appeared on national TV to announce that the bureau was offering a million-dollar reward for information leading to the arrest of the Unabomber. This was the largest monetary reward the bureau had ever offered to the public, with a portion coming from the three participating agencies. Members of the task force were charged with raising the remainder of the funds through private donations from universities, airlines, and other related firms that had been targeted by the Unabomber.

"Bob Pocica and Bucky Cox were the point men, and they went to the universities, airlines, genetics research firms to get the money committed," Webb recounted. "He and his team got a lot of pushback, as a number of them didn't want to participate. The team also had to involve attorneys from the bureau to prepare promissory notes to ensure the firms would actually pony up the funds as promised.

"The FBI tried to time the announcement so as to get the best possible reach from broadcast and print media," Webb recounted. The bureau had offered monetary rewards in the past, but it never hit the million-dollar threshold. "We wanted to shock the public, if you will—get people's attention.

"We had to have trained operators, bureau employees to answer the phones. The first day it was like eighteen people answering the calls, and by the end of about two months it was two guys on the night shift. The 800 number was out there, and it was being shown regularly during public service announcements. It lost momentum immediately after it was offered, because this is America, and some things count bigger than other things, and the day it was offered NBA star Magic Johnson announced his retirement from basketball, completely pushing the UNABOM story off the front page.

"We were watching. We had our televisions on, and we had the phones ready to go, and headquarters made this big deal. Inspector Clow flew back to DC for it to answer any questions, and he basically got run over by ESPN, because the Magic Johnson announcement just cut the wind from our sails."

During his on-camera segment, Louie Freeh directed viewers to the 800 tip line. He also revealed a clue—the indented writing FBI lab examiners had found on the letter sent to the *New York Times*—"Call Nathan R. WED at 7 PM." They hoped someone might recognize the words and link it back to the Unabomber.

The task force also printed up more than fifty-four thousand reward posters featuring the million-dollar reward and listing the sixteen UNABOM crimes and their locations. The task force had the posters hung in post offices around the country.

Even with Magic Johnson's newsy revelation, the tip line phones started ringing within minutes of Freeh's broadcast. Over the next several days, hundreds of leads came flooding in from across the country, with people turning in their exes, their neighbors, even the "weird" guy at the trailer park.

To coincide with Freeh's announcement, the bureau embarked on an all-out publicity campaign, targeting media outlets, both print and television, with the goal of garnering as much press coverage of the case as possible. Stories appeared in *People, American Journal, Gentlemen's Quarterly,* the *Washington Post,* even *Playboy.* Television news programs such as *Inside Edition, Connie Chung Eye to Eye,* and *America's Most Wanted* also aired stories about the serial bomber. The bureau wanted to get the word out to as many people as possible. Their hope was that people would feel the 800 number offered callers anonymity.

Despite the voluminous number of calls, no new lines of inquiry were established, and sorting through the unending leads quickly became a dreaded—and fruitless—task. At one point or another, every member of the task force was assigned to a shift. Postal Inspector Paul Wilhelmus was on deck the day a woman called from Florida to report her "creepy" neighbor, convinced he could likely be the person the task force was seeking. She explained that he had been acting suspiciously and provided Wilhelmus with his name. It turned out the man she suspected was the postal inspector who had recruited Wilhelmus into the Postal Inspection Service. Not only were people calling in to report possible suspects, they were also eager to share possible theories with members of law enforcement. Wilhelmus had one tipster who became a regular, and over time, the two struck up a kind of odd friendship. According to Wilhelmus, the man had a map of the United States on which he had plotted the different locations where the Unabomber had struck. "From those events, he would somehow connect the different locations, drawing lines to predict where we should do additional investigations." He didn't have any money to do the legwork himself, so he implored Wilhelmus to visit certain locations on his behalf, among them a site in Tulsa, Oklahoma. He wanted Paul to go armed with a witching rod, typically used to detect water, convinced the device would help point the team in the right direction. He even went so far as to mail a homemade witching rod, which he fashioned from a wire clothes hanger bent in a ninety-degree angle and attached to a piece of copper tubing to serve as a handle.

"In his defense, when it all happened and Kaczynski was finally tracked down and arrested, two of the points that this guy had identified on his map turned out to be relevant; one was in Texas where Kaczynski's brother had lived, and one was in Montana, where we found Kaczynski."

Eventually, the staffing of the phones fell to the agents in the office, and it got to a point where nobody wanted to answer the calls. Often the callers were elderly and likely bored. They seemed lonely and eager to talk to someone—but they offered absolutely nothing of value to the task force. Indeed, they wasted valuable manpower and time.

"We would get these phone calls from all these lonely elderly people from Florida," Webb recalled. "They saw somebody in a sweatshirt. We'd categorize the info that came in, follow up on some, and put others aside for consideration at some future date, and reject others."

Because there was a reward involved, task force members also had to decide if callers were entitled to share in the reward money if and when the Unabomber was identified and arrested. (A number of tipsters came forward at the end of the investigation convinced they were entitled to monetary compensation; task force members had investigated their claims and were able to say definitively that the information they had provided did not qualify them. Still, a handful of people insisted they were entitled.)

Despite task force members interviewing 3,300 callers and 55 businesses, nothing came of the hotline.

"That lasted for a little while and then it just became a phone," Webb said of the tip line. The initiative had seemed like a smart idea at the time, but ultimately it proved worthless.

In addition to the tip line, the task force attempted to use the Internet to bring in leads. The Internet was still in its infancy, and this would be the first time the bureau used it to seek the public's input on a case of this magnitude. The FBI had first employed the Internet several months earlier in the Polly Klaas kidnapping investigation, using it to distribute the wanted posters featuring Polly's photograph and information about the case to millions of users around the world. The UNABOM Internet project was assigned to victimologist Bill Tafoya, whose role was to monitor traffic and respond to leads that seemed promising. According to SSA Webb, the site received one million hits, with about thirty people responding with potential information—stunning numbers at that time. Unfortunately, much like the telephone tip line that preceded it, the Internet experiment ultimately proved ineffectual. Tafoya checked out a few of the more viable leads, but nothing was panning out. Some were concerned that he was not being efficient with his time and that he was spending too much of his day hand-holding those with possible leads.

It was time to move on. Task force members would have to find another way forward.

CHAPTER 16

"WHAT IS UNABOM?"

Though the UNABOM task force enjoyed extensive visibility, serving on it was not a plum assignment. Investigators and support staff rotated into the team and then back out. Some members stayed longer than others, and some were actively looking for a way out. The UNABOM investigation was still regarded as a dog of a case, and the failed tip line and failed million-dollar reward only reinforced that image.

Postal Inspector Paul Wilhelmus, who joined the task force three months after its creation, laughed in the summer of 2018 when recalling his first day meeting the team. Sitting in his newly remodeled home in the San Francisco Bay area, he told me how he had started his career with the postal service in Cincinnati, Ohio, in 1986. Three years in, he was transferred to the field office in Oakland, California, where he worked external crimes—basically investigating people stealing the mail. His next position was in the Audit Department, where he worked until 1989, when he was supposed to be reassigned to the mail fraud team. But the transfer never happened. "I came back from vacation and I was told, 'You are going to UNABOM.' And I said, 'What is UNABOM?' And my boss said, 'You are going to a meeting, and you'll find out.'"

On his first Monday in the office, Paul was invited to attend the morning meeting, which was held around a conference table on the thirteenth floor of the federal building on Golden Gate Avenue. After a brief explanation of the various squads and their responsibilities, Paul quietly watched a presentation from each of the five groups, mostly using poster boards to illustrate their findings. He didn't know what to make of it. But one thing was clear: a lot of work had gone into reinvestigating the UNABOM incidents, but nobody felt confident they were any closer to finding the perpetrator.

Paul was assigned to the "old suspects" squad. "We had five filing cabinets full of stuff that came in from all over the place—Chicago, Oakland, all over—and that is what we started going through," he said. "It was all part of the historical knowledge of learning what everybody before had done."

Sifting through the files, Wilhelmus learned that the Postal Inspection Service had made mock-ups of all the different package bombs in hopes of locating an employee who remembered something about the person who may have dropped off the parcel, but no leads were generated.

Another line of inquiry had centered around the craft paper used to wrap the Northwestern device. Since the bottom part of this device had been wrapped in this paper, which was brown and featured big pink dots, a group of postal inspectors had gone out and interviewed the producers of the wrapping paper, Gibson Greetings, in Cincinnati, Ohio. "In an investigation, basically, this is what you do," Wilhelmus explained. "You try to track down any little lead, and you go to the source."

Inspectors had wanted to find out where the Unabomber might have been able to purchase this paper, and that meant tracing the locations where it may have been sold. They learned it hadn't been a popular seller, and ultimately, like so many of the other leads, that one, too, went nowhere.

"With Kaczynski, all of his stuff being homemade, it was really hard to figure out where he bought batteries or wrapping paper. We were really grasping at straws, to be honest."

Agent Max Noel stumbled over a lead in some of the case files from the Utah bombing. Noel hoped to interview the case agent who had led the investigation into the mail bomb found by the janitor at the University of Utah's School of Business. Noel was one of the only agents on the task force whom Inspector Clow allowed to travel outside of the Bay Area in search of a lead. Others who identified possible lines of inquiry had to reach out to agents in the local field office to enlist personnel to follow up for them. But not Noel. Clow trusted him. He and a young ATF agent named Tom Atteberry were dispatched to Salt Lake City to follow up.

The Utah case was an oddball one. None of the federal agencies had been called in to assist in the investigation because the device had failed to detonate. The incident wasn't even linked to the UNABOM investigation until nearly a year later. It was only when postal inspectors following up on the bombing at Vanderbilt University traveled to the mail facility in Salt Lake City to retrace the Vanderbilt package that they learned of the Utah device. Noel hoped they could unearth something police may have missed.

In recalling the episode, SSA Webb rolled his eyes and laughed as he told the story of the Utah trip. Nothing went quite as planned, starting right when the agents hit the ground. The FBI field office was supposed to have set aside an office for the agents to use, but when they got there, nothing had been done, and there was no space for interviews. However, the men learned that there had been unconfirmed reports of a red Fiat seen leaving the parking lot where the device was found. There was a notation about the car in an officer's notes, but nothing further.

Max decided the lead was worth pursuing, so he arranged to meet with the old case agent, who was now retired and living in a suburb outside Salt Lake. The meeting started off amicably, with Noel asking the agent if he could recall any observations from his time on the case.

"What about the red Fiat?" he probed.

"You know, we never put much into that," the agent replied. "You know what, I got all this UNABOM stuff that I never got to. Let me go get it."

Noel watched as the retired agent sauntered over to his garage, lifted the door, and walked inside. A couple of minutes later, the man emerged with a dusty box packed full of UNABOM case files that quite literally hadn't been seen in years. By all rights, the material should have been sitting in the UNABOM task force offices in San Francisco, the reports digitized and part of the case file. Instead, here they were sitting in a dusty garage. The box contained dozens of leads that had never been followed up on. The agent claimed that another more important case had come in and so he'd put the material aside. When he retired, he simply collected his files and took them home.

To be clear, it was a different time, and clearly the FBI's policies and procedures today preclude such casual treatment of law enforcement materials. Unfortunately, the agent had unwittingly precluded others from tracking lines of inquiry that might have been relevant to the investigation. It was another example of how a lack of coordination had failed investigators. What if the Unabomber really had been driving a red Fiat and the lack of follow-through on the part of investigators in Utah was to blame for the injuries victims had sustained as a result?

"I was surprised Noel didn't deck the guy," Webb recalled.

The following day, Max walked into the office and exploded—yelling and cursing at people, Webb recalled. "Did you know your guy retired and he took the effing files with him?" Max asked agents in the Salt Lake City office.

The cursing only made things worse because many of the FBI office's staff were Mormon and quite unaccustomed to any foul language. "The SAC, Gene Glenn, who used to be in the Oakland field office, pulls him aside and says, 'You can't come back here. Everybody is offended by your language. You are going to have to work out of your hotel room.' The young agent who was with him was just so embarrassed."

Max didn't think much about it and figured the matter would blow over. These were FBI agents, after all. But the following morning, he arrived at the Salt Lake City FBI office only to discover his key card had been deactivated.

Max was incensed when he phoned San Francisco that afternoon.

He was livid that he had been locked out of the field office. Worse, he couldn't wrap his head around the fact that the case agent had taken the UNABOM files home with him when he retired. "I am not coming back tomorrow!" he barked. "It's going to take an extra week to run down all these leads, and I may need extra people."

That week, Noel and Atteberry, who had accompanied him to Utah, went to the local Department of Motor Vehicles office and had employees there run a report to determine how many red Fiats were in the area around the time of the Utah bombing. They then went around and checked out all forty-nine of them; their search took them to junkyards and used car lots, and in some cases they found the owners. One had been repainted, but they managed to locate it too. "They did a lot of follow-up work there, but in the end, nothing panned out," Webb sighed.

For task force members like Noel and Wilhelmus, downtime did not mean kicking back and taking a break. If there were no leads to follow, they were expected to help out another squad.

The Unabomber profile had remained basically unchanged until 1987, when the witness in Salt Lake City, Utah, claimed the man she saw in the parking lot behind the computer store appeared to be in his mid- to late-twenties, prompting investigators to refocus their search for somebody almost a decade younger. Still, the prevailing theory was that the bomber was a blue-collar worker in his early to mid-forties with a grudge against the airline industry. Now, five years and two new attacks later, the FBI wanted to update its profile, and they tasked Special Agent William "Bill" Tafoya, a behavioral scientist "who'd recently transferred to San Francisco from Quantico," and Mary Ellen O'Toole, "a field representative of the FBI Profiling Unit at Quantico," an FBI profiler, with revisiting the files to uncover possible links between the Unabomber's many victims.

Tafoya assumed leadership of the victimology team. Tafoya had a PhD in criminology, had been through the FBI Academy, and had trained as a behavioral scientist. During his tenure at Quantico, he and two colleagues, one with a PhD in social psychology who could work with statistics and the other a PhD in electrical engineering who had written an AI software program, attempted to address complaints from agents in the field in need of a criminal profile ASAP.

Time was of the essence, and investigators were frustrated having to wait while all pertinent materials were reviewed. To address their concerns, Tafoya and his colleagues set out to create an "automated profiler" that could provide a cursory review of files coming into the bureau. It was a major undertaking and required the threesome to examine every case file the National Center for Analysis had on serial killers in order to identify patterns. And, more specifically, patterns to explain how killers chose their victims.

Tafoya and O'Toole's review of the UNABOM files was not for the purpose of creating a profile, but rather to prepare a protocol for interviewing living victims of the elusive bomber.

O'Toole's career trajectory and her decision to pursue a career in law enforcement were vaguely similar to my own. Her father had been an FBI agent, and her mother had worked off and on as a personal assistant to J. Edgar Hoover. She began her career in the San Francisco district attorney's office as a criminal investigator before becoming an FBI agent. During UNABOM she was promoted to full Profiler status and transferred from San Francisco to Quantico. She ultimately spent nearly half her twenty-eight years with the bureau in the behavioral analysis unit (BAU), where she developed an expertise in criminal investigative analysis and offender behavior.

Both O'Toole and Tafoya got right to work upon arrival from Quantico. They and other members of the victimology team spent several months designing an eight-page questionnaire to be filled out by the living victims of all sixteen of the Unabomber's attacks. By August, the surveys were in the mail to the intended recipients with instructions to complete and return them to the San Francisco Division, where they would be entered into a computer database (which was still being created) for analysis.

When the surveys were returned to the office that fall, agents from the various squads were recruited to assist the victimology team with the second phase of their work. The task force made arrangements for all those who had completed the survey to come to San Francisco to be interviewed by members of the victimology team in hopes of finding that missing thread. The victims were haunted by their experiences, and at some point, they had all begun to ask themselves, *Why me? What did I do to bring this on?*

These sorts of questions are natural and typically afflict those who have been targeted in such a way. But with the Unabomber still at large, there were no answers—and the behaviorists trying to find a common denominator among them failed to establish any links or connections.

——

In late December 1993, SSA Bob Pocica traveled back to DC for the holidays. His trip included a stop at FBI headquarters to visit his old boss in the Criminal Investigations Division—one of a number of higher-ups there who was supposed to be reading the daily summaries Webb and the team had been dutifully creating on the Unabomber case.

Everyone on the task force was aware of the painstaking work that went into the summary—a task that often kept Webb at the office until way past 7:00 p.m. Every day, a new report had to be prepared. Everyone knew and appreciated that the report had to be done on a daily basis; the summaries ensured that everyone involved in the investigation across the US was kept current. Headquarters had insisted on the daily reports, and task force members had simply assumed that everyone in DC had been reading them.

Over the months, the daily summary had become a kind of ritual for Webb, Clow, and Clow's number two guy, Bruce Gebhardt. Webb would type it up, then Gebhardt would go through it line by line. Next, it was Clow's turn to give it a final read.

"Okay, let her fly!" he'd say when he was satisfied.

That was Webb's cue to walk it over to the teletype machine (e-mail was virtually unknown then) where Mary Cardenas, one of the office secretaries, would send it out to every UNABOM office in the country, including headquarters.

"Bob, what are you doing here?" his former supervisor asked.

"We're off for Christmas. I've got five days. I have to be back on January third."

"How's that UNABOM case going?"

"Oh, we're plugging along."

"Are you making any headway?"

"Don't you read the summaries?" Pocica replied, flashing his former boss a bewildered look.

"Summaries?" his former boss quizzed.

"Yes, we send you a summary every day."

Glancing around the office, Pocica noticed a huge stack of UNABOM summaries in the corner, clearly unread and gathering dust.

Webb recalled that Pocica was furious when he returned to San Francisco that January. He watched as Pocica marched past him and into Clow's office. "Headquarters doesn't care about this," he complained, before launching into a diatribe centered around the pile of unread UNABOM summaries on the floor of his old boss's office.

Now he had Clow on the warpath. "We will keep it going," he told Pocica, then proceeded to call the assistant director of the FBI. "What are we doing spinning our wheels out here?!" he yelled into the receiver.

Webb reminded me that the UNABOM investigation was separate and distinct from the rest of the work being done by the San Francisco Division of the FBI. San Francisco had no authority over any of it, and the task force was under the direction of the inspector, in this case Clow. Agents couldn't go to their own SAC and ask for time off; they had to seek permission from Clow. And he reported directly to headquarters.

Beginning that January, a couple of temporary staffers, or "rents," as Agent Webb referred to them, left the task force. The bureau used the somewhat derogatory term for those agents who were "inspection" staff, or on temporary assignment. There was the permanent staff, and then there were the "rent-a-goons," or "rents." And the task force was staffed mainly with rents. Even SSA Webb, who was based in San Francisco, was considered a rent, as long as he was assigned to the task force.

The rents who started to leave had either gotten better assignments or they'd requested a transfer and couldn't turn it down.

In early spring, news began to spread that headquarters, specifically FBI director Louis Freeh, was thinking of giving the UNABOM case back to the San Francisco Division. There hadn't been an incident in nearly a year, and the task force, despite its tremendous efforts and unlimited resources, had made very little headway.

In March 1994, word of the impending change of status reached Jim Freeman, the new SAC of the San Francisco Division, who immediately agreed to take over the UNABOM task force. It seemed as though he was the only high-ranking leader in the whole of the FBI willing to step into the role. Everyone else viewed the case as a career killer, but Freeman was confident he could turn things around. His experience with the bureau had included counterintelligence both foreign and domestic, kidnapping, extortion, and other criminal cases. He wanted to build a team of people from the Bay Area who could commit to the case for the long haul.

In selling himself to Director Freeh, he pointed out that the task force was pretty much up and running, and it was expensive to have all these people living on TDY (temporary duty year) in apartments. Additionally, people from two other federal agencies were also temporarily residing in the Bay Area.

Freeh appreciated Freeman's sense of commitment, and he greenlighted the change in leadership for the UNABOM task force.

April 1994 marked a changing of the guard, with UTF members in leadership roles returning to their field offices. Most of the rapid response team supervisors were being promoted and moving on to new positions in the bureau. John Loudon was sent back to headquarters as an instructor, and Inspector Clow was elevated to assistant director of the training division at the FBI Academy in Quantico, Virginia.

Even Webb was told he could reassume control of his old counter-terrorism squad. But he would never fully leave the investigation. Instead, he was designated the "go guy," meaning he was on duty call. If there was a bombing with a similar MO, Webb was called to go to the location to determine whether it could be the work of the Unabomber. Over the next year, he would be called to a handful of scenes, once from his sick bed—he was down with the flu—to be the eyes and ears for UNABOM.

Ted Kaczynski in 1967 on the campus of University of California, Berkeley. At twenty-five, he was the youngest professor ever hired by the university. He resigned from his position after just two years. (© George M. Bergman, Berkeley; GNU Free Documentation License; Oberwolfach Photo Collection)

In 1971, Kaczynski moved to a remote, one-room cabin near Lincoln, Montana, built with the help of his younger brother David. He lived there for the next twenty-five years. (Elaine Thompson/AP/Shutterstock)

Crime scene investigators photographed debris from one of Kaczynski's pipe bombs. (FBI)

FBI bomb technicians recreate one of Kaczynski's bombings. (FBI)

An eyewitness to a bombing in Salt Lake City, Utah, provided authorities with a description of the suspect, resulting in the now-famous police sketch of a mustachioed man wearing a hooded sweatshirt and dark sunglasses.

$1,000,000 REWARD

call
UNABOM Task Force
1-800-701-BOMB
(1-800-701-2662)

UNABOM CRIMES

1.	University of Illinois at Chicago, IL 5/25/78	**(1 injured)**	
2.	Northwestern University, Evanston, IL 5/9/79	**(1 injured)**	
3.	American Airlines, Flight 444, Chicago, IL 11/15/79	**(12 injured)**	
4.	President United Airlines, Chicago, IL 6/10/80	**(1 injured)**	
5.	University of Utah, Salt Lake City, UT 10/8/81		
6.	Vanderbilt University, Nashville, TN 5/5/82	**(1 injured)**	
7.	University of California, Berkeley, CA 7/2/82	**(1 injured)**	
8.	Boeing Aircraft Auburn, WA 5/8/85		
9.	University of California, Berkeley, CA 5/15/85	**(1 injured)**	
10.	University of Michigan, Ann Arbor, MI 11/15/85	**(2 injured)**	
11.	Rentech Company, Sacramento, CA 12/11/85	**(1 death)**	
12.	CAAM's Inc., Salt Lake City, UT 2/20/87	**(1 injured)**	
13.	Physician/Researcher, Tiburon, CA 6/22/93	**(1 injured)**	
14.	Professor, Yale University, New Haven, CT 6/24/93	**(1 injured)**	
15.	Advertising Executive North Caldwell, NJ 12/10/94	**(1 death)**	
16.	President California Forestry Association Sacramento, CA 4/24/95	**(1 death)**	

Explosive devices have been either placed at or mailed to the above locations. This activity began in 1978, and has resulted in three deaths and 23 injuries. The last device was mailed in April of 1995 from Oakland, California.

The **UNABOM** Task force will pay a reward of up to $1,000,000 for information leading to the identification, arrest and conviction of the person(s) responsible for placing or mailing explosive devices at the above locations.

Do you know the UNABOMBER?
Please contact the UNABOM Task Force at 1-800-701-BOMB / 1-800-701-2662.

In October 1993, the FBI announced a $1,000,000 reward for information leading to the arrest of the Unabomber, funded by contributions from the FBI, ATF, USPS, United Airlines, and some other "involved" parties. This was the largest monetary reward the bureau had ever offered to the public. (FBI)

UNABOM Task Force members SSA Joel Moss, SAC Terry Turchie, and SA Kathy Puckett, FBI Behavioral Analyst. Puckett's analysis of the Unabomber's words and her interviews of David Kaczynski and his wife, Linda Patrik, were instrumental in the capture of Ted Kaczynski. (Kathleen Puckett)

SSA Patrick Webb (center), one of the longest-serving members of the UNABOM investigation, with Task Force members and support staff at the FBI headquarters in San Francisco. L to R: Unidentified FBI Agent; Cindy Aiello, UNABOM secretary to ASAC Terry Turchie; FBI Media Representative Rick Smith; SSA Patrick Webb; SAC Jim Freeman; and Sue O'Brien, clerical staff. (Florence Webb)

On Tuesday, September 19, 1995, the Unabomber's 35,000-word manifesto was published in the *Washington Post* and *New York Times* after intense discussions involving Attorney General Janet Reno, FBI Director Louis Freeh, *New York Times* publisher Arthur Sulzberger Jr., *Washington Post* publisher Donald Graham, and members of the Department of Justice. (AP/Shutterstock)

The ultimate break in the case came when Ted Kaczynski's younger brother, David, reluctantly came forward to authorities after he and his wife, Linda, recognized similarities between the manifesto and some of Ted's writings. (Rich Pedroncelli/AP/Shutterstock)

In mid-March of 1996, FBI agents began surveillance of Kaczynski's cabin as they awaited a warrant for his arrest. (Elaine Thompson/AP/Shutterstock)

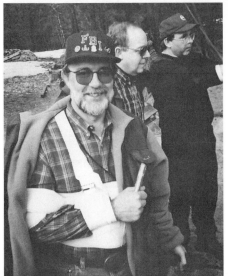

SSA Patrick Webb injured his arm as he and other law enforcement authorities attempted to prevent a television crew from filming Kaczynski's cabin on the eve of the Unabomber's arrest. (Florence Webb)

Kaczynski used a simple wood stove to keep warm in his cabin. Behind the stove are the floor-to-ceiling shelves where he kept provisions and bomb-making materials. (FBI)

Kaczynski built shelves adjacent to the cabin's door, along with a workbench where he fabricated some of his improvised explosive devices. (FBI)

During a search of the cabin, investigators found a package containing a live bomb under Kaczynski's bed. (FBI)

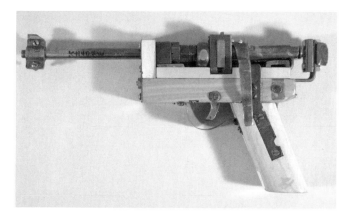

Law enforcement officials found this homemade pistol while searching Kaczynski's cabin. (FBI)

Kaczynski used this Smith Corona portable typewriter to type his manifesto and other documents. The FBI seized the machine during the search of his cabin. (FBI)

US Postal Inspector Paul Wilhelmus outside of the Unabomber's cabin after Kaczynski's arrest. (Paul Wilhelmus)

Booking photo of Kaczynski taken by authorities after his capture on April 3, 1996.

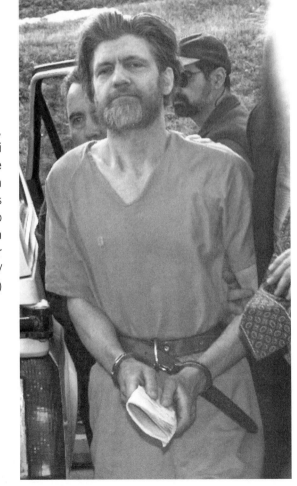

On Thursday, April 4, 1996, Ted Kaczynski was escorted into the federal courthouse in Helena, Montana. He was ultimately sentenced to eight terms of life in prison without possibility for parole. (Elaine Thompson/ AP/Shutterstock)

PART V

CHAPTER 17

A NEW DIRECTION

Jim Freeman's choice of Supervisory Special Agent Terry Turchie, a counterintelligence agent in the Silicon Valley resident agency, to head the UNABOM task force was met with surprise and skepticism by those in the FBI's Criminal Division. While there is no rule precluding an agent from the "intelligence side" of the bureau from working on the "criminal side," it was a barrier that was rarely, if ever, crossed.

The decision was one SAC Freeman did not make in haste; he was aware that intelligence officers are trained to take a long-term strategic view of an investigation, and he believed this was essential to solving UNABOM. He also knew Turchie was highly regarded throughout the San Francisco Division and the FBI at large.

In his early years in the bureau, Turchie had pursued timber thieves in the Oregon forests. By the 1980s, he was tracking Soviet spies at the United Nations in New York City. On one memorable occasion, depicted in *New York Magazine*, he and two colleagues wrestled Soviet spy Gennadiy Zakharov to the ground in a Brooklyn subway station. After a year at FBI headquarters in DC, Turchie took over a counterintelligence squad in San Francisco and was working out of the field office in Palo Alto when Jim Freeman tapped him for UNABOM.

Terry Turchie agreed to sit for a marathon, nine-hour-long interview in August 2018, during which he admitted he thought his supervisor was teasing when he contacted him out of the blue in March 1994 to suggest he take over the UNABOM task force.

"Thanks for considering me," Turchie replied. "I'm standing here looking out the window onto High Street, and I kind of like it here."

Turchie was happy in Palo Alto, and he was not interested in being reassigned to San Francisco. His home was just a few miles away from the office, and at lunchtime he looked forward to walking the couple of blocks to the center of town to grab a bite at one of the dozen or so eateries, where students and professors from nearby Stanford University tended to gather. And having an office overlooking the downtown area made him feel a bit like a king.

"Actually, the transfer isn't really a choice."

Turchie bit his lip and frowned. "You're joking, right?"

"Freeman needs you to come in and run the UNABOM task force. When can you get up here to San Francisco?"

"Well, I've got a few cases going on, so it will probably take me three or four weeks."

"How about this afternoon?"

As Turchie recalled, he felt himself turning pale. Upset, he phoned his wife, Joy, who had always been supportive of his career in the FBI and the inevitable transfers that came with the job. Joy had single-handedly cared for their kids when he was off on assignment. "I think I've been transferred to San Francisco," he told her.

"On what case?" she asked.

"UNABOM."

"What's that?" Joy listened as her husband provided an overview of the investigation.

"Why you? You don't know anything about bombs."

That was a good question, and one Turchie was unable to answer.

Turchie spent much of the thirty-five-mile drive north along US Highway 101 formulating an argument against the transfer. *How can they do this?* Relocating to another field office meant walking away from his cases and his colleagues.

He was a skilled professional with some deeply honed skills, but searching for some bomber who'd been in the wind for years certainly wasn't his specialty. It was hardly a secret that UNABOM was a dog of a case. He was pretty fired up by the time he marched into his supervisor's office that afternoon, but before he could raise a strong objection, Jim Freeman joined the meeting.

"Jim, you realize I haven't done criminal work in many, many years, since Portland," Turchie said. He was referring to his time chasing timber thieves in the Oregon forest, an investigation that turned into a federal corruption case. "That, and a bank robbery case."

"That's good enough," Freeman replied. "We'll expect you here tomorrow morning to meet your team."

Freeman's vision was to populate the task force with agents from both the Criminal and Intelligence sides of the bureau and draw on their unique and vastly different skills to track down the suspect. Before departing the meeting that afternoon, Turchie was told he had one week to present Freeman with a plan outlining how he was going to catch the Unabomber. This was Freeman's way of determining whether he had selected the right guy for the job.

Turchie was headed out of the building when he decided to pop in on the task force members unannounced and introduce himself.

"It was quite a motley crew," he recalled. "All they wanted to do was complain."

Turchie was savvy enough to recognize that coming in and immediately wielding power wasn't going to win over this group. Morale was low after so many months without a breakthrough, and pressure from headquarters to solve the case continued unabated. He informed the group that he would be spending the next week meeting with each of them privately, so he could get their feedback, thoughts, and suggestions. No one seemed particularly excited.

Turchie invited Agent Max Noel out to lunch with him, the first of many such invitations. The two men had radically different backgrounds. Max had worked criminal cases throughout his career and had plenty of experience in bombings. Turchie, of course, had none. Yet the two men had a great conversation.

"I will do everything I can to help you until I leave," Max told him.

Turchie was confused. "Leave?"

"Yes, I put in a transfer request. I've been here a year, and Clow promised I could go back to organized crime and back to my squad in Oakland so I won't have to commute into the city every day."

Turchie learned that Max was in striking distance of retiring, and he was set on spending his last days in Oakland.

"I will get you a copy of my transfer," Max said. "This has nothing to do with your arrival; I did it a couple of days before I knew you were coming, and I would appreciate it if you would support my transfer back to Oakland."

Terry fell silent. "I really need you to stay, and in all due respect, I can't support the transfer."

Max grew agitated. "I am not that easy to handle."

He continued, "I feel like I have done my time, but if you think I should stay, I am not going to fight that. But I am still going to put my request in and then you and Jim are going to have to decide."

Turchie knew that Noel was one of the most capable agents on the UNABOM task force, and he didn't want to lose him. "I want you to know for all the right reasons, I am not going to change my mind, and that is what I am going to tell Jim. I am going to tell him I won't sign the transfer."

Once back at the office, Terry went straight to Freeman's office. "Jim, Max wants off UNABOM. He can be a tremendous asset here. He works hard, he is dedicated. I told him I couldn't come in and tell you to sign his transfer." As Turchie spoke, he noticed Max's transfer memo on Freeman's desk.

"Okay, I won't sign it," Freeman said. He flashed a very brief smile, then turned his attention to the other papers on his desk.

In my sit-down with Turchie, the special agent grew animated as he recounted his lunch meetings with the various task force members. I had stopped at a bakery near my hotel to pick up a treat for us to share during the interview, and the mini pies there had caught my attention. I bought two of them and brought them along to my meeting. I had no idea at the time that Terry was a pie lover. As it turned out, he conducted many of his meetings at his favorite pie shop on Van Ness Avenue, not far from headquarters.

Turchie explained that, for the most part, his meetings with task force members proved fruitful. Most of the team already knew him and his work ethic. The majority just wanted off the case. They were pessimistic and secretly believed the Unabomber would likely never be caught. Still, they committed to working with Turchie to advance the investigation.

"A lot of them saw that when they got close to something that looked promising, the management guys would move in and take over, so there was some of that. And there was a lot of bickering between agencies too," Turchie recalled. "It just seemed like it was a desperation-type thing, nothing was going to work, everybody was just doing something so they didn't get stuck when the next bomb went off. They all felt that, 'Hey, we are going to be the ones who are going to get in trouble if there is another bombing, and we are doing the best we can.'"

It seemed inevitable that when a case goes on for so long, with no breakthroughs, it would be easy for investigators to lose interest no matter what the circumstances. "It's not so unique to see that happen," Turchie explained. "So, of course, we had to come up with an answer to that. We had to figure out how we could solve this thing."

At the end of the first week, Terry reported to Jim Freeman's office with the action plan he had created. He explained that after the June 1993 simultaneous bombings, the bureau established the task force in San Francisco and immediately embarked on a reinvestigation of all the events that had taken place since 1978.

"That's fine, but here's the problem," he said. "The real vulnerability, what I think kept that from being effective, is that the guys did all that reinvestigation from their desks. What we did is what the bureau always does: it sends out leads so agents who would review previous incidents would go through a file, they'd learn to become an expert on that particular bombing, but then they'd send leads to another field office to get the information to see what they might have missed.

"Sending leads out to other offices works for us in a lot of ways, but it is not working for us in this case; this case is just different."

"So what are you proposing?" Freeman asked.

"I propose that we reinvestigate these cases."

Freeman sat silent for a moment. "Reinvestigate them *again*?"

"Let me finish," Turchie said. "I think we should reinvestigate them again, but we need to let the guys go out to the field offices and be there, hands-on reinvestigating with their counterparts in these offices.

"Why do I say that? Because one of the things Max Noel told me was that he was the only agent George Clow allowed to go to other field offices to look at some of those previous events, and he has actually turned up some stuff. Plus, let's face it, it's more exciting to do that. You get on an airplane and you are vested in the case in a different way. If you are really enthusiastic, you can start showing the guys in the other field offices, 'Hey, I am really pumped up about this.'

"So our guys need approval from the bureau to be able to travel all over the country and further, if need be, to look at these leads."

Freeman nodded and smiled, although he didn't offer an immediate response.

Undeterred, Turchie forged ahead with his next point. "So we get all this information back. What do we need? Something we never had in Unabomber at all, even with the strategy the past year.

"In counterintelligence we always have an analytical angle to all we do. You collect all this information, but then you analyze it too. We have done UNABOM without any analytical component at all. We don't study things, we don't look at patterns, we don't find trends. So right now, UNABOM just looks like this scattershot of bombings from all over the country with no connection.

"Well, clearly, they don't have a normal connection, but there has to be something there tying them together. So instead of not having an analytical component, I think we need a major analytical component, meaning we need more people who are analysts."

"We don't have any terrorism people who are analysts," Freeman interrupted.

"Well then, I think we might want to train people from other places in the bureau, like in counterintelligence."

Convinced his ideas were worthy of implementation, Turchie launched into an explanation of the last part of his three-part strategy. He had made his case for reinvestigation, with the added caveat of permitting task force members to follow leads wherever they may take them. And his belief that analysis was also a necessary element to the investigation had not yet been shot down by Freeman. His third idea was for a running document titled "Known Facts, Fiction, and Theory About the Unabomber" to be regularly updated by task force members.

"The way I am looking at it," Turchie told Freeman, "the way we will manage this case is when we bring everybody together each week. The 'Known Facts, Fiction, and Theory' will change, and everybody working this case will always know what your 'Known Facts, Fiction, and Theories' are."

Turchie conceded that he didn't want to work leads based on "theory," but he was convinced that if task force members knew all the facts, when they started putting them together, one of the theories would emerge as worthy of follow-up.

The way Turchie saw it, Unabomber was kind of like taking a dozen jigsaw puzzles with thousands of pieces and going to somebody's house and dumping all the pieces on the floor and throwing away all the pictures. "We had thousands of pieces of crap, but we didn't even know what the ultimate picture looked like," he concluded.

CHAPTER 18

THREE-PART PLAN

The following Monday, the UNABOM task force had its first meeting with Turchie at the helm. The newly reconfigured team had thirty-one FBI, ATF, and Postal inspectors permanently assigned to it, as well as one Postal Inspection police officer, one person from the behavioral science unit, an Oakland police officer, one supervisory special agent from the headquarters laboratory, two secretaries, five intelligence analysts, two special clerks, and a computer specialist.

Turchie recalled being nervous that day, and a bit fearful of walking out in front of a group of trained—and professionally frustrated—agents to present his plan. He had to convince them to accept him as leader and to run with his strategy after so many others had proven unsuccessful. Turchie also knew that what happened next would set the tone for the days, weeks, and months ahead. He steeled himself and faced the team members who had gathered around a large oval conference table. All the agents' eyes were on him.

"I have talked to each one of you," he began, striking a casual tone and making eye contact with each of the men and women. "I have been staying late. I have been reading all the files. I think I have put together what I'd like to see us do. I am just going to throw it out there and see if it is at all viable, or if you guys hate it so bad I am going to have to come up with something a little better."

Turchie outlined his three-part strategy, which called for reinvestigating all the cases, using analysts to make sense of the investigative material they had gathered, and updating the known facts of the case on a regular basis. The men and women seemed okay with most of the plan, though Turchie drew a mix of sighs and grunts when he raised the idea of reinvestigating the fourteen bombings yet again. The negativity slowly dissipated when task force members learned they could take field trips to the various bombing sites and other locations deemed relevant to further their investigations.

The idea of bringing intelligence analysts onto the team pleased Agent Noel, who had long felt the profilers were not doing enough to flesh out their suspect. The concept of keeping a running list on the "Known Facts, Fiction, and Theory of the Unabomber" piqued the interest of some, but for the most part it seemed that those in attendance were adopting a wait-and-see attitude. Spirits were low and positive results were needed to boost morale.

Turchie wasted no time implementing his strategy. He explained that in addition to reinvestigating cases and keeping track of the facts, fiction, and theories, he was also going to implement a buddy system: "We are going to restructure the way we relate to each other. From now on, instead of going out and just working as an individual, I want everybody here to pick a partner. You are going to be a team with that one person. We are going to have a lot of ups and downs and there are going to be some really severe bounces in UNABOM as we go forward from here, and what I need to be sure of is that each of you is pumping up the other when we have those bad times."

Turchie had picked up this investigative idea while at the bureau in New York. "You can bring double the creativity, double the brain power, double everything, but more important than all that, I found very seldom when you are working together that you both get depressed at the same time. There is something about working together when a little lever goes off, and even if you are hogging all the depressive moments, some-body is going to switch the lever and act to balance it, and it does work."

"It doesn't matter if it is someone from the FBI, ATF, or Postal, I don't care," Turchie told task force members. "Just get with somebody and that is who you work with for the duration of UNABOM."

Postal Inspector Paul Wilhelmus picked John Conway, the longtime UNABOM case agent, who for years had worked alone on the investi-gation under SSA Webb's supervision. Although UNABOM had once been Conway's case to solve, he was just fine with having all these people brought into the investigation.

Conway had become close with the Epsteins—the family of Charles Epstein, the geneticist who had almost been killed by the package bomb sent to his home in Tiburon. In one of the first interactions Conway had with Turchie, he took Turchie to meet the Epsteins to introduce them to the new guy running the case. Terry recalled that they had a lot of faith and trust in the FBI because the agency had committed the resources and the background to move the investigation forward.

Postal Inspector Tony Mulijat and his partner proved to be another productive two-man team. Tony wanted to stay on with the task force for a second year, but he was up for mandatory retirement from the Postal Inspection Service. Members of the task force all liked Mulijat, and nobody wanted to see him leave. They recognized his rough-and-ready demeanor contrasted sharply with that of his Postal colleague Paul Wilhelmus, who approached his work with a methodical but soft touch. Mulijat, on the other hand, was a bull-in-a-china-shop kind of guy. He could be heavy-handed when it came to following leads, but his dedica-tion to the task force was unwavering, and everyone wanted him to stay, prompting Jim Freeman, Terry Turchie, and even FBI director Louie Freeh to advocate on his behalf.

Their efforts won Mulijat another year on UNABOM, and he quickly got to work on what would turn out to be a very fruitful project focus-ing on the Unabomber's attack on Dr. James McConnell, the psychology professor at the University of Michigan in Ann Arbor. McConnell's package, the tenth UNABOM device, had been sent to his home, where his research assistant, Nick Suino, had attempted to open it, suffering severe burns and lacerations from the ensuing explosion.

Mulijat was convinced that there were important clues to be found in the typewritten letter that had accompanied the McConnell device. It had been signed by someone named Ralph Kloppenburg, who was supposedly a PhD candidate at the University of Utah specializing in the "history of science." Kloppenburg, according to the letter, wanted Dr. McConnell to review his thesis. Mulijat was convinced there was something to this "history of science" angle, and he wanted to explore it further.

In reading up on Professor McConnell, he learned that he was known for his research on learning and memory transfer in planaria or flatworms, which he had conducted in the 1950s and 1960s. His research had led him to something called memory RNA, which he proposed in the 1960s as a way of explaining long-term memories stored in the brain. His theory was initially discounted by scientists in the field, but later revisited and again debated. One of his experiments had involved training flatworms to unscramble an extremely simple maze. Once they had mastered the maze, he ground them up and fed them to a second group of untrained planaria, to observe if they would be able to learn the maze more quickly based on the transfer of knowledge by ingestion.

McConnell claimed the experiment had shown such an effect, but his findings were later discounted for various reasons. However, future experiments seemed to prove his hypothesis. In spite of its controversy, McConnell's concept gained popularity in science fiction circles, with the idea of "mind transfer" appearing in short stories and TV episodes at the time.

Mulijat noted Professor McConnell was one of the men in the field whose work made people think. "Could somebody have become inflamed enough by his experiments to make him become the Unabomber?" he asked.

Mulijat and the team decided to do a deep dive into the "history of science," basically the study of science and scientific knowledge and what it generally meant to people, including both the natural and social sciences. Their first stop was UC Berkeley where, according to Turchie, the universe's supposed expert on the "history of science," Charles J. Susskind, was employed. Susskind was a professor emeritus of electrical engineering and cofounder of bioengineering studies at Berkeley.

"He was the nicest man," Turchie recalled of the balding scientist with the handlebar mustache. Through their meetings with Susskind, task force members learned that the history of science was not a big discipline, and that only a few major universities had the program—basically Harvard, Yale, Northwestern, the University of Utah, and Berkeley.

Mulijat's ears pricked up when he heard the names of three of the Unabomber's targets among the list of colleges. Clearly he was on to something, and his team members agreed.

"It was unbelievable," Turchie recounted. "All of these are places where we have bombs, and all these universities were biggies in the history of science. We felt we were on the right track."

Mulijat next learned that the history of science would be up for discussion at the upcoming 4S meeting for the Society of Social Studies of Science, an international, nonprofit association founded in 1975 that fosters interdisciplinary and engaged scholarship in social studies of science, technology, and medicine. The society's upcoming convention was slated for the fall of 1994 in New Orleans, and Mulijat wanted to attend. "All the experts are going to be there in one place," he told Turchie. "Can we get authority to go down and do a UNABOM history of science presentation at this convention?"

With his boss's okay, Mulijat got ahold of the guy putting the conference together. "I don't want to force my way in," he told him. "But we would like to come down. We would like to give a presentation on the Unabomber."

Mulijat's request was met with excitement. "You would like to come to our convention?" the organizer posed. "Oh my gosh, we are going to help solve a crime. The FBI is coming to New Orleans to give a presentation!"

Arrangements were made, and several members of the task force traveled to Louisiana to address the group. Mulijat was convinced that networking with the members could help get the word circulating on college campuses where the history of science was taught, and perhaps jar memories that might lead them to the Unabomber. While in New Orleans, Mulijat decided to show the Unabomber's early writings to one professor. He was curious to see if his allusions to certain works or his choice of words might spark something.

To the postal inspector's delight, the professor recognized some of the phrasing. "I get the feeling this guy is a disciple of Jacques Ellul and his book *The Technological Society*," he told Mulijat. The revelation was added to the task force's running list of known facts, fiction, and theory.

———

Turchie was determined to develop a full understanding of all the elements of the investigation—including the all-important computerized database that held promise for advancing the agents' work and potentially providing the team with some lead that would allow them to finally get closer to their elusive suspect.

He had been informed about the new computer system the bureau had acquired, and during his first weeks in the office, he made a point of introducing himself to Casey Henderson, the man in charge of getting the data scanned in and the database up and running. Casey Henderson was an independent contractor the FBI had hired to build the database in the Sun SPARC computer. Henderson and his wife and young daughter lived in Washington, DC; he'd opted to move to San Francisco on a temporary basis to do the job for the FBI. Henderson regularly flew into and out of San Francisco International Airport, returning home to visit his wife and daughter.

Task force members had been bringing all this information into the division from all these years of investigation and had been told that as they fed all the material into the massive parallel processor, or MPP, they were going to have an answer. The cutting-edge computer was going to analyze all the data, find the commonalities, and throw out the name of the Unabomber—or at least that was the theory. Just about everyone in the San Francisco office figured the likelihood of that happening was on par with the building getting hit by a meteor.

For the past seven months, Henderson had been working brutally long hours—routinely working until late in the evening and sometimes through the night. He'd limit himself to fifteen-minute breaks when he couldn't continue.

"He worked in that office for a solid year on this data," Turchie told me. "His whole deal was to make the computer network work." In addition to all the case files, Henderson was also inputting videotaped footage into the MPP. For instance, the postal service had issued a number of subpoenas over the years to universities such as Northwestern where bombings had occurred and where CCTV was operational. Postal and other agencies had those tapes in their UNABOM files, and Henderson was charged with inputting them into the Sun SPARC system. If all went according to plan, the system was expected to be up and searchable by June, less than two months away.

Turchie had taken that June completion date into account when drawing up his own strategic plan for the UNABOM investigation. He figured that by that point, the team would be proactively identifying suspects—and Henderson would put his massive machine to work.

"We were going to start giving him specific kinds of computer runs to do," Turchie said. "The database would allow us to better track individuals, pull together facts from diverse sources, and ultimately allow us to hone our searches."

But as so often happens in life—and in investigations—things didn't go quite as planned. About two or three months after Turchie arrived in San Francisco, Henderson walked into his office to deliver some bad news.

"There is no good way to put this," Henderson blurted out. "I have been working on this for the better part of the past seven or eight months

163

before the inspectors left, and here is the bottom line: all of these data-bases and all of these computer files that we have collected from '78, '79, '82, '85, most of them, the data is corrupted."

Terry laughed recounting the conversation. "I was a computer idiot. All I knew how to do was to conceive of what I wanted from computers, so I said, 'Casey, tell me what all this means.'"

"We have to start over," Henderson said glumly. "I have to go through each of those tapes, and I have to make it incorruptible."

"Can you do that?" Turchie asked.

"I can either do that, or I can tell you we can't use that one, and you will have to make a judgment as to whether or not you want the data entered."

The glitch with the corrupted data set the timetable back significantly. Everyone had thought they would have the database ready by late spring 1994. Now it was looking like early summer 1995. Yet another delay.

CHAPTER 19

REFOCUSING THE INQUIRY

Turchie learned of two fundamental issues that task force members were confronting during his initial round of interviews. Members said they were dissatisfied with the profiling unit's work on the case. They wanted a profiler who was cognizant of the latest information coming in and willing and able to revise the profile of their unknown suspect accordingly. Agents complained, too, that their work with the FBI lab in Quantico had become a constraint. The agents had been working with countless bomb fragments, all of which were being sent to the FBI lab for analysis. But the agents were barred from doing anything more with those key pieces of evidence. They wanted to be able to talk with manufacturers and industry experts too—and not worry about being fired if they did so. In a way, the FBI lab was "running" the UNABOM investigation; the agents wanted the task force to be in control and have the lab available as a resource.

Bill Tafoya and Mary Ellen O'Toole had been involved in their victimology project for more than nine months when Turchie came on board, so he was interested to hear their assessment. Not long after he arrived in San Francisco, he invited them to join him at his favorite pie shop on

Van Ness for a debriefing. The three discussed the findings over coffee and warm apple pie.

"Tell me about profiling," Turchie asked his tablemates.

"Terry, we have already told you all you need to know," Tafoya replied. He was talking about the profile the behavioral unit at Quantico had put together on the Unabomber early in the investigation—that of a male in his thirties or forties who'd attended but not finished college or trade school and who was likely connected to the airline industry. The only change that had been made to the profile had come after the Unabomber sighting in 1987. The eyewitness had said the man she saw was likely in his twenties or early thirties, prompting authorities to revise the profile and start hunting for a somewhat younger man.

"What does that mean?" Turchie probed.

Tafoya jumped in to respond. "Well, people don't change, and profiles don't change, so what our unit said and what we agreed with in 1978, 1979, 1985, and we even did one when the inspectors came here . . . a profile is a profile. Nothing's changed."

Turchie felt himself growing frustrated. "The problem with that is that we haven't gotten any closer to arresting the Unabomber," he said. "There has got to be more to profiling."

To which Tafoya responded, "Well, you just don't understand profiling."

Turchie decided to push the conversation further. He pointed to the 1980 device that had been sent to the Lake Forest home of American Airlines president Percy Wood. "A week or two before that bomb arrived, Wood got a letter from a guy who identified himself as Enoch Fisher, who said he was writing to alert Wood to a book that would be arriving in the mail in the coming days." In reviewing the UNABOM files, Turchie learned the name of the supposed book, *Ice Brothers* by Sloan Wilson, and its premise. "It was about these guys who worked on the crew of a coast guard vessel in the Northern Atlantic off the coast of Greenland during World War II." In the letter, the bomber referred to the book as being for men like Wood "who make decisions of great social significance."

Turchie highlighted that this device, which had been disguised as a book, arrived six or seven months after the bomb in the cargo area of the American Airlines flight out of Chicago. "Anyone would figure there is a connection here, so for a long time, the FBI and the other federal agencies investigating the bombings worked the airline connection. We had more and more information that started building. That, 'Uh-oh, this is definitely connected to an airline employee,' and there was a lot of fact to back that up. So we need to know—how do that letter and Enoch Fisher and Sloan Wilson and the *Ice Brothers* all factor in with the profile?"

Tafoya reiterated, "The profile is the profile."

"We just have to have more than that," Turchie insisted. "I need you to give me an assessment of this book, *Ice Brothers*."

"Well, that is not what we do," Tafoya replied.

Turchie was dumbfounded. He was aware of the effort Tafoya and O'Toole had been making as part of the victimology group. It was a massive undertaking that included the creation of an exhaustive survey that Tafoya had created for the victims to fill out. The idea was to find any potential links between them, whether it was that they had bought a car from the same dealership, traveled to the same city, stayed at the same hotel. Once completed, the answers were to be fed into a computer that would then find the commonalities and provide investigators with new lines of inquiry. Tafoya had also brought all the victims to San Francisco, where they were interviewed individually. Those responses were also going to be entered into the computer system.

"Well, where is that survey?" Turchie inquired. "You must have spent quite a bit of money bringing all these people out here. When will it be ready?"

Tafoya brushed the question aside and instead made a startling declaration. "Terry, we already know who the Unabomber is."

"Oh, who is the Unabomber?"

"Buckley Crist," Tafoya replied. "Crist is probably the Unabomber."

Crist was the professor at Northwestern University whose name had appeared on the return address of the package containing the first bomb left in a parking lot at the University of Illinois Chicago Circle campus.

Turchie was incredulous. "What are you telling me?"

Tafoya believed that Crist had deliberately listed himself as the sender of the package and left it on the ground next to a mailbox instead of posting it. He figured it would be found with ten dollars in uncancelled stamps and end up "returned to sender," which would take the heat off him and make him a victim in the eyes of authorities.

"I agree with Tafoya," O'Toole chimed in. "We feel pretty positive that Crist is the Unabomber."

O'Toole had begun her career as a criminal investigator in the San Francisco district attorney's office before joining the FBI in 1987. Since then, she'd become a highly respected field representative for the Profiling Unit at Quantico and was the only SA in the field considered likely to become a profiler following her training with the famed Behavioral Analysis Unit (BAU). It was during her time with the BAU that she developed an expertise in criminal investigative analysis as well as offender behavior. O'Toole pointed out that Crist's particulars fit the profile—he was the right age and had the right educational credentials. She claimed he had provided some questionable answers during his in-person interview.

"He came out here willingly," Turchie reminded them.

"Yes, but his wife was very ill at the time and in the hospital, and he *still* came."

"That is probably because he was trying to please us; he wanted to help," Turchie suggested.

Tafoya pushed back. "But he wanted to be here too badly. We want you to approve us opening a suspect case on him."

Turchie could barely disguise his horror. "I have not seen anything that convinces me to open up a suspect case on him. You are going to have to tell me a lot more before I do that."

Turchie explained that the task force was very cautious about who it identified as a potential target. UNABOM was a massive case, and the bureau needed to be pretty certain before it would support opening an official investigation into someone.

"Give me a timeline on Crist," Turchie asked the duo. "Evidently you have been doing some work on him, so let me see if he even gets past square one."

Several weeks later, O'Toole provided Turchie with a timeline of Buckley Crist's whereabouts during the times of the various bombing attacks. On paper, the case against Crist simply didn't make sense, because he had multiple alibies and his movements didn't track with those of the suspected bomber. But O'Toole insisted it was still possible for him to have done the bombings under a series of circumstances that made sense only to her.

In light of her findings, Turchie declined to open an official case on Crist, saying he did not see any reasonable grounds to do so. His refusal created a split between the three, with Turchie deciding he could no longer work with them.

That October he called a meeting with SAC Freeman. "We need our own profiler," he told him.

Freeman looked up from his desk. "The bureau will have a fit if we tell them we are going to replace the profiler," he replied, pausing to allow to Turchie to absorb the magnitude of his request. "Do you have any ideas?"

Terry suggested his old friend and colleague Kathleen "Kathy" Puckett, an FBI special agent who had worked with him on Squad 12, the Bay Area counterintelligence squad he led. Turchie had already recruited another counterintelligence agent from Squad 12, Joel Moss, to UNABOM, so bringing Kathy onboard would be a reunion of sorts. The three spent so much time together, Turchie's wife had affectionately dubbed them "the three musketeers." Turchie recalled that back then, Kathy had expressed an interest in psychology, and after he took over Squad 12, she decided she wanted to go back to school and earn a degree in clinical psychology. He told Freeman that based on the work she had done while on his squad, her skills were unmatched.

"Kathy hasn't been trained to be a bureau profiler, but she makes the bureau profilers look like Mickey Mouse," he boasted. "And she will give you her last mile."

"If she likes the case," Freeman replied. "But I've heard if she doesn't like it . . ."

Turchie cut him off. "She will be there all the time until the end."

"Let me get this straight. You want me to assign a nonprofiling agent to UNABOM to be the profiler and to offend the bureau and the profiling unit at the same time."

Turchie grinned. "Well, I wouldn't put it that way, but I guess that is the effect of it."

"It will probably be interesting," Freeman replied. "Okay, go find Kathy and see if she's interested."

———

When I contacted Puckett to ask for an interview in summer 2018, she was preparing to present expert testimony at a trial in Los Angeles. We arranged to meet in Northern California the following week.

I was pleased when she agreed to sit down with me. We set a tentative date for early August, when her trial was expected to end. In a crazy twist of fate, the area where she lived was engulfed by a wildfire and authorities were ordering evacuations. Thankfully, she didn't cancel our meeting; instead, she suggested an alternative. She agreed to travel three hours to the coast with her two dogs in tow to meet at a seaside hotel, providing her and her pets some much-needed relief from the smoke and me with immeasurable insight into her work on the case. Between 1988 and 1994, she'd been a principal in "Project Slammer," an interagency espionage study that involved extensive interviews with individuals convicted of espionage. She was just completing the study when Turchie tapped her for the UNBOM investigation.

As we sat staring out at the Pacific through the hotel room window, Puckett recalled with humor the day Turchie ambushed her outside the federal building on Golden Gate Avenue as she walked in the rain to her favorite neighborhood restaurant. After getting the go-ahead from Jim Freeman to bring her onto the task force, he'd immediately raced down the hall to her office, eager to give her the news.

"Where's Kathy?" he shouted when he didn't see her behind the desk.

"She's gone to lunch," the secretary replied.

Turchie did an abrupt about-face and headed down the hallway toward the elevator. He arrived in time to glimpse her shoulder-length blonde hair and black raincoat before the doors closed. Rather than waiting for the next elevator, Turchie bolted for the stairwell and ran down twelve flights of stairs, hoping to catch her in the lobby. He was out of breath when he finally caught up outside on the sidewalk and invited himself to lunch.

"Where are we going?" he asked.

"The vegetarian place."

He'd forgotten that Kathy was a vegetarian; he'd just doomed himself to a salad.

Over bites of lettuce he told her, "I need you to come to UNABOM."

She was intrigued, and by the end of the meal, he had convinced her to join the team.

"What's my first assignment?" she asked.

"I want you to read a book, *Ice Brothers* by Sloan Wilson."

———

With the new iteration of the UNABOM task force in place, ASAC Terry Turchie also began aggressively pushing for more local control when it came to following investigative leads based on evidence that had been collected at the various bombing crime scenes. Agents Joel Moss and Max Noel had been promoted to supervisory positions and called upon to lead two of the three squads that made up this new iteration of the task force. Moss was put in charge of the suspect evaluation squad; Noel was now leader of the bomb incident/special projects squad; and Penny Harper, who had also been a counterintelligence agent for most of her career, was tapped to head up the administrative squad, which handled the UNABOM hotline, subpoenas, recruiting new people, management of all temporary duty personnel, space management and logistics, and other analytical and administrative needs.

In his meetings with Agent Max Noel, Turchie had learned of Noel's dissatisfaction with the results the task force had been getting from the FBI lab in DC.

Noel's issue with the lab was complicated. Its technicians had examined the forensic evidence from all fifteen UNABOM devices, as is typical in bombing cases. With bombings, forensics is usually what solves the case, so over the many, many years the investigation had dragged on, it was understandable that the FBI lab had become the almost de facto case agent in the bombings.

When it came to bombing cases, the FBI lab would receive all the forensic evidence, and then agents would go back out to the field to look for other relevant clues based on the lab's findings. In most cases, they would already have an idea of who they were looking for—either from a fingerprint or some other forensic evidence—and pretty soon they would have a name.

But that hadn't been the case with UNABOM. Because the suspect fabricated all his devices with discarded and random pieces of wood, metal, wire, and other objects, there weren't any connections the lab examiners could make as they examined fragments from the various exploded bombs. It's not that the FBI lab technicians were somehow missing something. The technicians couldn't find anything because there was nothing there to be found. The UNABOMER had found a way to successfully obscure his bomb-making trail.

Turchie wanted permission to do something the agency hadn't done in the past. He wanted to let the FBI bomb techs do their work and prepare their reports. But he wanted to go a step further and reach out to outside experts. Turchie and his team had a gut feeling that there were people outside of the lab in Quantico who could potentially help them break the case.

Turchie put it this way in my meeting with him: "If we have aluminum, we ought to go to the foremost experts in aluminum in the country and have them look at it and tell us what they think. If we have green paneling nails, then we need to find the foremost expert on green paneling nails. If we have chrome, or a piece of evidence that looks like chrome from a car, we ought to go there, and if we have fragments of wood, then we ought to go to the experts in that particular kind of wood. If we need to go to the National Weapons Labs, then we should go there."

Jim Freeman agreed to lobby FBI director Louie Freeh for the approval Turchie needed. The men were cautiously optimistic that Freeh would approve the unusual request. Freeh was new to the bureau and eager to move the investigation forward. Hopefully, that would make him open to trying a new investigative technique. Ultimately the team was given a green light, and task force members hit the ground running.

CHAPTER 20

LINES OF INQUIRY

With Terry Turchie at the helm, Task Force members were now working on some fifty different projects—essentially fifty different lines of inquiry. They all stemmed from the information gleaned from revisiting the old case files.

There was a project focused just on the nails that had been recovered from the various crime scenes, with investigators reaching out to manufacturers and trying to find any clue that might lead them somewhere. Teams were also looking at wood, paint, and tape—all elements of the Unabomber's improvised explosive devices.

Task force members were dispatched to the offices of the *New York Times* in Manhattan to learn if anybody in the building had handled the letter and if possibly one of them had written "Nathan R." Investigators also committed to interviewing anyone with the name "Nathan R" in the Chicago, Salt Lake City, Sacramento, and San Francisco areas. The team identified 8,589 candidates, and investigators interviewed 3,363 of them, including one "Nathan R" who had a talk show in Salt Lake City.

In the end, a tremendous amount of work went into the "Nathan R" project, but ultimately, it turned out to be nothing more than a red herring. That became another of literally thousands of dead ends pursued by investigators.

Over the years, task force members had compiled public source documents from every place they knew the Unabomber had ever been. This information had been loaded onto a mainframe computer at FBI headquarters in Washington, DC. At that time, the bureau did not use computers, so all those records—over eighty-five million names drawn from drivers' licenses from Illinois; students at the University of California, Berkeley; the University of Utah; Brigham Young University; University of Illinois, Chicago Circle Campus; Northwestern University; Vanderbilt—all of them were manually entered into the database in the appropriate timeframes. There were also names of all of the contractors and subcontractors working on those campuses at those times, their employees, and on and on. The problem was, the mainframe computer was unsearchable, so all this data had to be entered into the new Sun SPARC computer system that contractor Casey Henderson was working to get up and running with the goal of creating a database that would be searchable.

Other suspects included people linked to the Weather Underground and other anarchist groups with ties to the Bay Area. The bomber's last twelve devices had originated on the West Coast, and investigators suspected he was operating somewhere in the vicinity. People with ties to these groups and any other person or persons who fit the criteria remained suspects until they could be ruled out. That meant determining where they were on certain dates when the attacks had occurred; if they had an alibi, they were crossed off the list. If not, the team would keep them in their sights until they uncovered something that would eliminate them.

At one point, Wilhelmus and Conway were dispatched to re-interview the American Airlines pilot who had been forced to make an emergency landing when a bomb went off in the cargo hold of his 727, just as he'd reached cruising altitude. There was something weird about the incident that bothered investigators. They'd learned that the pilot had failed to promptly deploy the evacuation chutes, even though there was a cutting-edge computer readout in the cockpit that alerted him. Why hadn't the pilot taken prompt action? Wilhelmus and Conway learned it was because he felt it wasn't necessary, as deploying the chutes often led to countless injuries among the deplaning passengers.

With all the new information coming in, the team needed a way to assimilate it. Monthly meetings became mandatory for case agents and even some assistant district attorneys in field offices across the country involved in the UNABOM investigation. That meant those from Salt Lake City to Sacramento to Newark needed to attend.

The meetings were held in the conference room on the thirteenth floor of San Francisco's federal building on Golden Gate Avenue and typically spanned two full days. Each event would begin with presentations from different experts discussing any new developments with relation to the bomber's sixteen devices. The afternoon included remarks and updates from Kathy Puckett, followed by the forensics folks, members of the projects squad, and so on.

Now that Kathy Puckett was on board, the victimology project was discontinued and O'Toole and Tafoya were reassigned. Before she transferred permanently to Quantico, O'Toole was put on the crimes against children squad to better use her talents there, and Tafoya chose to retire from the bureau.

There were now mandatory weekly meetings just for members of the UNABOM task force, as well as smaller group meetings with the individual squads to thread everything together and keep everyone informed. It was at one of these meetings that team members stumbled on a breakthrough—one that came from a simple question.

During the weekly meetings, Terry liked to stand at the whiteboard at the front of the room, marker in hand, and jot down ideas, leads, and other relevant information. Puckett was among those who were attending the meeting.

"Today we are going to talk about the first event," he announced, drawing complaints from nearly everyone at the conference table.

"Come on, Terry, we've talked about the first event a thousand times," one agent yelled out.

"We are going to talk about it again," Turchie retorted. "But we will combine it with the second event, and maybe we will figure something out." He motioned for Agent Conway to take the floor. John was now the longest-serving member of the UNABOM investigation, and he and Postal Inspector Paul Wilhelmus had been assigned to reinvestigate the first several attacks.

Supervisory Special Agent Joel Moss liked to keep track of what was being said, so he jotted down notes as Conway launched into his remarks. Conway's recitation of the facts included nothing new. Still, Moss furiously recorded his words. Conway was heading back to his seat when Moss momentarily put down his pen and asked, "I have one question. Why did the bomber choose to spend ten dollars on stamps and then not mail the package? Do we know if the bomb might have been too big for the mailbox?"

"The bomber might have made a mistake," Puckett chimed in. She was a new face at the table and people were just getting used to her. "From a behavioral standpoint, if you can figure out where the serial criminal makes his mistakes, that is probably the early days of his embarking on a criminal career, so if you can take yourself back to the very first crime and be sure of it in the very first moments, you might find things that you never thought you'd find, because maybe there would be more mistakes."

"Well, let's try and figure it out," Turchie said. "What can we do to see if maybe the bomb was too big for the mailbox?"

Wilhelmus raised an idea: "From the data we have from that first event, John and I can build a model, a mock-up of the bomb, and then call back to the post office archives to confirm that mailboxes are still the same size as they were back in the seventies."

"That is where the Unabomber definitely tried to do his first device," Kathy proclaimed. "He made a mistake. That was his first bomb."

That afternoon Inspector Wilhelmus headed for home, more specifically his garage, where he excitedly began constructing a mock-up of the first package based on the specs provided by the lab examiners. The bomb was a very crude device, constructed of a three-quarter-inch galvanized pipe measuring approximately nine inches in length.

The charge used by the Unabomber consisted of two types of smokeless gunpowder and matchheads. An anti-opening mechanism utilizing rubber bands and a nail served as an improvised firing pin to help trigger the device, which was hidden inside a box carved from a wood block. The box had a wooden lid, too, and looked much like the ones that people use to keep personal mementos. The box was long and narrow, measuring three by three by twenty inches, and had been sanded, polished, and stained with great care. The bomber had wrapped his package in three and a half layers of brown craft paper and affixed ten one-dollar Eugene O'Neill US postage stamps to the top. The white gummed mailing label stuck to the front was hand-addressed in blue ballpoint ink to Professor E. J. Smith at the Rensselaer Polytechnic Institute's School of Engineering in Troy, New York. A second gummed mailing label in the upper left-hand corner had Buckley Crist's Northwestern University address.

When the mock-up was complete, Conway and Wilhelmus headed to the airport to board a flight to Chicago. Their first stop was a parking lot for the engineering building at the Chicago Circle Campus. To their dismay, there was no longer a collection box there. In response to the Unabomber's sustained campaign, it and others around the country had been removed. Undeterred, the two went to the main post office just three blocks from campus, where they reviewed postal records and identified not only the mailbox that had been in the vicinity of the Chicago Circle Campus but also the exact model. They were able to find a warehouse containing all the old mailboxes, some dating back to the early days of the postal service. Among them was a mailbox identical to the one that had been on the corner of the university's parking lot in 1978.

Conway and Wilhelmus unsuccessfully tried to slide their mock-up into the box through the snorkel catch. The package went in a bit but then got stuck; they couldn't push it through. Moss's supposition had been accurate. At nearly twelve inches long, the mock-up was simply too big to go into the box.

That afternoon Paul phoned San Francisco. "Terry," he exclaimed into the receiver. "It won't fit! It didn't fit!"

Turchie excitedly shared the news with the other task force members. "But what does it mean?" he asked.

"Well, maybe it means that this is where the Unabomber is from, because we have four bombs with a nexus to Chicago, Illinois," Turchie theorized.

Moss's question had unlocked an important new clue in the case—not just about the size of the bomb but about the Unabomber's behavior and location at the time. More importantly, it was a breakthrough—and the task force members had been desperate to get a break. This was the first one they had had since linking the writings about the history of science to the universities that had been targeted—Northwestern, Berkeley, and the University of Utah. To be sure, the task force was still a long, long way from solving the case. But at last the agents were starting to see some small, incremental movements forward, and that was good for morale and a hopeful indicator that they were slowly but surely getting closer to their unknown suspect.

Eight months into Turchie's tenure, the unthinkable happened—the Unabomber struck again, this time in North Caldwell, New Jersey. It was Saturday, December 10, 1994, just fifteen days before Christmas, and Turchie had been out picking up his son from a friend's house after a sleepover. The two were just walking in the front door when the phone started ringing. An agent from headquarters in San Francisco was on the line, patching through a call from Special Agent in Charge Barry Mawn at the FBI's office in Newark.

Turchie and Mawn had worked together in the past. They'd met when Mawn was the assistant special agent in charge of the criminal division in the San Francisco office where they had worked on several investigations together.

"Terry, there's been a bombing inside a house here in North Caldwell," Mawn said. Turchie tensed up and grabbed a pen and paper to take notes.

Thomas Mosser, an advertising executive who worked in Manhattan, was killed when he opened a small, white cardboard box containing a pipe bomb that had been sent to his house, Mawn said. Mosser had been away on a business trip when the package had arrived at his house, and the family had put it aside for him to open when he got back. When Mosser began opening the box, the device exploded, sending shrapnel everywhere.

Based on an initial look at the crime scene and other information, agents determined that the package had most likely come from the San Francisco Bay area. A piece of debris from the remnants of an envelope found on the floor of the kitchen seemed to indicate the return address was for a company in the bay area called Closet Dimensions. Mawn told Turchie the FBI was already working with local police at the scene. "How do you think we should we proceed?" he asked.

"Based on what we know to this point, the bureau should treat this as a suspected UNABOM attack, and we should assume responsibility for the investigation until we prove otherwise."

Mawn concurred and agreed to handle the jurisdictional issue with local police. Meanwhile, Turchie reached out to Thomas Mohnal, an explosives expert at the FBI lab in DC, and instructed him to get on the next plane to Newark so he could process the scene. Then he called headquarters in San Francisco; he wanted to locate his supervisor, Jim Freeman, and advise him of the latest development. He found Freeman on the eighth hole of the golf course and quickly apprised him of the situation, with the two keeping in close touch throughout the afternoon.

Just three hours after Turchie had reached out to Mohnal, he learned that the explosives expert was on the scene in North Caldwell. It took Mohnal less than twenty minutes to make his assessment.

"Terry, this is a UNABOM event," Mohnal confirmed in a phone call from the scene. "I went in and almost immediately saw remnants of hickory wood fragments." The FBI had previously determined that their suspect had a habit of hand-carving wooden switches used in the improvised explosive devices. The presence of the hickory wood meant that it was highly likely that this was another UNABOM incident.

Turchie spent the next several hours working the phones, coordinating with his office, keeping SAC Jim Freeman advised, and relaying bits and pieces of information to others. By late afternoon, he and Freeman were at the headquarters in San Francisco, where they remained late into the evening.

Back east, the investigation was accelerating, and agents worked throughout the night at Mosser's house. Mosser had been standing in the kitchen when he opened the package. His wife, Susan, their two young daughters, and a teenage neighbor were also in the house at the time of the explosion, but only Mosser was injured. When police arrived, they found Susan Mosser at her husband's side, trying to comfort him as he lay mortally wounded on the kitchen floor. In addition to the two daughters at home, Mosser had a son and a daughter from a previous marriage, neither of whom was at the residence at the time of the incident.

The investigation unfolding on both coasts rolled into Sunday. In New Jersey, agents continued to process the crime scene and to interview witnesses. Investigators were eager to learn whether Mr. Mosser's work as an ad executive, first with Burson-Marsteller and more recently as general manager of Marsteller's parent company, Young & Rubicam, one of the largest public relations and advertising companies in the world, might be why the Unabomber had targeted him. One of Mosser's areas of expertise at Burson-Marstellar had been crisis communications. Perhaps his work in this area had shone a spotlight on him?

Back in San Francisco, Turchie and Freeman continued coordinating their efforts from headquarters. Investigators had learned of a phone call that Mosser received in the hours before the attack from the Monterey, California, area, and agents were assigned to follow up. Task force members were able to trace the number to Callaway Golf, a golf club manufacturer in Carlsbad. Thomas Mosser was an avid golfer, and someone at the company had simply been getting back to him about the purchase of some new clubs.

FBI Agent Don Davis and US Postal Inspector Paul Wilhelmus, both members of the UTF, were tasked with tracking down the address in San Francisco that had been listed on the envelope and determining where in the Bay Area the Unabomber had mailed his bomb. They quickly determined that the package had been processed at the US mail facility south of the San Francisco Airport, where they found witnesses and gathered physical evidence.

On Sunday afternoon, Turchie and Freeman sent two agents from the UNABOM Task Force to New Jersey to meet up with the investigators from the FBI's Newark office at the scene. Together they began building the framework that the task force would use to complete the North Caldwell bombing investigation and then integrate the findings into the broader effort.

Investigators learned that the cardboard box sent to Thomas Mosser concealed a homemade wooden box with the Unabomber's explosive device hidden inside. The aluminum pipe had been secured at both ends by metal and fastened with metal-locking pins and a steel collar.

Mosser's death marked the Unabomber's second fatality. He had now claimed two lives and injured twenty-three others. Inside the FBI's San Francisco office, morale was in the toilet. Another bombing had occurred that the team had been unable to stop. In spite of all the manpower dedicated to the investigation, the Unabomber was still out there and operating with impunity. Sensing the team's despair, FBI Director Louie Freeh arranged to travel to San Francisco to address the task force members directly.

FBI agents are trained to set their personal feelings aside and concentrate on the work at hand. Still, Turchie struggled to get over Mosser's death; it happened on his watch, and he felt personally responsible for what had happened—even though it wasn't his fault. "I got sick in the shower one morning," Turchie admitted. "Mr. Mosser had been murdered. It was too much. That is why Director Freeh's trip out here was so important."

Upon learning of Freeh's impending arrival, SAC Freeman contacted the director's office in DC to alert them that he would meet Freeh at the airport; someone would be at the gate to pick him up and carry his bags. He would also arrange for the two to have dinner together in Little Italy after the meeting at headquarters in San Francisco.

Freeh's office responded immediately to dispense with the formalities. The director didn't need anybody to carry his bags, and he would come down to the curb to meet the car. The office also said there wouldn't be any time on this trip for having dinner out; this would be all business.

Freeman was also informed that he was not invited to the meeting at headquarters. The director wanted to meet only with investigators on the task force—no supervisors would be allowed. Freeh wanted to hear from team members in the field without any management there; he wanted to know what people were feeling and what they thought. "That is how he was, and that is how he remained the whole time he was with the bureau," Turchie said.

It was the first time Turchie would meet the director. Freeh attended a brief meeting with all the managers of the three participating agencies: ATF, FBI, and the Postal Service. "It seemed everybody and their brother showed up to that meeting," Turchie recalled. "Everybody wanted to have a roundtable and tell the director how they felt, to give their opinion. I just listened."

"Louie Freeh already had the strategy we had drawn up, from reinvestigation to investigators traveling in the field to analytics to scratching victimology to the new computer to the Known Facts, Fiction, and Theory document," Turchie said. "But he didn't know that the team was having trouble with the profiling unit and the FBI Lab in DC—and that was a real concern to people on UNABOM."

The meeting was brief. Turchie had been invited to sit in, and while he was offered the floor, he chose to remain silent. When the discussion was over, Freeh signaled Turchie to walk with him to the next meeting. He wanted only working agents in the room—no supervisors other than Turchie—a directive that upset Freeman.

"It was the longest walk I think I've ever had," Turchie recalled. "We walked from the managers' meeting and down the hall into the squad. And there in the squad meeting, Max, in particular, just told him, 'We really have a problem with profiling.'"

Freeh told them that he understood and supported their strategy. As Turchie recalls, the director said, "I think these cases are going to get solved with a strategy rather than any one thing, and I think you'll solve it."

Hearing the director's clear statement of support meant more to the group than Freeh could have ever known. As Turchie recalled, "That was a turning point in the UNABOM investigation, when all the people on the UTF saw that the FBI director was really committed to this. We'd been trying really hard to make sure people's morale was high and improving, and his visit and the meeting he held with just the agents went a long way to addressing that."

Not surprisingly, within minutes of the meeting's completion, Jim Freeman received a call from a member of Louie's security detail. "The director has changed his mind. He wants to have dinner in Little Italy."

———

Moving forward after the Mosser attack proved difficult. Task force members worked to integrate the results of the Newark bombing into the overall investigation and proceeded from there. Wilhelmus and Conway's discovery that the first UNABOM package had likely been left on the ground at the University of Illinois, Chicago, Circle Campus, because of a mistake—the package was too big to fit in the mail chute—had provided the team with its first real clue about where the Unabomber may have lived early on and gave investigators a jumping off point from which to work. Mapping the various attacks provided team members with a pattern. The bombs had begun in the Chicago area, moving west over time. So it stood to reason that the Unabomber himself may have also followed this path westward. Determined not to let the Mosser attack slow the team's progress, Turchie proposed a new and daring strategy, one that he knew would be frowned upon by the bureau. "We need our own messaging with the public," he told his boss, Jim Freeman. "We have to do something that makes me almost squirm here; we have to have an alliance with the news media, so we can use them as our medium to get a message to the American public to help us solve UNABOM.

"That means we have to go out to them and give them facts, which they can start putting together in their own heads. Eventually somebody is going to listen and get the message, and we are going to get the right call that, in the end, is going to bring all this together.

"No fugitive is ever caught without the help of the public," Turchie insisted. "Why have we missed that all these years with UNABOM?"

Freeman did not immediately respond. Turchie was once again asking to break protocol, this time in a very public way. "What are you proposing?"

"I propose you be the voice of the UNABOM task force, because every day you are going to see the latest and you are going to know what we want out there, so we can recommend what we want out there and what we don't," Turchie said. He wanted his boss to go before the news cameras and appeal to the public for help in the case. The FBI was looking for someone who was likely born and raised in the Chicago area and had been in that area from 1978 to 1980, the Salt Lake City area from 1981 to 1985, and the San Francisco Bay area from 1985 on.

For an investigation of this magnitude, Turchie's approach was both shocking and unprecedented for a federal law enforcement agency that prided itself in keeping tight control over leads and always playing investigations close to the vest. But it also held promise. The FBI database contained some 85 million names, a staggeringly high number. The entire US population in 1995 was only 266.5 million. The reality was that the FBI could use a little help from the public. But would the agency's leadership be willing to go for such an idea? The team now had a bare-bones timeline they wanted to put before the public. They also had a new police sketch of the Unabomber they wanted to put forth.

When Jim Freeman had assumed the role of overseer of the task force, he had suggested they hire Jeanne Boylan, the artist whose sketch of Richard Allen Davis had helped capture the kidnapper and killer of little Polly Klaas. Her portrayal of Davis had been so dead-on that Freeman was convinced a new rendering of the Unabomber by Boylan was in order. He arranged for her to re-interview Tammy Fluehe, who had seen the bombing suspect in the parking lot in Salt Lake City, in hopes that Boylan's unique system of psychological interviewing might produce a more accurate rendering. The results were remarkable, and the newly commissioned drawing was widely distributed across the nation.

In early spring 1995, Jim Freeman stepped before the cameras and issued a public plea. "When you think of UNABOM, think of 1978, 1979, 1980, and think of the Chicago area," he announced. "Think of the 1981 to 1985 timeframe and think of Salt Lake City and then after 1985, think of San Francisco. And think of the sketch: the hooded man with the aviator sunglasses."

Turchie's plea to go public had been heard by the highest levels in the FBI, and they'd decided, in effect, to throw a Hail Mary pass. Would some American recognize this travel pattern? Would Freeman, Turchie, and the task force get a break? Only time would tell.

———

As they waited for new information from the public, task force members continued reviewing old case files, searching for anything that may have been overlooked. Another path of inquiry was opened after team members began revisiting the bureau's case files on the 1980 Percy Wood bombing and learned the United Airlines president had failed to tell investigators fifteen years earlier about thousands of airline employees he had fired during his tenure with the company.

When asked by agents in 1980 if he had ever "ticked anybody off," Wood had responded, "Everybody really liked me." He also claimed he had "never made any decisions of great social consequences." At the time, agents had simply taken Wood at his word.

But a shocking call to the historian at United Airlines from one of the task force members revealed that Percy Wood "was not remembering everything" about his time at the helm. The historian recalled that Percy laid off about five thousand United Airlines employees the year before he received the bomb in the mail.

"So, where did all these people go?" the agent asked the historian.

According to airline records, at least one thousand of the employees had gone to another airline, Western, to its headquarters in Salt Lake City. The information was eyebrow raising and prompted Turchie to dispatch a team to Salt Lake, where they learned that Western had since folded and been absorbed by Delta, and that a good portion of the Western employees had ended up at the United maintenance facility in San Francisco.

It was truly an astonishing moment for the entire task force. How could all the investigators at the FBI—and all the other investigating agencies—not have looked at the layoffs back in 1980? How was it possible that everyone had simply taken Wood at his word and moved on? Even a cursory search of newspaper archives would have turned up headlines about the layoffs at United. It would have been a major business story at the time. (And it sure affirmed the value of going back over case files as Turchie had insisted.)

Suddenly the task force had five thousand new suspects who had a clear and obvious reason to be angry at Wood—getting laid off and having their lives upended. In theory, any one of them could have become upset enough to put a bomb in the mail. Was Wood the primary target for the Unabomber all along? Had all the other bombs been sent merely to throw them off? There was only one way to find out—investigate each one of the five thousand workers who had been laid off. It was a massive undertaking, and nobody knew if it would lead anywhere or not.

"We start by trying to trace them," Turchie recalled. "We had no computers. We got the names of the United Airlines employees who had been laid off, who had gone to Western. Western went out, and the files went to Delta, and they were in a warehouse in Atlanta, where you have dust and dirt covering the boxes. Delta agreed to give us all these records, so we go through them one at a time to find out which of these people went from United to Western to the maintenance facility in San Francisco."

Meanwhile, the postal service learned that the package sent to the home of advertising executive Thomas Mosser in Caldwell, New Jersey, Bomb Number Fifteen, had been mailed from South San Francisco near the United Airlines maintenance facility where some of the laid-off workers had gone. That lent more credence to the notion that one of Wood's former employees was responsible. There was another piece of evidence that also had the FBI looking at airline industry employees too.

The task force, Turchie explained, had talked to experts who believed that some bomb components could have been fabricated from aircraft components. The NTSB also had reason to suspect someone from the industry, because some of the bombs used redundant detonators to ensure that if one failed, an alternate detonator would still cause the bomb to explode. Aircraft manufacturers built redundancies into their systems too—to better ensure passenger safety.

The kicker was that investigators had found that fifteen of the laid-off and twice-transferred airline employees had clocked out of the maintenance facility in south San Francisco at the same time the Unabomber had dropped off his parcel at the postal facility in town there. "You don't know whether to have chills. Is one of these people the one who did this, or none?" Turchie said. "You have to go and knock on the doors, and you have to make the judgment and move along. You cannot help but be tense, or admit you have no idea what you have left behind."

Task force members wound up spending the bulk of their time doing a deep dive into airline personnel, with an emphasis on disgruntled employees. The agency wound up investing hundreds, if not thousands of hours of investigators' time looking in the wrong direction. It was, unfortunately, a waste of time.

In the spring of 1995, the FBI's deputy director at the time, William Esposito, and the criminal division section chief, Robert Conforti, came to San Francisco for a full updated briefing on the UNABOM investigation and the team's strategy and plans for the future. Both SSA Terry Turchie and SAC Jim Freeman were invited to attend.

The meeting took place in the SAC's Conference Room and lasted several hours. "I laid out all the ideas we, as the most recent group to attack the UNABOM case, had for moving ahead and how confident we were in so many of the small facts that we had identified during our short time together," Turchie recalled.

"Bill Esposito asked whether we had everything we needed from the FBI to implement our strategy, and I answered yes, other than the fact that we had so many investigative projects stacked up on the runway. The only hurdle was that we had to base our time projections on completing all those projects one at a time, due to manpower and priorities."

Esposito then asked how the team could solve that issue. Turchie suggested that UNABOM's work had far exceeded the workload for any one squad. The team had finally put itself in the position to begin analyzing the thousands of pieces of information already collected over the previous sixteen years and to initiate investigations into possible suspects based on that analysis. But even that list was long.

Turchie proposed expanding the UTF and dividing it into three different squads—one for management, logistics, and all support; a second for all the "reinvestigation" of each UNABOM event (to include lab forensics and more); and a third for assessing all the possible subjects that had been identified to date. In order to accomplish those goals, he argued that they would need to double or triple the current squad's manpower as well as add more people to the UTF mission in Salt Lake, Chicago, and Sacramento.

Esposito looked across the table at SAC Freeman, who was in attendance that day, and told him he wanted to see him in his office and he also wanted to call Director Freeh. Turchie waited in the conference room for a while, but there was no sign of the men emerging. He grabbed a quick lunch and promptly returned to the conference room. After about an hour, the office door opened and the men emerged. Turchie and other members of the team could only guess at what the outcome might be.

Esposito looked at Turchie and said, "I spoke with Louis and here is what we are going to do. We are going to create the three squads you recommended. We are going to start transferring more agents, analysts, and support employees into San Francisco from other offices and from the New Agents classes currently at Quantico. That will mean the UTF will expand from its current thirty-plus agents, support, and other agency personnel to nearly one hundred.

"We are going to approve full-time analysts round the clock for the database projects, and we want you to implement all the investigative projects simultaneously to get them moved along as quickly as possible.

"We are also going to designate UNABOM across the bureau as the major case of the major cases. And finally we are going to create in the San Francisco office the UNABOM DIVISION instead of a UNABOM squad and promote you to become its ASAC. Now, can you solve this damned case?"

CHAPTER 21

"GO GUY"

SSA Pat Webb was no longer a full-time member of the UNABOM task force, but he was by no means off the investigation. "Once I went back to my squad, Joel Moss or Max Noel would regularly call me and say, 'Do you want to stop in today? We are onto something interesting; come in for the last fifteen minutes of our meeting,'" Webb recounted.

As the resident "go guy," Webb was expected to drop whatever he was doing and board a plane at a moment's notice to be the eyes and ears of UNABOM. "I was kind of the traveling expert on UNABOM," Webb said with a smile.

He was down with the flu when he was directed to board a flight to Edmonton, Canada, via Denver, to assess a bombing event that technicians on scene suspected might be linked to the Unabomber. He made it as far as Denver. His flight was pulling up to the gate when an announcement came over the PA system: "Please, no one leave the plane until Mr. Webb comes forward."

Airport security personnel were waiting in the terminal to escort him to the service desk, where he was advised to call the office.

"False alarm," Joel Moss told him. "They've already got a suspect in custody. You can turn around and go home."

The trip wasn't a total loss. Webb's twin brother, Peter, an investigative television reporter, lived in Denver, so the two shared a drink at the airport bar before he boarded a flight back to San Francisco.

Webb also represented the San Francisco Division and UNABOM at bomb squad liaison meetings, where bomb techs from around the country met to discuss anything unusual that had been found in a device, from explosive powders to components to triggering devices and more. And he ran training sessions for bomb techs all across California.

When new equipment became available, Webb was sent to Redstone Arsenal in Huntsville, Alabama, to learn how to use it. He and several other technicians from across the country were chosen to receive training in how to use the bureau's new Total Containment Vessel, a trailer-mounted, lead-and-steel sphere capable of containing a blast with the power of up to twenty-five pounds of TNT. Unbeknownst to Webb, this device, along with another newly invented bomb tool, would soon play a critical role in the UNABOM investigation.

Today, the Total Containment Vessels are used by bomb squads around the country to transport live devices. According to the vessel's manufacturer, "inside the vessel a bomb can be transported through city streets without the need for evacuation. If an explosion does occur, the fragmentation and shock wave will be contained while pressure escapes from a series of small vents."

Task force members were just regaining their footing after the latest UNABOM attack on Thomas Mosser in Caldwell, New Jersey, when they were blindsided by another domestic terror attack—this one unrelated to the Unabomber.

On April 19, 1995, Timothy McVeigh and Terry Nichols launched a bombing attack on the Alfred P. Murrah Federal Building in downtown Oklahoma City, and bomb techs from across the country were dispatched to the scene. Early suspicion that the Unabomber might be responsible was quickly dismissed.

Within ninety minutes of the attack, McVeigh, a Gulf War veteran and a sympathizer of the US militia movement, was in custody, having been pulled over by an Oklahoma highway patrolman for driving without a license plate. During the traffic stop, the officer, Charlie Hangar, discovered McVeigh to be in possession of illegal weapons and placed him under arrest.

Federal authorities quickly determined that it was McVeigh who had parked a Ryder rental truck packed with 4,800 pounds of ammonium nitrate fertilizer, nitromethane, and diesel fuel mixture in front of the Alfred P. Murrah Federal Building, then detonated it, killing 168 people and injuring hundreds more. The blast demolished one-third of the federal building and left behind a crater measuring eight feet deep and thirty feet wide. Another three-hundred-plus buildings within a sixteen-mile radius of the explosion were also damaged.

Unlike UNABOM, where forensics had failed to identify a suspect, lab examiners were able to definitively link the attack to both McVeigh and Nichols, based on forensic evidence collected at the bombing site. The two men were charged with what remains the largest domestic terrorist attack ever perpetrated on US soil. On June 11, 2001, Timothy McVeigh was executed by lethal injection; Nichols is serving a life sentence on "Bomber's Row" at the Supermax in Colorado, where, ironically, the Unabomber is also being housed.

Bomb squad techs from Webb's counterterrorism squad were among those being directed to Oklahoma City to assist in the processing of the massive crime scene. At that time, there were less than one thousand trained bomb technicians in the United States, and with the bombing in Oklahoma City, resources were stretched. Webb was on his way to a training conference of the International Association of Bomb Technicians and Investigators (IABTI), when he learned of the bombing on the Alfred P. Murrah Federal Building. Bomb tech Dave Anthony was at the airport that Wednesday morning to meet him and bring him to the fire department training academy where he was scheduled to give a presentation. The two men arrived at the location to find forty people clustered around the television sets looking at the Oklahoma City bombing coverage. "They are looking at fire and smoke," Webb remembered. "Dave Anthony got called to Oklahoma City while I was speaking."

Teams working the bombing investigation, code-named "OKBOMB," collected nearly one billion pieces of evidence from the scene and interviews conducted with relevant parties.

Perpetrator Timothy McVeigh claimed he was angered at the federal government's handling of the Ruby Ridge incident in 1992 and the Waco siege at the Branch Davidian compound in 1993. The standoff at Ruby Ridge, as it has come to be known, began on August 21, 1992, when self-proclaimed white separatist Randy Weaver, members of his immediate family, and close family friend Kevin Harris resisted agents of the US Marshal Service, FBI, and the FBI Hostage Rescue Team attempting to affect a bench warrant for Weaver's arrest after his failure to appear in court on firearms charges. The confrontation, which lasted eleven days, occurred outside the cabin Weaver had built on Ruby Ridge, located about forty miles from the Canadian border, near Naples, Idaho.

The confrontation turned violent in the first two days, beginning with a shootout between US Marshals and members of the Weaver family that resulting in the death of Deputy US Marshal William Francis Degan, the Weavers' fourteen-year-old son, Samuel, and the family's dog, Striker. Weaver's wife, Vicky, was also killed by an FBI sniper during a second exchange of gunfire.

McVeigh hadn't liked the way federal authorities had handled the two events and admitted he had timed the Oklahoma bombing attack to coincide with the second anniversary of Waco. Ironically, several of the agents and investigators on the scene in Oklahoma City had worked Ruby Ridge and/or Waco, so emotions were raw.

Five days after the bombing in Oklahoma City, Agent Webb received a call from ASAC Terry Turchie. San Francisco's mayor, Frank Jordan, was concerned about security at the fiftieth United Nations celebration, marking the signing of the Charter of the United Nations in San Francisco in 1945. President Bill Clinton and UN secretary general Kofi

Annan were expected to attend the commemoration at the opera house on Van Ness Avenue, and security concerns were heightened in light of recent events in Oklahoma City. The mayor was calling a meeting for Monday morning to discuss an action plan.

"You and I better go to that," Turchie told Webb.

The two men were on their way to the meeting when Webb received a call from Don Thurman, the chief of the FBI's Explosives Unit who had taken over from Chris Ronay. Thurman was dispatching people to Oklahoma, so Webb asked if it would be okay for him to bring a few bomb squad guys from the Bay Area to observe and see what they could learn. This would be an excellent way to prepare his team for the upcoming event, he thought. Thurman gave him permission to bring four bomb squad officers to the site.

Mayor Jordan was thrilled that the FBI was stepping up and gave Webb the okay to take just one bomb technician from his force, the San Francisco police commander. Webb agreed, and went ahead and invited the bomb guys from San Jose PD, San Francisco PD, and the Alameda County bomb squad, so there were a total of four bomb techs on the one-day excursion.

Webb had just arrived back at San Francisco headquarters a little after one that afternoon to find the phone on his desk ringing. "Can you run down here quick?" Joel Moss barked into the receiver. The task force and the counterterrorism squad were on the same floor, but on opposite ends of the building, which spanned one entire city block from Polk to Larkin Street. Webb knew it wasn't good when he saw the cluster of task force members assembled around Terry Turchie.

"Pat!" Turchie yelled over their heads. "I just hung up the phone with Dick Ross, the SAC in Sacramento. There's been a bombing at the California Forestry Association, an industry lobbying group in Sacramento. The victim recovered a package at the front desk, opened it up, it detonated and killed him. The receptionist was injured. They think it's UNABOM. Can you go and confirm? Manage the crime scene?"

This sounds just like what happened with Mosser and Gelernter, a package delivered like this, Webb thought. "I'm on it!"

Webb had a brand-new bureau car, and it was in the garage having "wigwags" (flashing lights) installed on it. He grabbed his briefcase and had somebody take him to the garage, which was eight blocks away. At 3:00 p.m., he started driving toward Sacramento. "I just drove like a madman going up Interstate 80 at seventy-five miles per hour, siren and wigwags going," Webb recalled. "It took like ninety minutes. I was jamming."

The brick building that housed the offices of the California Forestry Association was on I Street in a leafy neighborhood north of the capital. "I start getting toward the scene and the streets are blocked. They are calling me on the radio saying, 'Where are you?'"

"As I am getting toward the scene, I go by the headquarters of the Sacramento Fire Department, park my car, grab my bomb gear and coveralls, and I say to the battalion chief in charge, 'I need to change clothes; I am with the FBI.' I get to the scene about 5:00 p.m., badge my way in, and I find Dick Ross, who was the agent in charge."

"Pat, Sacramento PD wants to get in there and tear things apart," Dick railed. It had been a couple of hours since the bombing had occurred, and the officers from Sacramento PD wanted to get to work. But the FBI was also concerned about preserving the scene to ensure that evidence wasn't contaminated.

Webb observed some bomb squad guys on the scene, but the FBI bomb tech in the Sacramento field office was in Oklahoma City, so he was basically on his own to run the bombing crime scene investigation. He took a few minutes to orient himself, but soon found himself under assault from a young homicide detective who was becoming unnecessarily aggressive. The officer was all about getting upstairs and taking care of the crime scene, and he was nonstop in Webb's face. "Why is this the most important case?" he demanded. "Why are we delaying?"

"Be careful what you wish for," Webb retorted. "If this is UNABOM, this is bigger than you are."

The head of the local bomb squad, Jack Souza, was standing to one side watching the situation with the detective unfold, and he finally stepped in. "Back off!" he warned the officer. "This is Supervisory Special Agent Pat Webb, he knows Unabomber, and if I need to call the chief to put you in your place, I will."

Turning to Webb, Souza said, "Let's get the core people together that you want to work on this crime scene and take it from there." He made the decision to have the three people accompany him inside: Jack Souza, a second bomb-scene tech, and a video crime scene guy. "We'll go and make an initial assessment, and then we will divide up the rooms," Webb told them. Then he went off to one side to change his clothes. He put on his jumpsuit that read FBI across the back and a hard hat, because he was about to enter a building that had just sustained a bombing, and in which the ceiling was likely going to collapse.

Webb's phone rang just as the team was about to head inside. It was San Francisco; the bureau was going to send its Evidence Response Team (ERT) to the scene. Sacramento didn't have one, so Webb was relieved. He knew they would get there with their trucks and help establish order.

It was 6:30 p.m. when the foursome entered the crime scene. By 6:45, Webb was convinced: it was UNABOM.

"In the reception area, I found small pieces of lead mosaic, just like the one that had been used in the Mosser bomb in New Jersey the December before," he recounted of his initial walk-through. "So, the bomber was adding, making his own shrapnel and wrapping it to the outside of the pipe bomb. This was new; we had also seen it in the Mosser device just months before. The intent was to kill people. Shrapnel goes everywhere.

"There was a big hole in the reception counter. The victim was behind on the floor facedown and terribly injured. An officer from the Sacramento Police Department was there standing guard over the body. The concussive blast from the bomb had blown the victim's suit pants off. They were found yards away. The receptionist suffered ear damage."

Damage around the office's reception area was fairly extensive, Webb recalled. The artwork had been blown off the wall, and nearby rooms showed signs of damage too. There was dirt everywhere, and the walls showed signs of buckling—which is common in that sort of scenario.

Webb remembers walking into one office where he found a pair of red women's shoes on the floor. When the bomb went off, someone had literally run out of her shoes to safety. It was in that room, he said, where they found a cast aluminum disk that the bomber had used to seal the pipes. Investigators had seen the very same sort of disk in three other bombings—Epstein, Gelernter, and Mosser.

"In another office, I found a little piece of filament tape that had a piece of bug screen attached to it. I had seen that in Epstein. And the wood [bomb fragments] had craft paper glued to it, old grocery bags. We now know it was homemade glue; he didn't wrap it, he really packaged it." The investigators were now putting together a bomb signature that went all the way back to the device that went off in 1982 at Vanderbilt.

"And then there was an end plug. The Unabomber used a particular type of end plug, a metal piece with two ends in it he would drill into the pipe at cross angles, and he'd insert this end plug and then put a cross hatch in through the end plug and hammer them across. And that held the powder in. That end plug was surprisingly resilient. We recovered it in a lot of the devices."

Webb vividly remembered using gloved hands to pick up the end plug he found on a bookcase. After fifteen minutes, he walked back outside to alert the other bomb techs. The plug fit the Unabomber's signature perfectly. Webb knew he was dealing with the suspect he'd already been tracking. Outside, he relayed his findings to other investigators on site.

"This satisfies me," he said, holding up the end plug in his gloved hand. "This is UNABOM."

Webb's first call was to Terry Turchie. "It's UNABOM."

"Okay, it's yours," Turchie told him.

Webb knew that the San Francisco evidence response team (ERT) would be arriving in half an hour, so he went to speak to the FBI agent in charge. "He was not elated," Webb recalled. "Who wants a UNABOM? He's already had one UNABOM killing in his town. But the task force was running it, so he didn't have to worry about it."

Webb's next notification was to the homicide detective who had given him grief when he first arrived. "You can go home," he told the young officer, who was huddled with several other detectives by some patrol vehicles. "It's UNABOM, so this is an FBI case. You just went from top of the rung to the bottom."

Now the real work was about to begin. The evidence response team and its trucks had arrived with five agents on board. It was time to begin the methodical search of the crime scene. Webb and the five-man ERT joined with the search guys, and the evidence collection got underway. The next few hours were spent moving from room to room, photographing, measuring, and wrapping up the evidence.

As the evidence collection team got to work, inspectors from the postal service and ATF agents were outside the building setting up the sifting screens. Members of the Sacramento County Sheriff's Department were taking the lead in handling the perimeter. California state fire marshals and local FBI agents were also on the scene.

At a briefing at the local fire department that evening, Webb learned more details about the circumstances surrounding the package's arrival. The receptionist told detectives that she found the package on the counter after it was apparently delivered to her area by someone in the company's mailroom. She noted it was addressed to the company's former president, William Dennison—which was odd. Not sure what to do, she had called out to Dennison's newly arrived replacement, Gilbert Murray, to see what he wanted to do with the parcel. Murray walked up front to have a look at the package himself.

The receptionist said she waited at the reception desk until Murray arrived. When he did, she asked if he could stay at the front desk for a minute or two while she went to use the restroom. As the receptionist walked away, she noticed Murray pulling a pocketknife out of his pants pocket. It looked like he intended to open the package. The next thing she knew, there was a massive explosion, and she was knocked off her feet. When she returned to the reception area, Murray was on the ground.

Webb said death likely came instantly to Murray. "His jaw was blown off, he had a huge hole in his chest, because the bomb was right at chest height when he opened the package. The victim was facedown and exsanguinated, blood just everywhere," he recalled.

As Webb and his team continued their sweep of the office, the coroner's team arrived to remove the body. Emergency responders "rolled his body out to the coroner's van, right in front of all these news teams," he said.

One of Webb's great regrets was not handling that part of the scene differently. He hadn't anticipated wheeling the body out of the building in full view of the news crews. It was only later that he thought about the impact on Murray's wife, family, relatives, and friends. With hindsight, he would have erected tall privacy screens to limit what the news crews could video. But it was too late.

Webb recalled the team leaving the crime scene around 3:00 a.m. "At some point, everybody gets tired. Bomb techs from the sheriff's office, ATF, all kinds of people were helping."

Only later would the team learn that Gilbert Murray may have not been the intended target. The company's former president, William N. Dennison, had served as chief executive officer of the National Forestry Association from 1980 to 1994. He'd been a prominent figure on a number of different contentious issues—including the "timber wars," a struggle that pitted ranchers, loggers, and the timber industry against environmentalists over the development of private and public lands.

Investigators also learned that several employees had flagged the package, which was about the size of a shoe box and wrapped in brown craft paper, as suspicious and had even alerted Murray to their concerns. They noted the box was particularly heavy, and several people even shook it, trying to figure out what was inside. One even joked that he was going to hurry back to his office before the "bomb exploded." Even the woman at the reception desk that day had been suspicious enough that she deliberately asked Murray what he wanted to do with the package. Tragically, Murray didn't seem as concerned as others on staff.

"Let's not send it on; let's open it," Murray had reportedly told her.

Webb noted that with the Murray device, the Unabomber appeared to be returning to his previous technique of making bigger devices. The bomb was similar to the one sent to Mosser in New Jersey, but there were also a few key differences.

"He'd added more explosives, and he'd added the shrapnel," Webb explained. They were both well-built devices, able to withstand the jostling that takes place when a package is sent via the postal service. Mosser's device had been mailed from Sacramento to New Jersey, so investigators knew it went through the postal service and got tumbled and sorted along with hundreds of other packages. In theory, the bombs could have blown up in mail-sorting facilities or at some other point in their journeys—but they didn't.

"We could see, with the Murray device, that the Unabomber went back to big devices because you could put more powder in them and make them more lethal," Webb told me. "Murray's box was twelve by twelve by twelve, and it was sent in a white cardboard box. Mosser's device was also in a white cardboard box, and it was a pretty good size, but not as big as Murray's."

Webb said the shift in the Unabomber's technique told him that the suspect was learning and improving his bomb-making skills. He appeared determined to make the devices more lethal than before. "He'd learned things. In Mosser's device, he kicked up the [quantity of] powder and he put four batteries in it, rather than two. He did four batteries for Murray too, which causes it to function that much quicker."

Webb was quite aware that he was tracking a killer, and he was determined to take him down as quickly as possible. Law enforcement officers never forget crime scenes where people get killed. But as a bomb expert, the agent admitted that he had to admire the bomb maker's methodical and meticulous work. "The minute Murray took the pressure off that flap, it detonated," he stated. "He died instantly, and it blew the crap out of the reception room."

The Unabomber was honing his craft, learning to make bombs that were ever more lethal, ever more vicious. He'd begun to mold his own shrapnel and add items including razor blades and nails on the outside of the pipe bomb as a way of increasing their lethality "because he just wanted to harm people."

On the forty-six-year-old's death, prosecutors wrote, "The bomb so badly destroyed Gil Murray's body that his family was allowed only to see and touch his feet and legs, below the knees, as a final farewell."

That June, Terry Turchie and Pat Webb attended a memorial for Murray, who left behind a wife and two teenaged sons. The City of Sacramento planted a big redwood tree on the grounds of the Sacramento capital in remembrance, followed by reception at the Capital Hyatt. Both of Murray's boys were there. "It was a heart-tugger," Webb recalled.

PART VI

CHAPTER 22

PROFILING A KILLER

There was a growing suspicion among some experts that the Sacramento bombing had occurred because the Unabomber was angry that the spotlight had been taken away from him with the Oklahoma City bombing, and that he wanted to shift the media's focus back to him. To be sure, it was an attractive idea. It would suggest that the Unabomber was a narcissist. But a majority of the investigators on the UNABOM task force weren't convinced. For one thing, the Unabomber's devices were made by hand with excruciating attention to detail. It's likely that they took weeks or even months to construct. And most of the devices were sent through the US mail system—which added even more time to the process. More than anything else, the calendar dictated that the events were unrelated.

"I don't think he could have made the timing," SSA Webb said, arguing that five days—the time period between the Oklahoma bombing and the Sacramento attack—simply wasn't long enough for the Unabomber to fabricate a bomb, package it, and mail it.

Behaviorist Kathy Puckett agreed. Investigators had determined that the bomb that killed Gil Murray was already in the mail stream by

April 9, rendering this theory erroneous. "The Sacramento attack wasn't because he was feeling eclipsed by Timothy McVeigh," Puckett reasoned. "He had his own schedule, his own agenda."

Since joining the task force five months earlier, Special Agent Puckett had been familiarizing herself with the bomber through his sporadic correspondence. Puckett noted that the early communications had been very brief and had a specific purpose—to ensure that his bomb was opened by the recipient.

The Unabomber's fourth device, sent to the home of United Airlines president Percy Wood, was preceded by the letter from "Enoch Fischer" urging Wood to be on the lookout for a book of "great social significance" that would be arriving in the mail in the coming days. His seventh bomb, discovered by Professor Diogenes Angelakos in the coffee room at UC Berkeley, was purposely left with the odd note aimed at enticing the finder to interact with the device taped to its handle: *"Wu, it works. I told you it works. I told you it would . . . FC."* The tenth bomb, sent to Dr. James McConnell, the psychology professor at the University of Michigan, had also arrived with a typewritten letter affixed to the outside of the package expressly written to invite the recipient to open the parcel.

Unlike in prior bombing cases, the Unabomber never made any demands for money or other action, Puckett continued. There was never any apparent cause for his attacks, and they all seemed quite random in nature. The Unabomber's sole intent was to cause injury and death. That was part of what made him so difficult to profile and ultimately identify.

"The only writing before the 1993 letter to the *Times* was the one that induced the recipient of the letter at University of Michigan in Ann Arbor to open it by saying 'this is a dissertation; I want your opinion.' Or, in the case of United Airlines president Percy Wood, 'I am sending under separate cover a book that will be very interesting to you.'"

Puckett noted that in addition to enticement, the Unabomber's writings also indicated he was a person with a desire to be "accurate" and "precise."

The Unabomber, Puckett continued, "wanted to ensure that what he wanted to happen happened. He didn't want a random statement. He wanted a statement against the psychology professor at the University of Michigan who was doing experiments on worms and the president of United Airlines who had fired a lot of people. There was another element here too—the Unabomber's ego," she said. "He also doesn't want to humiliate himself by having a bomb go wrong, like it has before."

She pointed to a remark he made in the letter to assistant managing editor Warren Hoge of the *New York Times*:

> Notice that the postmark on this envelope precedes a newsworthy event that will happen about the time you receive this letter, **if nothing goes wrong.**

"It's the precision, the attention to detail; he always needs to be precise," Puckett pointed out during a meeting with task force members. She had no idea how prophetic her remark would prove.

Investigators executing a search of the Unabomber's cabin after his capture in 1996 discovered passages in journals he kept about his bombings. In one handwritten entry entitled "How to hit an Exxon exec," he plotted out an attack similar to the one he carried out in the Percy Wood attack:

> Send book-like package to his home preceded by a letter saying I am sending him a book I've written on oil-related environmental concerns—attacking environmental position—and I'd like to have his comments on it before preparing final version of manuscript.
>
> For return address: Get names and addresses of several big-time business execs and call direct [unreadable] to get their numbers, until you hit one who has an unlisted number. . . . Thus you'll have a real return address, but the Exxon exec can't get his number to call for verification.

With little else to go on, Puckett, with the help of a new FBI profiler named James Fitzgerald, was analyzing every word the Unabomber had written to date. Fitzgerald, or "Fitz," as he liked to be called, had been sent out by headquarters to assist the task force in the area of behavioral analysis.

Fitzgerald had been a police officer in Bensalem, Pennsylvania, before applying and gaining admission to the FBI training program that would ultimately land him a position as a criminal profiler. Remarkably, UNABOM would be his first profiling assignment with the bureau, and Turchie and Puckett were convinced he'd been chosen because of his minimal connection to the team at Quantico. Everyone at the profiling unit in Virginia was angered by Turchie's decision to replace profiler Mary Ellen O'Toole with Kathy Puckett, a counterintelligence agent who was *not* an FBI-trained profiler.

"They were not talking to me at all," Puckett recalled. "They had a real problem with me. I needed to consult with other people, but they didn't want to send anybody who already had a record of going against the task force or against me, so they brought Fitzgerald out and we started working together."

At first, the two focused almost exclusively on the limited writings from the Unabomber, looking for spelling errors, unusual word usage, grammar, and anything else that might provide a window into the person composing these letters and enticements. There was precious little in their "library" when they started, but that was about to change.

On April 26, 1995, just two days after the attack on Gilbert Murray, the *New York Times* received a second correspondence from "the terrorist group FC" offering to "desist from terrorism" if the newspaper agreed to publish a manifesto the group was working on. The author had included the group's *identifying number*—the secret code to prove the letter's authenticity.

Task force members had commenced an investigation into the nine-digit number when it had first appeared in the 1993 letter to the *Times*. They had determined it was a social security number belonging to a petty criminal who had been in and out of the prison system in the state of Ohio. Investigators suspected the bomber had found a piece of paper with the social security number on it in a parking lot somewhere in Ohio and had decided to use it as his group's digital identifier. Perhaps as a way to throw investigators off his trail?

FBI agents in New York were dispatched to the newspaper's offices on Forty-Third Street, where they were able to confirm that the identifying number included in this latest correspondence matched the one provided in 1993, thus confirming its author was the Unabomber.

Unlike the earlier correspondence, however, this latest installment, which stretched to 1,600-plus words, included a possible motive—"Opposition to the industrial-technological system." It also included a demand—"We have a long article, between 29,000 and 37,000 words, that we want to have published." More intriguing was that the Unabomber was offering up a deal—"If you can get it published according to our requirements we will permanently desist from terrorist activities."

But, there was a catch. According to the letter, the group would halt the bombings if three of its conditions were met.

First: Our promise to desist will not take effect until all parts of our article or book have appeared in print. Second: If the authorities should succeed in tracking us down and an attempt is made to arrest any of us, or even to question us in connection with the bombings, we reserve the right to use violence. Third: We distinguish between terrorism and sabotage.

By terrorism we mean actions motivated by a desire to influence the development of a society and intended to cause injury or death to human beings. By sabotage we mean similarly motivated actions intended to destroy property without injuring human beings.

We reserve the right to engage in sabotage.

After all the bombings, why was the Unabomber suddenly writing this long letter, and what did the suspect hope to gain with the publication of a far longer piece? The letter to the *Times* wasn't the only missive either: the suspect had penned three more letters, one to Richard J. Roberts, an English biochemist and molecular biologist who was awarded the 1993

Nobel Prize in Physiology or Medicine for the discovery of introns in eukaryotic DNA and the mechanism of gene-splicing; a second to Phillip A. Sharp, who shared the Nobel with Roberts; and a third to David Gelernter, one of his previous victims.

To be sure, Puckett and the team suddenly had a good deal more to go on, but where would this lead? In a way, the case had just become more like other serial bombing cases in which demand letters and elaborate manifestos were more common. What did it all mean, and what could be taken from his words to the *New York Times* and the three men?

In his letter to the *Times*, the Unabomber offered rationales for a number of the bombings that had already taken place. He claimed the reason he had waited so long to come forward—seventeen years to be precise—was that his early bombs were ineffectual and not powerful enough. But he finally felt that he and his alleged group had perfected their techniques and were now capable of crafting "small, light" devices that packed more destructive force than anything that had been done in the past. "With a briefcase-full or a suitcase-full of explosives, we should be able to blow out the walls of substantial buildings," he wrote. ". . . Clearly we are in a position to do a great deal of damage. And it does appear that the FBI is not going to catch us any time soon. The FBI is a joke."

The Unabomber's letters to Richard Roberts, Phillip Sharp, and David Gelernter varied in their content. Two were simple threats, while the third was meant to taunt. The ones to Roberts and Sharp were nearly identical: "It would be beneficial to your health to stop your research in genetics. This is a warning from FC."

The letter to David Gelernter was longer and more aggressive and explained his rage against those in technical fields. "People with advanced degrees aren't as smart as they think they are," the letter began. Calling Gelernter a "techno-nerd," he went on to attack the foundation of the doctor's work in modern computer science.

In the epilogue of your book . . . you tried to justify your research by claiming the developments you describe are inevitable . . . that

212

any college person can learn to compete in a computer-dominated world . . . being informed about computers won't enable anyone to prevent invasion of privacy . . . genetic engineering . . . environmental degradation through excessive economic growth . . . and so forth . . . If there were no computer scientists, there would be no progress in computer science.

The Unabomber was on a writing tear, which was good for investigators, particularly Kathy Puckett. She immediately got to work analyzing this fresh batch of evidence.

CHAPTER 23

"WARNING"

The Unabomber's letter-writing campaign exploded onto the front page of newspapers across the US after a letter arrived at the offices of the *San Francisco Chronicle* on Tuesday, June 27, 1995, threatening to blow up a commercial aircraft.

"WARNING. The terrorist group FC, called Unabomber by the FBI, is planning to blow up an airliner out of Los Angeles International Airport some time during the next six days. To prove that the writer of this letter knows something about FC, the first two digits of their identifying number are 55," it read.

The editorial team at the *Chronicle* wasted no time informing the FBI, and almost immediately Turchie and Freeman were on their way there. The two men reviewed the letter and quickly alerted their superiors in Washington, DC.

Investigators were unsure whether the Unabomber intended the six days to begin on Saturday, June 25, when the parcel had been postmarked, or Tuesday the 27th, the date the package had arrived at the newsroom. No matter; the bomb—if indeed there was one—was timed to go off during one of the busiest travel weeks of the year, the Fourth of

July. More than 50 million passengers were expected to travel across the nation during the period.

A crisis management center was immediately set up at Los Angeles International Airport. It would be manned twenty-four hours a day by teams from the Federal Aviation Administration, Postal Inspection Service, ATF, Secret Service, Airport Police, Los Angeles County Sheriff's Office, Los Angeles Police Department, and Los Angeles Fire Department. Authorities tried to reassure the public with news that federal, state, and local law enforcement agencies were forming a task force to deal with the situation, which they were deeming a "credible threat." News of the crisis drew Federico Pena, the US secretary of transportation; Los Angeles police chief Willie Williams; California's lieutenant governor Gray Davis, and Los Angeles mayor Richard Riordan to the scene at LAX, and security at airports around the state was stepped up to the highest levels since the Gulf War.

Departing passengers were asked for their tickets and photo identification. They were politely detained if the names on the tickets and IDs did not match. Security workers at metal detectors were increased to help ensure that there was sufficient staff to process the countless suitcases and handbags that had to be screened. Security outside passenger terminals was increased too, and uniformed police kept vehicles moving. Because of the stepped-up security, passengers were told to anticipate delays of up to two hours. Still, most of the flights departed on time and delays were few.

SSA Webb and others were calling bomb technicians from all over the country to go to Los Angeles. "We were going to do a giant search on fifty-four containers an hour of airmail coming in, just a ridiculous number, and they had to get to LAX," he explained. "LAPD and LA Sheriff's Office and Orange County and everybody assembled at the airport started examining these airmail containers in the event that the Unabomber actually had put a bomb in the mail."

At first, the search orders affected virtually all the mail that was being sent from California to other states across the nation, including letters, checks, and other items that were being sent in business-sized envelopes with first-class postage. But later that day, authorities allowed letters under eleven ounces in weight to be transported by air. But the searches continued for larger parcels and those slated for ground transport.

Logistics were a nightmare at Los Angeles Airport, which handled fully half of the parcels delivered in California daily. X-ray scanners were set up in a hangar at the south end of the airport and staffed by dozens of technicians from a multitude of law enforcement agencies.

In the middle of his coordination efforts, Webb learned that he was being tasked with delivering the Unabomber's latest letter to the FBI lab in Washington, DC, so examiners there could begin their analysis. "I had the actual letter, and I flew the redeye from San Francisco to Washington, DC. A car was waiting for me at the airport to take me to the J. Edgar Hoover Building at Ninth and Pennsylvania to have them look for fingerprints and indented writing and compare the typewriter. We knew it was authentic because it had the secret number on it."

The return address on the letter was listed as one Fredrick Benjamin Isaac Wood, and the address, 549 Wood Street, Woodlake, CA 93286, which seemed to tauntingly carry on the Unabomber's "wood" theme, was determined to be fictitious. Woodlake is a small city in California's San Joaquin Valley, but the street address simply did not exist. Investigators assumed that the name of the sender would also prove to be made up; it was not lost on them that the supposed sender's initials created the monogram FBI.

Webb was at headquarters for only a short time when a call came in from the New York office saying that the *New York Times* had just received a packet from the anarchist group FC, claiming the bomb threat at LAX was just a hoax: "Since the public has a short memory, we decided to play one last prank to remind them who we are," the letter stated. "But, no, we haven't tried to plant a bomb on an airplane (recently)."

The letter was oddly apologetic, with its author expressing relief that no one had been killed as a result of Bomb Number Three, which exploded in the cargo hold of American Airlines Flight 444 from Chicago to DC in November 1979. He also expressed regret that Bomb Number Six, meant for Vanderbilt University computer scientist Patrick Fisher, had harmed Fisher's secretary instead.

> The idea was to kill a lot of business people . . . But, of course, some of the passengers likely would have been innocent people—maybe kids, or some working stiff going to see his sick grandmother. We're glad now that that attempt failed.
>
> We do not think it is necessary for us to do any public soul-searching in this letter. But we . . . are not insensitive to the pain caused by our bombings.
>
> A bomb package that we mailed to . . . Fisher injured his secretary when she opened. We certainly regret that.

The bomber's musings were interesting, but the importance of this communication was its demand—the publication of the group's fifty-six-page anarchist manifesto, which was enclosed in the packet to the *Times*. The author promised that the group would refrain from any further acts of terror—if and only if the manifesto was reproduced in its entirety and verbatim in either the *New York Times* or the *Washington Post*. But the group strangely reserved the right to commit sabotage.

Over the next few hours, the FBI got calls from others who had also received a copy of the manifesto from the Unabomber. In all, three media outlets, the *Times*, the *Washington Post*, and *Scientific American* magazine, received one. Dr. Tom Tyler, a professor of psychology at UC Berkeley, was also mailed a copy, which arrived with an accompanying letter, basically an angry reaction to Tyler's public comments about the type of person who might commit bombing attacks like Oklahoma City and the ones carried out by the Unabomber.

> Dr. Tyler . . . We read a newspaper article in which you commented on recent bombings, including ours, as an indication of social problems. . . . We apologize for sending you such a poor copy [of the

manifesto] . . . We can't make copies at a public copy machine because people would get suspicious if they saw us handling our copies with gloves.

FC

Soon, SSA Webb was back in the car with another agent and headed back to the airport—this time to pick up a copy of the manifesto that was being flown down from New York so headquarters could begin its meticulous examination and review.

"The first thing we wanted to do was to make copies so we could start analyzing its contents as soon as possible," Webb recalled. "We were all wearing white gloves and carefully running the Xerox machines." Techs there emphasized to exercise extreme care with the document lest some bit of evidence be contaminated. As the copies started coming off the machines, agents realized they needed to be careful, too, about who had access to the copies. No one had any idea what the manifesto said, and no one knew what turns the investigation would take.

At some point that day, Webb got a call from Terry Turchie, who was still back at the San Francisco office. "Have you heard about this manifesto?" Turchie asked.

"Yeah, we are xeroxing it now," Webb said.

"Can you get us a copy?"

"Sure," Webb told him, thinking that wouldn't be a problem. He was literally helping make the copies. But then an assistant director came into the offices and announced that no one outside of headquarters was allowed to see the document.

Webb put his fellow task force members first, picking up an extra copy of the manifesto and quietly sticking it in his briefcase for the trip back to SFO. "I called Terry and I said, 'When I fly back, you'll have a full copy.' And he said, 'Fantastic.'"

As Webb recalled, headquarters eventually relented on its tight control of the manifesto and faxed a copy to the FBI's San Francisco office. But Webb was already one step ahead, with the hard copy in his briefcase.

He boarded the plane to fly west, pulled out the document, and started reading. "The Industrial Revolution and its consequences have been a disaster for the human race . . ."

"I read this damn thing," Webb said. "I was looking for clues, and he was talking about industrialization of society and stuff; it was just mind-numbing.

"I mean, I got off the plane in a coma, and then I went to the office and gave Kathy Puckett my copy and told task force members what was going on," Webb continued. "We knew the Unabomber was an extremely intellectual person. But when you see what this guy had done—using a manual typewriter, putting this whole thing together . . . it had very few strikeovers, it was impeccably spell-checked."

Special Agent Puckett immediately tasked her team with reviewing the entire document, analyzing each and every word, and analyzing the document itself looking for hidden clues.

"I was just thirsting for it," admitted Puckett, who broke down the document line by line, blew it up, and tore it apart.

Everyone has his or her own writing style, special words that they use time and again, vocabulary sets and more. It all makes for something of a signature that can help identify a specific individual. Would the manifesto prove the big break in the case that everyone had been hoping for?

Jim Fitzgerald was back at Quantico, so someone faxed him a copy of the document. Fitzgerald immediately recognized the word parallels, as did Puckett and even Turchie, who was actually the first member of the team to start pointing out the parallel phrases. A request was made for Fitzgerald to return to the task force to help decipher the document, and permission was granted. Once in San Francisco, he was a little mystified as to what they were supposed to do, Puckett recalled. "He was looking at the document. It was a bunch of gobbledygook, and he said, 'I don't know what else to do with this, so first I'm going to count the words, and then I'm going to try and separate out the different themes.'" Fitzgerald and Puckett got to work, poring over every word.

Fitzgerald's focus on linguistics to decipher the manifesto was unique, an investigative technique that hadn't been used before. His linguistical analysis of the document revealed that its author tended to use British spellings, which he'd probably picked up from textbooks he'd read. He also observed that some of the terms the suspect had used were dated. For example, he referred to women as "chicks," which telegraphed to Fitzgerald that this was not a young man, but a person who was a certain age when this terminology was en vogue. He also found certain lingo in the text that indicated the author was likely from the Chicago area, which aligned with the task force's earlier findings.

"Fitz didn't know anything about document analysis, but he just dove in—first counting words, then counting themes and subjects," Puckett recalled. It wasn't long before Fitzgerald started to extract intriguing elements of the document. "He said, 'Do you know what is the most common theme? It is not technology; it is children, how they are raised, how they are schooled, how they are shaped, how they are forced to do things.'"

Among the details she and Jim Fitzgerald gleaned from this thirty-five-thousand-word manuscript was that the Unabomber was far more educated, far better read than had previously been believed. "He was perfectionistic, older, had some sort of university connection. We didn't know it yet that he was a professor at Berkeley. He was not a disgruntled airline employee from United, not a low-level worker at a machine shop; we had been running all these leads down for years.

"He was coming across as somewhat anachronistic in his language, somebody who read more than he talked to people. He was of a different generation. He was a mature person, who had been schooled in older literature than we had thought earlier," she explained.

The Unabomber's lengthy communiques were also chock full of new leads for task force members to investigate and explore. The manifesto, in particular, mentioned a handful of books and newspaper articles, prompting investigators to bring the authors of these various works to San Francisco to participate in a brainstorming session. More than forty authors accepted the invitation, and each was provided a copy of the manifesto upon his or her arrival. Investigators asked the group to read and analyze the lengthy document, then share their ideas on who they thought the Unabomber might be. Speculation was all over the map, with theories spanning the spectrum from high school dropout to PhD. A few of the titles were quite obscure and impelled investigators to dig deeper, hoping it might lead them in the right direction.

At that moment, Puckett realized the manifesto was autobiographical in nature, although its author probably didn't realize that he had been writing about himself. The Unabomber was unwittingly providing the world with a kind of self-portrait, and if published, someone was going to recognize him.

———

Within hours of the manifesto's arrival at the *New York Times*, FBI director Louie Freeh called out to San Francisco to hear the UNABOM task force's recommendation with regard to publishing the lengthy anarchistic document. There was already debate among senior officials about whether to accept the Unabomber's most recent proclamation that his supposed bomb threat at LAX was a prank. The consensus was to err on the side of caution, with most in favor of keeping the airport under heightened security, although baggage and mail screenings loosened in the coming days. Now, Freeh and others at the FBI and DOJ needed to decide whether to publish the manifesto. The task force's initial response was a resounding no.

A meeting was called, and Jim Freeman, Terry Turchie, Max Noel, Kathy Puckett, and Jim Fitzgerald reported to the conference room to share their thoughts. "This is a no-brainer," Turchie stated. "Of course, we're not going to take a chance of publishing the manifesto; he is not going to stop bombing."

Historically, the FBI had a policy: the bureau did not negotiate with terrorists, and the general consensus around the conference table that afternoon was in line with that sentiment.

"Go write it up," Jim Freeman instructed the team. Headquarters needed a memo outlining the task force's position, so the group headed to Turchie's office to begin drafting the document. The foursome began hashing out the memo when the conversation took an unexpected turn, and they started discussing the unlikely idea of publishing the manifesto.

"We all realized it right away," Turchie recalled. "We need to publish this manifesto."

Two hours later, the group was back in Jim Freeman's office. "We have good news and bad news," Turchie said as he led the team into the amply sized corner room.

"Don't play games with me," Freeman replied, a hint of agitation in his voice.

Turchie took a seat across from his boss. "We think we made the wrong decision."

Freeman put down his pen, looked up at the group, and smiled. "Well, that is interesting, because I was thinking the same thing."

The FBI director and the attorney general were waiting on the group's decision, so whatever they decided, they needed to be able to defend their position; they needed to be sure.

"We are going to recommend publication," Freeman affirmed.

When the director phoned back, Freeman stated the task force's position. "We are in favor of publication," he said.

Freeh wanted to hear arguments for why the task force was making the recommendation.

At one point, profilers at Quantico, Puckett, and several other task force members in San Francisco were conferring together via telephone. "There was this huge hoo-ha," Puckett recalled. "Everybody was saying, 'We don't relent to terrorists' demands.' There were a lot of people saying there is no way we should do this."

Mary Ellen O'Toole, the former profiler for UNABOM, was one of the people on the conference call with Puckett. "It's the unit's position that he is a man of words," O'Toole said, speaking on behalf of the profilers. "This is what he has been working for, to get his views across. We believe he will honor his promise."

Puckett was skeptical. She, too, agreed that the manifesto needed to be published. But she was troubled by the profiler's willingness to take the Unabomber at his word about future bombings.

"No, Mary Ellen, he is a man of bombs," she retorted. "And, I am not sure if he *can* stop, even if he wants to."

There was a flurry of phone calls between the FBI office in San Francisco, the profilers at Quantico, and senior officials at headquarters in DC. FBI director Louie Freeh was willing to entertain all the arguments for and against publication before he met with the attorney general, who would make the final decision. Ultimately, he decided the best way to do that was to get everyone around a conference table in DC. He told Jim Freeman, Terry Turchie, Kathy Puckett, and Jim Fitzgerald to catch a plane to Washington.

Amid all the debate, *Penthouse* publisher Bob Guccione stepped forward with an offer to publish the manifesto in his girly magazine. His invitation won him a copy of the fifty-six-page document, which arrived via US mail, along with a typewritten note from the Unabomber: "You can publish this, but since your magazine is so disreputable, I reserve the right to kill one more person."

Apparently the Unabomber had a sense of humor, albeit a twisted one.

CHAPTER 24

TO PUBLISH OR NOT
TO PUBLISH

The meeting with FBI director Louie Freeh was held in his private conference room at the DC headquarters. Task force members arrived to find FBI assistant director Jim Kallstrom from New York and a handful of other assistant directors seated around the polished wood table in the director's office. Before SAC Jim Freeman even sat down, he was fielding angry comments from some in the room. "You are out of your mind, Freeman," one of the execs said. "You are doing the wrong thing."

"Just listen to what we have to say," Freeman retorted.

Director Freeh heard the exchange and immediately called the meeting to order. "Terry, why don't you get us started?" he said, turning the floor over to ASAC Turchie.

As head of the UNABOM task force, Turchie was uniquely positioned to make a case for why the team was behind publishing the manifesto. During his thirty-minute presentation, he updated the group on some of the investigation's latest developments and made a case for why he believed someone was going to recognize the Unabomber's words and respond with a phone call to the FBI. As Turchie wrapped up his remarks, all the senior officials around the table were looking to Louie Freeh for how they should respond, all the while shaking their heads in disapproval.

"Let me hear from Behavioral about this, Jim," Freeh said, turning the conversation over to Jim Wright, a profiler from Quantico who was seated next to Puckett. "Well, at the unit, we have decided that these are long-held beliefs and we really think that this is what the Unabomber has really wanted all the while, from the time he was sending bombs and blowing up grad students at universities, and we believe if his demands are met, it will save lives rather than take lives. If we go ahead and publish, we can make that assurance; we believe he is likely to keep his promises."

"Kathy, would you like to jump in?" Freeh interjected, introducing Puckett by her first name.

"Well, here is where we differ," Kathy began. Out of the corner of her eye, she noticed that Jim Wright sat quietly, facing straight ahead and refusing to look at her. "I don't believe he could stop if he wanted to. I think he is a bomber. He is angry. This is what he does; he has been doing this since 1978."

Still, Puckett concurred with the team when it came to the decision of whether to publish the manifesto. "I think we should publish, because we want to get his words out to a large group of people—because he has written before, and someone is going to recognize his phraseology."

Kathy saw that Freeh was nodding his head as she laid out her reasons for publication. And when one or two of those present tried to rebut her argument, he cut them off.

"Okay," he said, "we are going to see Janet Reno in the morning, and I am taking Terry and Jim and Kathy to see the AG with our position, because that will be our position."

"I guess I am going back to Quantico," Wright said through clenched teeth. Puckett smiled to herself, watching all the other guys around the table agreeing with Louie.

In recalling the meeting, she remembered how excited she was at learning that she was going with the director of the FBI to actually meet with the attorney general, Janet Reno, for the first time. Relatively few FBI agents had that kind of opportunity during their careers. "I just couldn't believe my ears." She smiled.

The following morning, the task force members met in the hotel lobby, then crossed Pennsylvania Avenue to the old Department of Justice building, where Janet Reno had her office.

"I am carrying a briefcase, and it's summer; everybody is sweating," Puckett recounted. "We arrived at these big metal doors. It's the old Department of Justice building with the WPA murals from the Works Progress Administration from the 1930s on the wall. We go into this high-ceilinged conference room, and the AG comes walking in, and here is Janet Reno, bigger than life, and she just has this big smile—she has the big presence."

Turchie, Freeman, and Puckett were all surprised when Janet Reno began instructing the attendees on where to sit; they hadn't anticipated that one at all. Eric Holder, a lawyer for the DOJ who would go on to become the first African American US attorney general under President Barack Obama, was also attending. Louie opened the meeting with a brief introduction, then turned the meeting over to Jim Freeman, who in turn asked ASAC Turchie to bring the attorney general up to speed on the manifesto debate.

"Janet Reno was just tremendous," Turchie recalled. "She was just so into the details. She had been following the investigation and was up on all the facts."

About a quarter of the way through the discussion, Jamie Gorelick, the deputy attorney general, joined the meeting, making a commotion before plopping down in the empty chair next to Reno. Turchie waited for her to settle in, then continued with his presentation.

"Well, I have a question," Gorelick interrupted.

"You missed the first quarter of the meeting. He's already answered that," Reno barked to stifled laughter from those around the conference table.

Terry took the opportunity to introduce Kathy Puckett, who immediately found herself answering questioning from the AG.

"I have a question, Kathy. What is the difference between behavioral and behaviorist?"

"It is the same thing," Puckett replied, eliciting a chuckle from the attorney general.

All in all, the meeting was cordial but formal, with a couple of smiles from Janet Reno.

As the conversation wound down, Reno looked across the table at Louie. "Can I see you?" she asked, prompting all those in attendance to rise and exit the room. The wait in the reception office seemed an eternity. After what felt like hours, the two finally emerged. Reno was wearing a big smile as she said her goodbyes and returned to her office. No one dared ask Louie about the closed-door meeting. Instead, Turchie, Freeman, and Puckett followed him to the elevator.

When the elevator doors closed, Louie looked around, then asked, "Who is in here with us?" When he saw that it was just the four of them, he broke into a smile. "Did you see the AG slap the deputy AG down?" he said, referring to Janet Reno's dress down of Deputy AG Gorelick back in the conference room.

Everybody started laughing. It was a welcome relief to an otherwise intense few hours. As the group crossed the lobby, Louie explained what had gone on behind closed doors. He said that Janet Reno was on board and was arranging a meeting with the publishers of the *New York Times* and the *Washington Post* for the following day to discuss printing the manifesto. "She said this was the best briefing she'd ever had on any case. She was all in," Louie declared. Everyone breathed a sigh of relief.

———

The next day, Terry Turchie and Jim Freeman attended what would be a historic meeting with Janet Reno, Louie Freeh, *New York Times* publisher Arthur Sulzberger Jr., *Washington Post* publisher Donald Graham, and a handful of people from the Department of Justice. As Turchie put it, this was the only time in the history of the FBI that a meeting took place between the bureau and the publishers of two major newspapers thrown together in a situation that required mutual cooperation; the media and the G-men joining forces for a common cause—something that had never happened before and has not happened since.

The meeting took place in the lunchroom of the J. Edgar Hoover Building. And right from the start, both publishers were skeptical. The *New York Times* wanted a guarantee from the FBI that the Unabomber would stop his terrorist bombings and stop targeting people if the manifesto was published, so they could say they were doing it for the public good and not just acquiescing to the FBI. "He was pretty manipulative," Puckett said. "It really was an extortionate demand: 'If you don't publish this, more people are going to die.'"

Both Sulzberger and Graham wanted to know what kind of guarantee the FBI could give them that no one else would get hurt, that the bombing would stop.

"We can't give you a guarantee," Reno replied. "But you can say that, I, Janet Reno, recommend this so that you can identify and apprehend this bomber."

Those in the room remained skeptical as they listened to Turchie present the task force's plan. He explained that the team preferred the manifesto to be published in the *Washington Post*, but he stopped short of providing a reason.

"We think the Unabomber will want a trophy copy of his paper, so we would like to surveil newsstands that sell the same-day edition of the *Post*," he said. "There are only two newsstands in the city that carry it. Everywhere else, it is delayed."

Someone from the *Post* had a question. "How many copies of the *Washington Post* and how many of the *New York Times* are circulated in the Bay Area?"

This was an answer both Freeman and Turchie already knew: the truth was nobody read the *Washington Post*, whereas the *New York Times* sold hundreds of copies in a day, which is why the task force preferred publishing in the *Post*; logistically, it would be much easier to surveil the handful of people buying the *Post* than it would be to keep track of all the *Times* readers.

Turchie knew all eyes were on him, wanting to hear his answer. "Well, there are always fifteen copies of the *Post* at the newsstand we want to watch."

Louie chuckled. "Well, you can see that nobody else in the country cares what we think back here in DC."

There was another reason to go with the *Post*—the publisher had the ability to create a pretty lengthy insert with its printing equipment, while the *New York Times* did not. Ultimately, it was decided that the *Post* would publish the manifesto, and the *Times* and *Post* would split the cost. Both papers would also put out an article about the Unabomber and his manifesto on publication day, which the group decided, would be September 19, 1995.

———

As SSA Webb so aptly put it, the whole teeter-totter of this case was based on that manifesto being published, which is why the surveillance operation on the newsstands on September 19 was so important. SSA Joel Moss was in charge of putting it together and making sure the two newsstands were being carefully monitored. Two teams were out on the streets, each tasked with following every person who bought a copy of the *Post* that Tuesday. To prepare for the demand, the newspaper flew in twenty extra copies.

The newsstand on Geary was supposed to open at 8:00 a.m., and for extra insurance, task force members reached out to the guy selling the papers to alert him that his location was under surveillance. Agents were posted on all the corners, and at window tables at the luncheonette across the street. By 7:00 a.m. the two teams were in position. No one had anticipated the demand the manifesto would bring, and soon the phone at headquarters began ringing with agents from the field calling in to alert supervisors that there were already lines forming around the block with people waiting to buy the paper.

"We need more guys out here," one caller said.

The request sent everybody scrambling to try and get more agents to the scene. At one of the locations, investigators observed a somewhat disheveled-looking man waiting near the front of the line. When it was his turn, he purchased not one but a handful of newspapers. Agents followed him to the Bart station, where he boarded a train, traveled a few blocks, and stepped off. Then, he boarded a bus. He kept doing that for about an hour, shifting back and forth from the bus to Bart and vice versa. It was as if he knew he was being followed and was trying to dump any tail that he might have. The team stayed on him, eventually following him to Daly City and then to Pacifica, where he entered an apartment complex. They waited as he crossed the lobby, and carefully watched as he boarded the elevator.

"Who was that?" one of the agents asked the person manning the lobby.

"What was what?"

"The person who just came in, and where is he going?"

When the man being questioned hesitated, the agent pulled out his badge. "FBI, answer the question!"

"That's Joe, he's on . . ."

The agent directed the man not to say anything to Joe, then took off up the stairs to Joe's apartment with backup in tow.

Once upstairs, the team knocked on the man's door.

"Who is it?" the male occupant yelled through the closed door.

"We just want to talk to you."

"Who are you? I am not opening the door."

After a few minutes of back and forth, the man finally cracked open the door and peered into the hallway to see who was knocking, at which point one of the agents threw a foot in the door, and the team pushed its way inside. The apartment was small and dark.

"Who are you?" the man demanded.

"We are the FBI," one of the agents responded.

"You need to turn on a light," a second investigator directed.

The man fumbled about, finally illuminating the space with the flip of a wall switch, and the agents found themselves knee-deep in magazines, newspapers, books, and other assorted junk, a hoarder's place. "Why do you have so many magazines stacked around your apartment?" an agent asked.

"Why are you in my apartment?"

"We are here to talk to you."

One investigator stepped out into the hallway to confer with his colleague. "This guy is really squirrely. Who is he?"

It turned out that over the years, "Joe" had written letters to his local congressmen, state senators, even the sheriff. He had also written numerous letters to the FBI. All of them were complaints about one thing or another, because no one was paying attention to his concerns.

"The FBI is following me around, and they want to know what I am reading," he told the group, all of whom quickly realized he was not their man and they'd been on yet another wild goose chase.

The rest of the newspaper purchasers turned out to be regular everyday readers. There was one other man who had briefly raised suspicions when he, too, bought several copies of the *Post* and headed for a downtown office building. Turned out he worked for a brokerage firm, and part of his morning routine was to pick up copies of the newspaper for himself and a few of his coworkers. Case closed.

By day's end, it was clear the surveillance operation had yielded no new or viable suspects, although newspaper sales for that day hit a record high, with people across the country—and the world—anxious to see what the Unabomber had to say.

The decision to publish the Unabomber's lengthy manifesto sparked fierce debate. According to an article that appeared in the *New York Times* on September 20, 1995, the publishers of both newspapers, the *New York Times* and the *Washington Post*, "drew sharp criticism from some quarters" with some claiming they had "abdicated journalistic responsibility by giving in to a terrorist" and created a scenario in which news organizations might have to acquiesce to more demands from terrorists at some point in the future.

Others, including a number of journalists and terrorism experts, questioned whether the publishers could really stand by and ignore the plea from law enforcement while knowing that authorities were trying to catch a serial bomber who had eluded them for seventeen years and had launched multiple attacks resulting in three deaths and injuries to twenty-three others.

Several weeks after the Unabomber's manifesto appeared in the *Washington Post*, the *International Herald Tribune* (owned by the *New York Times*) printed a letter to the editor E. Chapman in Fontainebleau, France, essentially calling out the Unabomber for his denouncement of technology.

"Without modern technology, would the . . . manifesto . . . have reached the audience he seeks? No telephones, no electricity, no radio, no television—he wants to have his cake and eat it, too."

CHAPTER 25

55,000 LEADS AND
COUNTING

September 19, 1995, publication day, had come and gone. The 800 tip line had seen a brief spike in calls following the manifesto's appearance in the *Washington Post* that Tuesday. In fact, more than fifty-five thousand leads had come in since the phone lines were first opened in 1994, but none had proved viable, and printing the manifesto did nothing to change that.

Still, task force members remained focused, unwilling to let this latest disappointment deter them. Agents continued to talk to people at universities where the history of science was being taught; others followed leads the team was not yet ready to retire. One line of inquiry investigators had been chasing focused on a group of gamers in the Chicago area who regularly gathered to play Dungeons and Dragons. The group numbered nearly one hundred and were known to play in the hallways and classrooms in the building at Northwestern University where the first and second bombs had detonated. As late as July 27, 1995, FBI agents were keeping a list of "players and peripheral players involved in a loosely knit group of individuals commonly referred to as the Dungeons and Dragons Group." One FBI document references a visit with a gaming group in Fresno, California, during which members were shown a composite drawing of the Unabomber and asked if they recognized him. They were also shown pictures of some of his explosive devices. At some point, the members began talking among themselves, and word began to spread that the FBI was asking questions—and perhaps even looking for the Unabomber among their group. "Many of the members of the group became paranoid and began pointing fingers at one another," one agent wrote in his report.

According to ASAC Turchie, "the main suspect that was developed on the first bomb turned out to be on the long list of the Dungeons and Dragons players." In fact, at least forty to fifty players were still under suspicion in late summer 1995, and agents continued to look at them as persons of interest until they could rule them out.

The story got even weirder when task force members learned that several of the members had gotten together and decided they ought to write a book about how the Unabomber was operating among them. Turchie recalled that after Ted Kaczynski was arrested, "one of these guys calls the FBI and says, 'You have made a terrible mistake,' basically insinuated the bureau had arrested the wrong man."

Yet another angle the investigators had been unable to follow to its conclusion was the DNA found on the device left at the business school at the University of Utah. Lab examiners had discovered several hairs, but DNA testing was still in its infancy at the time, and they were unable to determine much from that specimen. But there had been a number of scientific advances in DNA testing in the ten-plus years since the evidence had been collected—new DNA tests, new microscopes—so the hair and fiber examiners at the FBI lab went back to have a second look, this time in a new light.

"They find a whole selection of hair and fibers, and it is a Caucasian hair, an African American hair, some mouse fur," SSA Webb recalled. "Nobody knows what it means. It was fun to redo that, but now what?" It wasn't until investigators discovered Ted Kaczynski's diaries during the execution of a search warrant on his Montana cabin that they learned the truth—that Ted had gone into both a women's restroom and a men's restroom and wiped the toilets at the University of Utah, then scattered the hairs in the package. He included them just to distract investigators."

By now, the team had taken various bomb components—aluminum, wood, paint, and green "avocado" nails—to Lawrence Livermore National Laboratory, Oak Ridge National Laboratory, the National Transportation Safety Board laboratory, the Underwriters Laboratory, Scotland Yard, Virginia Polytechnic Institute, Rohm and Haas adhesive consultants, Integrated Paper, the Aluminum Association, and others.

The explosives' unit had designed a questionnaire that the team sent out to every crime laboratory in the world, looking for similar construction techniques.

Cassie Henderson was hard at work on the computer analysis, and Kathy Puckett was updating the behavioral analysis. Task force members were even revisiting the million-dollar reward publicity campaign, yet again reaching out to the public through the media and emphasizing the suspect's westward migration from his beginnings in Chicago in the seventies to Utah in the eighties to Northern California in the nineties, hoping that someone, somewhere would recognize him. Calls continued to come in to the tip line, but few, if any, got past the initial screening phase.

In early fall, the task force had a new suspect in their sights. According to ASAC Turchie, the man had become known to them through one of the many projects being investigated. He seemed to check off all the right boxes, he was the right age, he had been to all the right universities, and he had been involved in a bombing on campus while attending college. His pedigree raised enough eyebrows to land him a spot on the short list of subjects now under surveillance. The undercover operation revealed that he was putting "wooden stuff" in his trash, including hickory wood, the same kind of wood found in several of the Unabomber's devices. A search of his rubbish yielded pieces of wood that agents collected and sent to the FBI lab in DC for evaluation. Agents also found the hair shavings amid the trash and were able to retrieve enough DNA for testing. The team was surveilling the man for a couple of weeks, and some of the investigators were convinced he was their guy. "There were some good specifics about time and place, but in the end, there wasn't enough evidence to link him to the bombings. Still, some on the task force weren't ready to give up on the lead.

"This was the hardest part of the investigation," Turchie explained. "They want so much for it to be the guy, and we just had to drop it and move on. You do have to make decisions to close things down at a certain time."

Task force members all agreed that there were points in the investigation where it all started to feel hopeless. Everyone was pretty deflated after this latest suspect had been ruled out, so when a new and promising lead came in, in early February 1996, people were circumspect. It was the middle of the month when the call came in to FBI headquarters in DC from an attorney on the East Coast. He didn't want to provide his name, or the name of the client he was representing, but he did drop a few hints, breadcrumbs, that he hoped would be titillating enough to grab investigators' attention.

"He was giving us information like, 'a guy who taught at Berkeley, who was from Chicago.' He didn't want to get into a lot of detail," Turchie recounted.

But what did it mean? And who was this mystery caller?

——

Unbeknownst to task force members, the attorney was attached to Ted Kaczynski's brother, David. But it was David's wife, Linda Patrik, who first raised the possibility that her brother-in-law might be the Unabomber. Linda was in Paris on sabbatical at the end of 1995. At the time, the French capital was experiencing its own bombing campaign, which was being carried out by members of the Armed Islamic Group of Algeria, one of two main Islamist insurgent groups fighting the Algerian government during the Algerian Civil War, which had begun in 1993. The group was using IEDs to blow up the city's public transportation system, and the terrorist attacks had rattled Patrik. She was at the time a professor of philosophy at Union College in Schenectady, a city in upstate New York about fifteen miles southeast of Albany, the state's capital. In an interview with a local newspaper some years later, she recalled using meditation to try and calm her nerves.

One afternoon she was in her Paris apartment reading the *Herald Tribune*, the international English-language newspaper, when she came upon an article featuring excerpts from the Unabomber's manifesto. The words seemed familiar, like she'd read them somewhere before.

Linda had never met her brother-in-law, but she had read some of the letters he had sent to David. She knew of Ted's preoccupations, but more important, she knew of her husband's despair over Ted's decision to cut off all ties with him after receiving David's letter announcing his engagement to Linda.

"David had the temerity to get married to Linda," Puckett explained. "Ted was absolutely disgusted that his brother would do that. Ted had never met Linda, but he didn't like the fact that his brother had succumbed. He even wrote a letter to David talking about how they were both virgins, intimating that by getting married, David was breaking that bond."

According to Puckett, who had seen all of Ted's writings, Ted was totally jealous of David. "Linda was with someone else when David met her, it was a difficult wooing apparently, and Ted just despised David for that, and also because David let him know that he wanted a life outside of what he and Ted had known."

The last time David had seen Ted was in Montana in 1986. After receiving news of David's engagement, he essentially cut off his brother. Linda and David were married in a Buddhist ceremony, and much to David's disappointment, Ted refused to attend the wedding. He basically shut his brother—and the rest of his family—out of his life and retreated into a world of his own.

When David arrived in Paris for a visit with his wife in late 1995, Linda told him of her suspicion, that the Unabomber's manifesto sounded a lot like his brother, Ted.

"Linda, you have never met him, you don't know anything about him," David replied. "Ted wouldn't hurt anyone, he is so kindhearted to animals." David was referring to his brother's early interaction with the rabbit their father had found and caged in the family's backyard, and the one he had shot during a hunting expedition in Indiana when Ted was a teenager.

"There is just no way," David insisted.

"Promise me when we get back home to New York you will read it."

"I will."

Once back in the United States, David's attempts to locate a copy of the manifesto proved impossible. The newspapers were all sold out, so he went to the local library and pulled it up on microfilm. The document popped up on the screen; by the time he got to the third paragraph, his jaw dropped. It sounded a lot like his brother's voice. Upon reading the manifesto to its conclusion, the phrase "cool-headed logicians" jumped out at David. This was a term he had heard his brother say many times before, and he worried that perhaps Linda was right.

David was in the process of packing up his mother's home in Evergreen Park and moving her to Schenectady to be closer to him. Wanda Kaczynski had saved many of her eldest son's belongings in a steamer trunk in the attic of the family's home in Lombard. Ted had left everything behind when he left for the final time to begin his solitary life in Montana. Wanda held on to the items, hoping that one day he'd reconnect with the family and want to reclaim them.

That night, David went to the attic and began sifting through the trunk, where he found an essay Ted had written in 1971. For the next several weeks, David and Linda vacillated back and forth over whether Ted could be the Unabomber. They would read Ted's writings, then read the manifesto and talk about it. "Well, this rules it out," David would say after comparing several passages from the two documents.

"No, it doesn't," Linda would argue.

They continued agonizing over what to do. Linda had a college friend named Susan Swanson. Susan was a private investigator, and she agreed to look into Ted's life a little bit to see what she could find out. But there really wasn't much out there, and her efforts did nothing to resolve David and Linda's quandary. Amid their back and forth, David had provided Swanson with a sample of his brother's writing; she decided to give it to a retired FBI profiler she knew named Clint Van Zandt. She was curious what he might have to say.

Van Zandt admitted to seeing some similarities between the writing sample Swanson had provided him and the thirty-five-thousand-word manifesto. He told Swanson he didn't think it was likely that Ted was the Unabomber, but he suggested the couple give a sample of Ted's writing to the FBI and let the bureau determine whether it warranted further investigation.

By this time, David had conferred with an attorney, who also happened to be a friend, Anthony Bisceglie, a well-regarded Washington-based lawyer. As luck would have it, Bisceglie had just finished an espionage case and had developed a good relationship with an FBI special agent named Molly Flynn, who had also worked on the case. Flynn had gone to law school, but she never actually practiced law. Instead, she joined the FBI and was now an agent based out of headquarters in DC. She eventually became a de facto member of the task force and case agent on UNABOM in Washington. (In any major case with a major case number assigned to it, there is always an agent at headquarters who serves as a liaison with whatever field office or resident agency is leading the investigation.)

After conferring with David and Linda, Bisceglie approached Flynn about the couple's concerns. He wanted to have the essay analyzed by the FBI. But he declined to disclose the name of his client or the location of the writer of the essay, wanting to wait until the bureau had made its evaluation. He also placed the call to the 800 tip line and provided only bare-bones details.

SA Flynn took the essay to the FBI for analysis. To her chagrin, examiners there ruled it "irrelevant" after determining it hadn't been typed on the "UNABOM typewriter."

From the lab's perspective, at least, the only thing that mattered was finding a match to the typewriter that the manifesto had been written on. Though trained experts, they weren't looking for similarities in word choice and writing style at all—that was well beyond their purview. Fortunately, Flynn wasn't ready to dismiss the matter just yet. She decided to reach out to the team in San Francisco to alert them to the document.

"She phoned the switchboard, but the call went unanswered," ASAC Turchie recalled. "She hung up and redialed three times before the operator finally picked up the line." By now, the task force had fielded more than fifty-five thousand calls and none of them had led anywhere, so a ringing phone had become simply a nuisance.

An announcement went over the office intercom: "Anyone on the UNABOM task force, dial the operator." SSA Joel Moss finally broke down and called the switchboard and directed the operator to patch the call through. He listened as Agent Molly Flynn told him about the document she had come to possess and how the guys at the lab had ruled it out as irrelevant because it had not been typed on the "UNABOM typewriter."

"I've read the manifesto," she explained. "And this writing is eerily similar."

"Fax it to me," Moss told her. "I will wait by the machine." When the twenty-three-page transmission arrived, the special agent took it back to his office to read. Within the hour, he and Kathy Puckett conferred and decided to call and ask Terry to lunch the next day.

"I can't," Turchie replied. "I have a lunch meeting with Jim Freeman tomorrow."

"Terry, you need to cancel," Moss told him. "You need to trust me, we need to have lunch."

The next day, Terry, Max Noel, Joel, and Kathy walked to Max's Opera Cafe, a New York–style deli. Turchie was a foodie, and according to him, Max's had great Russian cabbage soup and wonderful German chocolate cake, both of which he ordered that afternoon, along with his usual—a Reuben sandwich.

Joel pushed a folder with the twenty-three-page essay across the table to Terry and Max. "We think this is the Unabomber," he said.

"This is just a piece of paper with words," Noel declared, tossing the document onto the table. "We have better leads than this."

Max was a straight shooter. He wasn't buying the whole "language" thing that Puckett and Fitzgerald were peddling. He was old school and believed in good old-fashioned legwork to get the job done. As far as he was concerned, the team had expended enough time and manpower on the manifesto. He implored the others to stay focused on the strategic plan the task force had been following and not to get caught up in another wild goose chase. The team had just dropped one likely suspect, and people were disappointed and leery of immediately turning their attention to someone else. Nobody was ready to jump back in with two feet, even if the evidence was compelling. Besides, it was Friday, and the weekend was upon them. People were exhausted and looking forward to a two-day respite. Everyone around the table knew that if they showed the essay to SAC Freeman, he would demand they work the weekend to investigate it.

As they sat debating back and forth, Jim Freeman himself made an unexpected visit to the table. "So, this is who you blew me off for," he bellowed to Turchie, who offered an awkward apology, followed by a promise of an explanation.

That night, Terry joined his wife in the family's living room to watch some television. But he couldn't concentrate on whatever was on the screen. Instead, his thoughts were on the essay Moss and Puckett had presented to him at lunch. Skimming the pages, words and phrases jumped out at him—words that were eerily similar to those found in the Unabomber's manifesto. Springing from the couch, he exclaimed, "Joy, I think we've identified the Unabomber!"

The next morning, Terry had already learned from Freeman's

secretary that his boss was not expected back at the office that afternoon, so he left a copy of the twenty-three-page essay on his desk, thinking he and the others would have the weekend to relax. He barely made it back to his office when his phone began ringing.

"Get up here right away!" Freeman barked into the receiver.

"Where did you get this?" he demanded the minute Turchie appeared in his doorway. "Nobody's going home. We've got to work through the weekend on this!"

Turchie, Puckett, and Moss spent Saturday and Sunday around the conference room table with SAC Freeman, hashing out the possibilities. Don Davis and Tony Mulijat of the Postal Inspection Service, Mark Logan of ATF, and the FBI's Penny Harper and Jim Fitzgerald joined the discussions. Terry had given the essay a closer read on Friday evening, and when he arrived at the office on Saturday morning, he was desperate to share what he'd found. In comparing the essay to the manifesto, he'd found some identical wording. It was more than a simple coincidence.

After several discussions between Special Agent Molly Flynn and attorney Anthony Bisceglie in Washington, the FBI finally had a name—Theodore Kaczynski, who, according to Bisceglie, hailed from Chicago, was a mathematical genius who had attended Harvard at the age of sixteen, had earned a PhD at the University of Michigan, and had taught at UC Berkeley in 1978.

"By now, Cassey Henderson really had our databases up and going and with one entry, the name popped up—Theodore Kaczynski; he was deep in our case files," Terry Turchie recalled. "We sent two guys across the bay, and we found old catalogs from these years and that is where we found his name. He was in our database, where he'd been picked up on a list of people who had been employed at UC Berkeley, and his social security number, the first three digits, came back to Illinois, and then we ran a DMV check and he shows up in Montana."

A surveillance team was immediately dispatched to Montana, with task force members Jerry Webb (no relation to Pat Webb), Candace DeLong, and several others hoping to get a look at the man who quite possibly was the mysterious bomber who had eluded them for more than seventeen years.

Ted Kaczynski was UNABOM Suspect 2416, Kathy Puckett recalled. "We had a lot of people who we would get tips on so agents would come to me and say, 'I got this suspect. What do you have to say about this? What is the shrink way to look at this?'

"I would ask them to give me more information, because with indirect assessment you need more information. During my doctoral curriculum in clinical psychology, I'd been trained in direct psychological assessment methods, which are statistically validated, measured tests of various kinds. In indirect assessment, you don't have that luxury, so you need to know everything, you weigh everything, and you look at everything together.

"I always told my students when I was teaching forensic psychology, 'Suspend your judgment and hang out in doubt and uncertainty.' That is hard to do, because everybody is programmed to come to a conclusion."

CHAPTER 26

A BREAK IN THE CASE

I t was decided that Kathy Puckett, Joel Moss, and one other FBI agent from San Francisco, Lee Stark, would travel to DC to meet with David Kaczynski and his wife, Linda Patrik. Stark, a former army officer, had been designated the case agent for the Kaczynski file. He was a gruff, taciturn guy—not exactly the person to put a reluctant witness at ease.

The meeting was scheduled to take place at the law offices of Bisceglie and Walsh on Seventeenth Street Northwest. David Kaczynski couldn't get off work until late, so he and Linda flew down to DC on a Friday night; it was February 16, Valentine's Day weekend 1996. The next day was a blizzard, and the power was out in most of the city. Special Agent Lee Stark and Molly Flynn conducted the interview.

"It was cold," Puckett recalled. "The whole atmosphere was cold, in terms of the weather and the mood."

Puckett noted that while David Kaczynski was composed and low-key, both he and his wife were hesitant to talk. It didn't help that Agent Stark was leading the questioning. The couple was extremely conflicted about discussing Ted with the FBI, and Stark's abruptness made them even more uncomfortable.

Special Agent Puckett was supposed to do the next interview with the Kaczynski family. She felt the environment, a stark and cold office, was not the best setting for such a difficult discussion and suggested they hold the meeting back at her hotel. She and her colleagues were staying at the Grand Hyatt on H Street, which had a generator and partial heat during the power outage. She rented a suite and ordered in coffee and pastries to create a more welcoming atmosphere for David and his wife.

David wept as he spoke about Ted's reaction to their family tragedy. Theodore Kaczynski Sr. had been diagnosed with terminal cancer, and in 1990, he took his own life. Both David and his mother were home at the time, and David cried as he recalled hearing the fatal gunshot. David's attorney, a short man with dark hair, dressed in a suit and black cowboy boots, stood at the back of the room and watched the intense exchange. Linda sat awkwardly on the couch, clearly in emotional pain as she observed her husband.

Puckett recalled that as David spoke of writing to his brother to inform him of his father's death, she leaned forward. "David's eyes fixated on mine, and he said, 'Ted said that was an appropriate use of the mail.' I said, 'That was hard to talk about and I know it; we are going to take a break and have some tea.'

"Everybody gets up, and David is kind of shaky. Tony lights a cigarette and says, 'That was well done,' and I thought, 'I wish I could have a cigarette.' I had quit a couple years earlier.

"When the interview reconvened, I wanted to talk to David and Linda very specifically about what was in Ted's letters to them. I'd deliberately kept them with me so we could talk about them. Terry was furious that I was breaking the chain of evidence. He wanted me to send them right away to the FBI lab. But I wanted to ask David about some of the references in the letters."

Kathy was also curious about what kind of books Ted liked to read. David told her that his brother read numerous books, including *The Technological Society* by Jacques Ellul, and loved reading *Scientific American* magazine.

Though not key pieces of evidence, both items were noteworthy for Kathy and the task force. The Unabomber had wanted his manifesto published in either the *New York Times*, the *Washington Post*, or *Scientific American*. And Ellul's book was also referenced in the manifesto.

"We arranged that the next weekend, we were going to southwest Texas near the Rio Grande, where David had his own cabin and other letters from Ted."

The following Friday, Agents Lee Stark and Kathy Puckett flew to Texas with David Kaczynski. A driver from the El Paso FBI office was at the airport to meet them in a bureau car, a brand-new, four-wheel-drive Chevrolet Suburban. "He hits the accelerator and he is flying down that road at like a hundred miles an hour," Puckett recalled. "Lee thought we were going to crash, and David hears noise overhead. 'What is that sound?' he asked.

"'That is a plane,' I told him. 'That is actually our people; they are just watching out for us to make sure you are safe.'

"David felt completely surrounded by the FBI in the car, and in the air. From then on, it was just me and David and Lee. We are down in the desert, and pretty soon we are driving two miles an hour on this rutted road. And by this time we had seen Ted's cabin, because we had a surveillance team in Montana. And we go to David's cabin, and it is this cheerful little structure with pink eaves. And I said, 'Did Linda paint that?'"

"Yes," he replied.

"David makes some tea, then he opens a secure door to an underground storage area that he has dug in the ground, like a tornado shelter kind of thing with a padlock, where he had stored Ted's letters."

The cabin was in the badlands in southwest Texas where severe storms were common, and so it made sense that David would have kept his valuables safely stored away under lock and key. Ted's letters were stored along with foodstuffs and other supplies. It seemed as though David had kept virtually everything his brother had given him. The truth was that David had idolized his older brother; it was extremely difficult for him to live with the fact that they were estranged.

"He wanted Ted to be proud of him. Ted had this cabin in the woods that he'd built in two weeks, and David went out to southwest Texas, and for a while he lived in a hole in the ground, and he bought some land, and he built his own cabin. He was trying to get some kind of admiration from Ted for something he had done himself, emulating his brother.

"David always wanted to be in his brother's life," Puckett told me.

Puckett described the content of some of Ted's letters to David as "totally scathing condemnation." They included lines such as, "You are a slathering sycophant to that woman. You are a patsy," apparently referencing David's soon-to-be fiancée, Linda Patrik. Puckett remained convinced that Ted was jealous of his brother's relationship with Linda and viewed his decision to marry as the ultimate betrayal.

At the end of the weekend, David returned to Schenectady. The following Friday, he, Linda, Lee Stark, Kathy Puckett, Molly Flynn, and another FBI agent named Jim Wilson went to Chicago to see the family home in Lombard. Wanda had sold the modest three-bedroom blue-shingled house to a young couple and was just settling into an apartment in Schenectady.

By this point, task force members had been on the ground in Lincoln, Montana, for nearly two weeks, surveilling Ted's cabin and quietly interviewing townspeople to learn as much as they could about this reclusive man. The whole mission there was to do some really discreet investigation, to see Ted come out of his cabin, and so on. The operation was completely hush-hush; no one outside of Jim Freeman, Terry Turchie, and a few higher-ups back at FBI headquarters in DC were to know anything about it.

The assignment was so top secret that task force investigators Paul Wilhelmus of the Postal Inspection Service and Mike Grady of ATF, both of whom had been tapped to go to Montana, had been instructed not to reveal their undercover work to anyone in their respective agencies, not even their supervisors. In addition to Wilhelmus and Grady, Max Noel was also selected to partake in the surveillance operation, along with an FBI agent named Dave Weber. Weber was on the SWAT team and was the principal firearms instructor for the San Francisco field office. Weber was an outdoorsman, a wilderness-type guy who was able to provide the team with a lay of the land. The FBI senior resident agent in Helena, Tom McDaniel, was briefed on the team's impending arrival, as was Assistant United States Attorney Bernie Hubley. But the operation was so under the radar that even the SAC in Salt Lake City was not alerted until weeks later.

Once they'd landed in Montana, SSA Noel and Inspector Wilhelmus were directed to check all the hotels and motels in the Helena area to see if they could learn where Ted may have stayed during his trips to and from the bombing scenes. He had hand delivered some of his devices, and others had been mailed from letter boxes in and around the Bay Area, which meant he had to have left Lincoln at certain points over the years. Their first stop was the Park Motel, an old motel in the downtown area that had been in operation for decades. They told the owner they were looking to see if a guy named Theodore Kaczynski had ever stayed with them. "He has run into some problems with the tax man," Noel suggested. "So we need to find him."

The name did not ring a bell, but the Park Motel kept records that dated back for years. A search of the files revealed that Kaczynski had stayed there between 1978 and 1996, and the owner provided the agents with a list of dates and times that turned out to match the dates of some of the bombings.

"The dates were on either side of one of the bombings," Turchie recalled. "So he was either on his way to a bombing or coming back from one."

Agents also visited the tiny library in Lincoln, where they learned that Kaczynski had checked out some of the books that had been either listed or referenced in his manifesto. And they interviewed a cardiologist in Montana who had seen Ted during the period when he was writing his manifesto. The cardiologist told investigators that Kaczynski "was under particularly bad stress," Turchie recalled.

Someone had also spoken to Butch Gehring, whose father had originally agreed to sell Ted the plot of land where his cabin now stood.

Agents watching the residence had managed to glimpse Kaczynski on several occasions when they first arrived, but they had not seen him in nearly a week, and there was growing concern that the suspect was up to something nefarious. Uneasy over this latest development, Jim Freeman contacted Puckett, who was in Chicago with David Kaczynski, and issued a directive. "I want you to get David to write a letter and get in communication with Ted. We need some confirmation that he is still in Lincoln."

"Boss, we have an agreement with his attorney that Ted will not know that David is assisting us."

Max Noel was furious when he learned that Puckett was refusing to comply with Freeman's directive. "She is not being tough enough on David," he railed. "She is too soft on him; she needs to be more demanding on him."

Terry Turchie spoke up in Puckett's defense. But her unwillingness to push the envelope raised doubt in Freeman, and he worried that she might go rogue. The following weekend, Puckett and the others were scheduled to travel to Schenectady to interview Ted Kaczynski's mother, Wanda. Freeman wanted Turchie there to keep an eye on Puckett. He made it clear that Turchie was to be in the house when she was speaking to Wanda.

David Kaczynski had been put in the untenable position of brokering the meeting between the FBI agents and his mother. He had told the group that of the two brothers, Ted was more like their mother. "I am more like our dad," he said. "She is very protective of Ted—she is fiercely protective of Ted."

On Saturday, March 9, the group made its way to the apartment complex in Schenectady where Wanda Kaczynski was now living. It was a very cold day, with temperatures hovering at twenty-four degrees and dipping to a record low of eleven. David went to visit his mother first, with the understanding that FBI agents would show up later in the day. Everyone knew that it was going to be a difficult meeting: David had to tell his mother that he had been the one to contact the FBI about the possibility that Ted was the Unabomber. All the agents could do was guess about how Wanda would react to the horrific news.

Turchie had promised his boss that he would stay by Puckett during the interview with the woman. But now he was on the fence about the matter, wondering if his presence inside the apartment would cause even more anxiety for Wanda and David, neither of whom had ever met him. When they got there, he decided to stay outside waiting in the cold car.

Wanda Kaczynski greeted the FBI contingent—Kathy Puckett, Molly Flynn, Jim Wilson, and Lee Stark—with a polite, "Hello, nice to meet you."

David was just inside the front door, and Puckett recalled that he appeared stricken, as if somebody had stabbed him in the heart. Later, she learned that David had just gotten done telling his mother about how he'd reached out to the FBI. Wanda Kaczynski hadn't had any time to process or even react to the news that her firstborn son may be the Unabomber. David said that his mother had taken the news fairly well under the circumstances; she told him that he must have had a very good reason for talking to the FBI. Still, she couldn't comprehend the notion that it could be Ted who'd killed and wounded innocent people with his bombs.

"I don't believe for a minute that my son is involved in any of this," she told the agents that day. "But I understand you have a job to do."

The team spent three hours at the apartment, while Terry Turchie waited and shivered outside in the car.

Special Agent Puckett recalled that from the moment she met Wanda Kaczynski, she was certain that Ted's mother had absolutely no idea that her son could be the Unabomber. "She was completely unwitting," Puckett asserted.

Even David Kaczynski was having a hard time reconciling that his brother was capable of such violent acts. He'd routinely defend his brother during meetings with agents, often using a line like, "I understand you have not yet eliminated Ted as a suspect . . ." But then he would reread the manifesto, and his doubts would resurface. His mother, on the other hand, had no doubts about her son's innocence. "I don't think she was even persuaded at the trial when he pleaded guilty," Puckett said.

Wanda Kaczynski told Puckett and the others visiting her home that day people didn't understand her son. "He is different; he is a unique personality, but my son is not a killer. I know that," she insisted.

"I totally understand how you feel," Puckett assured her. "I hope you understand we are not here to pursue an agenda. This is a part of the investigation, and we have to run things out to their natural conclusion."

Wanda provided the investigators with more letters from Ted's steamer trunk, served the agents tea, and told them about Ted as a child. She recalled the episode when he was hospitalized with a case of the hives as a child and told them she was convinced that the event had changed his personality. "He's had a difficult time, he has problems with friends, and he is very solitary, but he is brilliant. He went to Harvard at sixteen—skipped two grades and went to Harvard," she boasted. "He was misunderstood; he was a sensitive boy. He is not like everyone else, but he doesn't have to be; he is a brilliant boy, but people think badly of him."

Puckett concluded that Wanda Kaczynski was a mother who was staunchly defending her alienated son. Even after Ted had repeatedly cursed her out, even after he had disowned her and his entire family, she still defended him.

CHAPTER 27

GETTING CLOSE

Supervisory Special Agent Patrick Webb had been one of the more consistent faces of the UNABOM investigation. He had been on the case since 1982, when the Unabomber attacked the UC Berkeley campus, and he'd had a foot in the door ever since. Although he'd been sent back to oversee the counterterrorism squad in 1995, after serving one year as a supervisor on the UNABOM task force, he had stayed involved in his role as the "go guy" for UNABOM.

In mid-March 1996, Webb was at a management retreat in Monterey. Terry Turchie was also in attendance, and during the event he approached Webb with some news. "We are getting close," he told him. "We've got some real promising leads in UNABOM, and we've already sent two agents to Montana to scope things out."

"We are getting to the point where we are going to need to do a search on UNABOM," Turchie continued. "We are going to need somebody to go into the cabin, and it is not going to be me. It is going to be you. You are going to have to get a crew together."

Webb alerted his number two guy, Don Sachtleben, who had taken over as acting supervisor of the counterterrorism squad while Webb was attached to the UNABOM task force, and they immediately began their strategic planning.

A couple of weeks later, Webb was in Sonoma County teaching a crime scene class titled "How to Blow Up Cars." At the end of the lesson, he and his team packed up their big truck and headed back to the city to attend a retirement dinner for an agent named Rick Smith; all of the local agents had received invites. Webb recalled Jim Freeman approaching him at the party. "He said, 'I think we are going to do this next week, so get your team together.'"

David Kaczynski had contacted the FBI the second week of February, and by the following week, a team was in Montana. The FBI had a ton of work to do—setting up surveillance, starting to track Kaczynski's movements, and continuing their investigation—all in preparation for securing a potential search warrant or arrest warrant by the end of April or early May. But a network news service threw a wrench in what was supposed to be a carefully crafted investigation.

As Turchie recalled, "On March 31 I get a call from Jim Freeman, who was in Montana. I was in San Francisco for my son's birthday. Jim told me that CBS News has found out that we are working on a suspect in Montana. They are saying Dan Rather has talked to the FBI director, Louie Freeh, and the bureau feels it has bought us some time. CBS is not going to say anything unless one of their competitors gets wind of it."

The fact that CBS knew about the potential suspect meant there was a clock on everything investigators were doing. Suddenly, time was of the essence. The agents had reason to trust that CBS would keep its word to stay silent for some period of time; media outlets do sometimes strike deals with law enforcement when it's in the interest of public safety or the solving of some significant crime. But the deal also meant that now CBS's producers, cameramen, and correspondents would also have to find a way of going undercover and not showing their hand to competitors such as NBC and ABC. Reporters and correspondents often keep an eye on their competition because each and every one of them is looking for a big scoop. No one wants to be left behind.

Suddenly, the FBI had agents quietly investigating agents as they tried to figure out who could have leaked the Montana lead to CBS. They suspected it might have been someone from headquarters who had been pushed aside from the investigation, but they didn't have enough evidence to prove it.

"So, on April 2 at noon, we fly our SWAT team and some agents on an FBI detail flight that goes to Salt Lake and makes a connection into Helena, and I am with them. We got into Salt Lake at midnight on April 2. Between noon and midnight, we probably moved a hundred people to Montana.

"We were still talking to DOJ, and they were telling us we didn't have enough to get a search warrant for Kaczynski's place," Webb explained. Even David Kaczynski's comments on the manifesto weren't enough—because David couldn't say for sure that it was his brother who wrote the piece. Everything the FBI had was circumstantial. "We were faxing back and forth, and they were telling us what we needed to change in order to secure a warrant. At some point, Louie Freeh went to Janet Reno and told her, 'Whether this is signed or not, I am going to authorize it.'"

The following morning at 7:00 a.m., Turchie and Bernie Hubley, the US attorney from Helena, went to see US District Court Judge Charles Lovell. Judge Lovell had served in the United States Air Force before graduating law school and going into private practice in Helena. In 1985, he was nominated to a new seat on the United States District Court for the District of Montana by President Ronald Reagan. "He was a great guy, he brought donuts, he had a big box of donuts in his conference room," Turchie recalled. "He was very cordial, very nice."

Judge Lovell told Hubley and the others he needed more time to review the documents before he could render a decision on whether to sign the search warrant. "Go have donuts and coffee," he told the team. "I'll get you in a couple of hours."

The agents were frustrated by the delay and by their own inability to act. The entire case was now resting on Judge Lovell's decision on the search warrant. What the FBI was asking for was highly unusual and without precedent.

In spite of all the work the task force had done over the years, the team had been unable to secure a single shred of physical evidence tying Ted Kaczynski to any of the bombing attacks. The request for the search warrant cited "language"—essentially the commonalities in verbiage and writing style employed by Kaczynski in his letters and the UNABOM manifesto—as the basis for entering the cabin. No law enforcement agency had ever attempted to link someone to a crime or series of crimes before based solely on language, and Judge Lovell truly did need time to consider its merits.

No one was ever as careful as Ted Kaczynski to not leave any physical evidence behind, SSA Webb asserted. The only thing that led the FBI to Ted's cabin in the woods were his own words.

That also meant that the FBI needed to recover from the cabin clear evidence linking Kaczynski to the crimes or he'd be free to go. The FBI was counting on two key issues to fall the agency's way: Judge Lovell green-lighting the search warrant and agents finding evidence in the cabin. (The notion that Kaczynski would somehow confess to being the Unabomber seemed unlikely.)

It was after 10:00 a.m. when Judge Lovell called Turchie, Hubley, and the others into his chambers. "He starts asking us questions about the affidavit, we all go through it line by line," Turchie recalled. "Everyone in the room feared the judge would rule there was not sufficient cause to sign the warrant, but he surprised us all."

"I've read this, and I think there is probable cause, so if you think this is the Unabomber, you go get him!" Lovell exclaimed.

Word was immediately relayed to Jim Freeman, who was in the forward command and close to Ted Kaczynski's cabin.

There was no radio service between Helena and Lincoln, so an FBI radio crew had already been dispatched to Montana. Two men, both radio techs, hired snowmobiles and drove the necessary equipment to the top of Mount Helena, where they set up a radio repeater with encrypted radio channels so agents in Helena could talk to those in Lincoln without fear of others listening in to those transmissions. There was no other way to communicate; Lincoln had just one public phone booth.

Task force members also arranged for a twenty-five-foot recreational vehicle to be brought to a vacant lot in Lincoln for use as a mobile command center. A female FBI agent, working undercover, approached a woman in Boise, Idaho, and arranged to rent the vehicle from her. The agents arranged for the vehicle to be driven from Boise to Lincoln, where it was parked in an out-of-the-way location and used by task force members, including Terry Turchie and Jim Freeman.

The intense pressure of the investigation combined with the secrecy needed for the entire operation weighed on everyone who was involved. But there were humorous moments, too, that helped break things up and provide a bit of levity for the agents. One came from the woman they'd rented the RV from.

The FBI agent had told the woman she was supposed to meet her husband at a fishing hole, and that was why she needed it.

"I don't want to be gamed," the owner told her.

Webb chuckled, recalling how after Kaczynski's arrest, the woman spotted her RV on television. News reporters were doing live shots from the FBI command center and she spotted her vehicle in the background; she immediately realized she'd been had. "She calls the television station and says, 'That's my motor home!'"

Lee Hayden, an FBI admin guy who handled logistics, was tasked with renting sixty rooms at the Best Western Hotel in Helena for the incoming team. He also had to procure transportation for all the staffers being flown in—and, because of the location, they all needed four-wheel-drive vehicles. Hayden scoured the rental car companies for four-wheel-drive vehicles and wound up renting just about every single one of them within a two-hundred-mile radius.

When the planeload of FBI agents arrived at Helena, Hayden was there standing on the tarmac handing out keys to personnel as they got off the plane. He'd tossed as many of the keys as would fit into an empty 7-Eleven Slurpee cup and handed a set to each agent as they walked by.

"We moved fifty agents up there," Webb remembered. "We rented just about every four-wheel-drive vehicle in the state, so when the press got there, they didn't have any four-wheel-drives left to rent."

Headquarters had alerted the Pentagon that the FBI had a special operation running in Lincoln, Montana, and it needed a top-notch bomb team to assist. The army handpicked EOD technicians from the West Coast, including from Yakima, Washington.

"There were six of them," Webb recounted, "all army guys, led by a captain and a sergeant major. They were told to get to the Best Western in Helena by 8:00 a.m. the following morning, and they drove like bats out of hell to get there."

The bomb techs knew the operation was covert and that they had to blend in, but they also needed to be recognizable to Webb and the others. Webb chuckled recalling the moment he arrived in the hotel lobby that morning to find six guys dressed in civilian clothes, all wearing bright-blue Seattle Mariners baseball caps. "It was brilliant!" he remarked, and the impromptu plan allowed all of them to maintain their undercover status.

The six men on the EOD team had all their tools, rope, pry bars, lights, gear, bomb suits, and X-ray equipment with them.

The agents in the field knew they had to expect the unexpected. There was no good way of knowing when their next hot meal or shower was going to come. From Webb's perspective, it was best if everyone ate before heading out on assignment, so he encouraged the group to enjoy breakfast before setting off for Lincoln to start their reconnaissance efforts. They needed to fully familiarize themselves with the terrain near Ted Kaczynski's cabin in the woods. Arrangements had been made for the teams to use the 7 Up Ranch, a former dude ranch in Lincoln, as a staging area, where they could wait while a search warrant was secured. The site's rustic seventy-seven-hundred-square-foot log structure became a hangout for law enforcement personnel during the days-long operation.

"We had enough tools to get into the cabin safely," Webb explained.

At one point, Jim Freeman and members of the SWAT team slipped into the woods, close enough to Kaczynski's cabin to view it through binoculars. The men gave the bomb technicians a briefing on the cabin. "It is a ten-by-twelve . . ."

The team learned there was a driveway up Stemple Pass Road, and then a huge saw mill, equipment, front-end loaders, and logs. Ted's cabin was a quarter mile up the hill from the sawmill. There was a logging road that went up through the woods about a half mile, and virtually nothing else nearby. There was one cabin about two hundred yards away that belonged to Glenn Williams and was used for elk hunting.

"We had snuck people in there to conduct surveillance, and they could tell if Ted was home because smoke would come from his chimney," Webb explained. "You could see the smoke from the Williams cabin, and they had. They could also glimpse the log trail, so if he walked out, you would be able to see him.

"We had two guys in there for two days, they just huddled in sleeping bags, no fire, because we didn't want to call attention to them." FBI agents Jerry Webb and Candace DeLong were among those watching Kaczynski to make sure he didn't go into town carrying any packages. The agents wanted to ensure that Kaczynski didn't slip any more improvised explosive devices into the US mail.

Early in the operation, the team was introduced to Jerry Burns, the local forest service ranger. Burns knew Kaczynski, he knew the area, and he provided the teams with an outline of the property. "We knew there was a root cellar nearby where Kaczynski kept potatoes; we knew there was a loft in the cabin because of the pitch on the cabin roof," Webb explained.

Burns also knew that Ted Kaczynski was very upset that the Kennecott mine company had copper mines in the area, and he was worried that they might reopen some of them. So Turchie, Freeman, Burns, and the others had come up with a ploy to get Kaczynski out of the cabin with a fabricated story about Kennecott. Since Ted knew Jerry Burns, Jerry agreed to be part of the ruse.

"The plan was for Max Noel to walk up to the cabin with Burns and Tom McDaniel, the agent from Helena who always wore a cowboy hat," Webb explained. "We only had a search warrant, no arrest warrant; we'd been back and forth with headquarters on whether we had probable cause to arrest him.

"Max was going to walk up with those other guys, get Ted Kaczynski, take him to the Williams cabin, and stash him there, and then it would be the bomb team's turn inside."

———

Seconds ticked by as the forward team anxiously waited for word on the warrant. To a man, everyone on scene wanted to ensure that everything proceeded according to plan. They also knew that nothing could happen until the court approved the warrant. Finally, Jim Freeman gave them word that Turchie and the others had secured a judge's signature and the operation was a go.

Once Freeman gave the go-ahead, the foursome—Max, Tom McDaniels, the resident FBI agent in Helena, and Jerry Burns—walked up the trail and banged on the door.

"Ted, it's Jerry Burns. We got these guys from the mining company, we are going to look around for posts and pins," referring to the devices used by surveyors to mark property lines. After all, no one wanted to intrude on Ted's land.

Ted Kaczynski mumbled, opened the door just enough so he could look out, and told Burns that his property lines were all clearly marked. But Burns said they couldn't see the markers because they were covered with snow.

"Let me get my coat," Kaczynski grumbled, turning and starting to move deeper inside the cabin.

Fearing that things could go bad, Jerry grabbed onto Kaczynski before he could take a step. There was a struggle between the two—made all the worse by the icy conditions that day. In one quick motion, Max pulled his Sig Sauer Model 226 from its holster and stuck it in Kaczynski's face. He told him that he was with the FBI and that they had a warrant to search the cabin. Kaczynski made no effort to flee and was placed in handcuffs.

The men started walking down the road to Williams's cabin for holding, and a call went out on the secure FBI radio channel, "Subject is in custody."

"And so, we were ready to go in," Webb recounted.

Everything hinged on the evidence team and bomb techs going into the cabin and finding some evidence that would allow the FBI to obtain an arrest warrant for Kaczynski. If they didn't find anything, the agency would have no choice but to let their suspect go.

"We drive up and collect the EOD team. This was before ATVs became really common. We didn't have a truck or anything to get up there, so we had to walk up. We could have brought a whole van load of equipment. But the team wanted to execute the search warrant quickly. We were all keenly aware that CBS knew of our presence here and could put a spotlight on the investigation at any moment if another network started poking around.

"We get there to the cabin, and the EOD people staged," Webb said. "You don't want to go in to a search like that and get blown away. So we had people staged at safe distances. The cabin had a wooden door with a single key deadbolt on it. It was ajar. We just pushed it aside, and Don Sachtleben and I stood there for a good five minutes. There was no point to go charging in; we were just slowly trying to assess what we were dealing with."

The team made a point of checking for booby traps in the cabin. They didn't expect to find anything because of the way they'd surprised Kaczynski and quickly pulled him out of the cabin; he didn't have more than a few seconds to potentially set something. And there was no electricity in the cabin, which reduced their risk.

"The first hour or two Don and I just observed, browsed," Webb continued. "We didn't collect anything; we just looked at stuff. The back shelf was just little bottles and cans and Quaker oatmeal containers, and perhaps sixty little baby food jars. On the other side there was some food and macaroni. We spent two or three hours just looking at things. We found the diaries up on the left-hand side, not only devices, but all of his testing notes, and I remember for some reason, there was a Spanish text book up there, but we are there trying to figure out: Who is this guy?

"We went in at 12:54. He was grabbed at 11:30. To the left was wood shelving and a small built-in desk, the back wall was wall-to-wall shelving. The right wall was an open firewood box under the window and the bed, a bunk. Above that was a bookcase with all the binders. A hatch up above that led into the loft. We moved the hatch and just climbed up there and looked; there were boxes, a suitcase, and a typewriter case right in front.

"At 2:00 p.m., FBI bomb tech Frank Doyle came in with us, he was running the evidence response team," Webb continued. They started looking through things in a more methodical manner and taking note of what they found.

Ted had numerous small metal cans that he'd reused, labeling each one with its contents. He had Calumet baking powder, Hershey's chocolate, Quaker corn meal, and Quaker oatmeal. Other cans contained zinc, brass, and lead. There were also cans holding lead tire weights, miscellaneous pieces of low-melting-point metal, tin, and aluminum. The agents also found one-foot lengths of copper tubing, miscellaneous pieces of copper pipe, solid-cast aluminum ingots, C-cell batteries, assorted pieces of electrical wire, hacksaw blades, hand drills, drill bits, and solder.

No doubt the agents were just starting to scratch the surface of what was inside the cabin. The team was also acutely aware that it needed to find something that tied Kaczynski to the Unabomber. So far, that piece of evidence was eluding them.

It was dark, warm, and smoky in the cramped cabin. Everything carried the smell of smoke from the open fires Kaczynski used to stay warm and cook with. There was no running water in the cabin, no bathroom, no sink, no toilet. It was easy to understand why their suspect was filthy dirty, disheveled, and covered with ash.

By 2:15 p.m., Webb said, it was time to halt their work. He asked that Terry Turchie and Jim Freeman come up to the cabin.

"Okay let's stop," he directed, and everyone stepped outside. Webb asked that Terry Turchie and Jim Freeman come to the cabin. "They hadn't been up there yet. It took fifteen minutes to get them there. They were looking around the place. I had this oatmeal box that contained a handful of [bomb] ignitors, and I had tears in my eyes, and I said, 'This is the guy.'"

The men collectively breathed a deep sigh of relief. After tens of thousands of hours of work by hundreds of different people across the US, they'd finally apprehended the Unabomber and made the nation just a bit safer for everyone. Their suspect, the one with the genius IQ and degrees from Harvard and the University of Michigan, looked harmless enough. There was nothing about him to suggest that he'd been the one to create such an extended period of terror.

"They said to me, you walk to the Williams cabin, we need to call the US attorney in Helena and tell him we have enough to charge him."

Postal Inspector Paul Wilhelmus and ATF's Mike Grady had been in the Williams cabin with Ted Kaczynski for nearly two hours. Ted had refused to answer any questions about the investigation, although he agreed to talk about anything other than the case. This was the only time he ever spoke to investigators. Once in custody, he closed down and simply stopped speaking to them. (One television docudrama about the case featured a reenactment scene in which Kaczynski is seen talking to Jim Fitzgerald during an interrogation. In fact, Kaczynski has never said a word about the case to any member of law enforcement.)

Wilhelmus was taken aback by the suspect's appearance. "His clothes had holes in them; his face was covered with ash; his hair was matted with ash; he smelled like dirt," he recalled. *This is the guy?* he wondered.

The agents had spent most of their time with Ted talking with him about living in the woods. "He had a garden, and we talked about how he irrigated it, how he lived on rabbits," Wilhelmus said. "He felt like he was the smartest person in the room. I was in there with Max, Mike Grady, and Candice DeLong. At one point, Max brought up how Ted was a math major—he taught at Berkeley, an outstanding math program."

"What kind of math did you teach?" Max asked him.

"Well, how much mathematics have you taken?" Ted replied.

"Calculus."

"Well, you wouldn't understand it if I told you. It would just be a waste of time."

Sensing Ted was hungry, someone offered him a Snickers bar. He grabbed the sweet and immediately began eating it—oddly biting right through the plastic wrapper on the candy bar.

After a short while, Ted asked to see a copy of the search warrant, so someone brought it down to the cabin, and he began pointing out inaccuracies in the document's description of his tiny A-frame home. "Well, that window should be on this side," he nitpicked. "Where is the affidavit?"

"That is sealed," Max told him. "You will get that later."

After Terry Turchie had toured Ted's cabin with SSA Webb, he came to see Kaczynski. Ted perked up the minute he realized who he was. "You are Terry Turchie," he said, seemingly pleased that he was talking to the head guy now. "You are the one who applied for the search warrant."

Wilhelmus laughed, remembering Mike Grady's fixation with the fact that Kaczynski's cabin didn't have a front step. "God, that guy's lived here for twenty years, and he never had a front step?" Grady observed. "You go right from the cabin in the mud."

By 3:00 p.m. the US attorney in Helena was alerted that the search team in Lincoln had found enough to charge Kaczynski. By that time, the news was out. Turchie and the others pulled out onto the road and there were three news vans and five reporters.

At that point, Max and Jim told Kaczynski they were placing him under arrest. "We are going to charge you."

They went to the Helena FBI office, where Turchie got on the phone with headquarters and there was a big fight over what they were going to charge Ted with; at some point, Louie Freeh got involved.

"We had pieces, but was it enough to charge him?" Webb explained. "We found all these test notes, he'd blow things up in the snow. He'd find paint and dry it out; if you dry it enough you can get the aluminum out of it.

"He was creating his own potassium by peeing and getting the aluminum out of it. He had a getaway kit, a go-to-town kit in his cabin—a pair of slacks, a sweater, and a pair of real shoes. And he would wear that when he would go west to Missoula or east to Helena and he'd have to clean himself up."

Of all the things Webb and the other bomb techs found that first day, the unopened letter with the red circle around the return address from Ted's brother, David, stayed with Webb. "He never opened the letter his brother sent to him on an arrangement he specified," Webb recalled, shaking his head in disbelief. Apparently the letter had been sent to apprise Ted of the memorial service planned for his father.

———

When Max Noel told Kaczynski he was going to be arrested, Kaczynski began to quarrel.

"For what?" he asked.

"He wanted to play lawyer and argue about it," Webb recalled.

A three-car motorcade was arranged to transport Kaczynski to the marshal's office. "We drive up the hill, and there are like two hundred people around the jail, and there are television cameras there," Webb recalled. "We take him over to the jail, and there were some college kids who showed up outside the office. They were all in the municipal parking lot when Ted was being led out of the building, and one of them snaps a picture of him and sells it for two grand to the Associated Press. You have to kind of admire his ingenuity." Webb laughed.

"We went back to the US attorney's office, and we are trying to figure out details on how to charge him. The bureau jet was arriving from head-quarters and nobody's eaten, so we drive over to Burger King. It was 10:00 p.m. in Helena, and we pull up to the window and the guy inside says, 'We are closed.' So, we bang on the window and yell, 'FBI, we need food. Give us thirty Whoppers and fries.'"

CHAPTER 28

THE UNABOM
TYPEWRITER

The following morning, Webb and his team drove the sixty miles back to Lincoln. Don Sachtleben had stayed behind because he had to write the affidavit for the charging agent. "I get a call on the radio, 'Headquarters called, and they want that typewriter case; it's really important.' Bill Tobin, the typewriter examiner, is coming to Montana, so let Tobin look at this typewriter."

The agency was still looking for something that would definitively link Ted to the Unabomber—and they were hoping the typewriter would be the single thing they needed.

The UNABOM typewriter had one unique characteristic that made the agency believe it could be used to potentially tie Kaczynski to the case: it had a twisted or bent letter *W* that left a very distinctive imprint. The agents had already seen a typewriter case during their visual search of the loft, and they all assumed it contained a typewriter. But there was also the possibility that the case contained an improvised bomb, so they needed to handle it with extreme care.

"We had to go get this typewriter," Webb said. "But we didn't want to go and just pull the case out of the loft. When you go to bomb school, you learn about rigging, basically how to pull things out of tough places.

"We set up this elaborate pulley thing to pull it out. Everything is suspicious, so we don't want it to go off. It takes us like two hours. There is some snow around, we are clomping around in the snow. We had to pull it out of the loft and down the stairs, and we have it hanging there, twist it, pull it out the door, and twist it to a location where we can put it onto this wood sheet. It takes like two, maybe three hours. We get the typewriter out at 1:00 p.m.; the guys bring out the X-ray [machine]. What do they find? It is not a UNABOM device; it is a typewriter.

"Bill Tobin, who had been the UNABOM typewriter guy forever, gets out a jeweler's loupe, he looks at the letter *W* meticulously. 'It's not it; it is not the UNABOM typewriter,' he declares.

"I just laughed. It was a combination of laughter and being furious, because we'd spent two or three hours moving this thing, and the *W* wasn't right. So Bill Tobin leaves, and we make a pact—that we will not take direction from headquarters again. It was my bomb scene; I don't care who calls out. We needed to do what was practical and safe.

"We worked the rest of that day. We started sorting stuff out of the cabin. I remember going down to the command post and I was furious. 'We spent three hours on this stupid typewriter!' I railed to Freeman and Turchie. 'I am not taking headquarters' direction again. It is my call, my cabin," I told them.

"We will tell headquarters to back off," Turchie assured me. "We will do what is practical and safe."

Webb and his team worked through the afternoon. "We'd had constant problems with press sneaking in. There was a logging road quite a ways from the cabin, where the property sloped down to a stream where Kaczynski got his water and then went back up toward the road. He had a little lean-to where he would hang his rabbits, and the root cellar his father had helped him build was there.

"The SWAT team was still around doing parameter security, and I get a call at about three in the afternoon—a TV news team had gone past the road guards and didn't come back out. 'We think they are taking that logging road above you,' the agent says over the radio.

"I go out and listen around. I can hear some voices, I had my radio, so I said to Don [Sachtleben], 'Keep going in the cabin, and I will see if I can figure out where these people are.' "The hillside is steep and snow-covered, and as I am climbing up the hillside, I fall backwards and dislocate my shoulder.

"Thankfully, I had my radio and I called Don, 'Can you come up here?' and he discovers me there on the ground. 'We have an injury,' Don radios.

"Agent Candace DeLong was a nurse. She was moonlighting as a nurse on the night shift when she was an FBI agent, so she was the first to render aid. Within five minutes, three or four agents show up. I am on my back, I say, 'I hurt my shoulder—just take a roll of duct tape and duct tape around my right shoulder.' They had to have two people on each side of me. They walk me down the creek bed toward the Williams cabin, and Jerry Webb—an agent not related to me—backs a pickup truck down this rocky path and takes me to the command center.

"Freeman says, 'Let's medivac him,' so I am in this ambulance. Don came down with me to the hospital and he calls Florence. She was in the Santa Cruz area on business and he tells her, 'Pat has been hurt, but he is okay.'

"They take me to the airport in Lincoln, all kinds of press people there, Rita Williams from San Francisco was there, and the helicopter takes me to St. Patrick's Hospital, sixty miles west in Missoula. It landed on the roof, and they roll me into the ER . . . Missoula, and I have an FBI bomb jacket on. I tell them, 'Whatever you do, do not cut this jacket! I had to wait like three years for this jacket!'"

Doctors popped Pat's shoulder back into place and put his arm in a sling. He was told he needed to do a follow-up visit with an orthopedic surgeon once back in San Francisco. It was after 10:00 p.m. by the time he was discharged that evening—but he had no intention of heading back to the West Coast with his broken wing. He was determined to get back to Lincoln and see this phase of the investigation through to the end.

Webb had transportation to get back together with the team that night, so he stayed at a hotel in Missoula. The bureau's plane was also being used for a mission to New Mexico.

"I find out that after I got hurt, Don went back up in the cabin, and they found this aluminum-foil-wrapped box under the bed. It is labeled to the Tan Aerospace Company in Dallas, Texas. It has a label on the top, because Ted's style was that he would wrap his devices in brown paper. The foil was to keep it dry and safe.

"They pull it out and x-ray and see it is a live UNABOM device. They shoot it from a couple of angles, and they know exactly what it is. Don says, 'This is enough; let's stop. Pat got hurt, we have a live bomb,' and he locked up the cabin."

That night the FBI sent the bureau plane to Albuquerque, New Mexico, to bring in a bomb expert named Chris Cherry and a team of researchers from Sandia National Laboratories. Cherry and his team had developed a device called a Percussion Actuated Non-electric, or PAN disruptor. It was designed to allow law enforcement to safely disarm improvised explosive devices like those from Kaczynski.

The FBI desperately needed to preserve the components from Kaczynski's unexploded bomb from the cabin, and the team hoped the PAN disruptor would allow them to do exactly that.

Webb was back on the scene by 7:00 a.m. Friday. Two agents from San Francisco who were in Montana for Kaczynski's arrest ferried him back to Lincoln by car. "I am in the same clothes I was in the day before; I've got this brace on my shoulder, and they put me in the back of a bureau car with nine hundred pillows they'd 'borrowed' from the Holiday Inn," Webb recalled.

Not even a dislocated shoulder could keep the FBI agent away from seeing the case through to its rightful conclusion. By now, a crew from the Los Angeles field office had arrived in Lincoln, including two highly seasoned bomb techs.

That Friday, Pat and the others spent the entire day deciding the logistics of getting that live bomb out of the cabin and down to a site where they could render it safe. Transporting the package in the front of a pay loader was one of the suggestions being considered.

Soon after the team from Sandia arrived, they began making plans to bring the bomb out of the cabin using a remote-controlled robot and moving it to a sheltered area where the PAN disruptor could be used. Roads were graded and wooden ramps were built between the cabin and a nearby open field where the PAN disruptor had been set up. The delicate operation took three full days, but it was successful. The cabin couldn't be searched, nor the crime scene processed, until the device was safely removed and detonated.

During the operation, one of the perimeter guards had caught an NBC producer, cameraman, and sound man who appeared to have deliberately ignored warnings to stay out of the area and surreptitiously gone in to shoot tape of Kaczynski's cabin. The guards brought the crew to Webb, who was furious and threatened to arrest them. Webb called headquarters and asked for counsel from his seniors before taking any action. Word came down from Janet Reno that the crew should not be arrested, and Webb let them go—along with the video tape they'd shot.

That night, as task force members ate at a local bar and restaurant, Webb watched as NBC News aired "exclusive video" of Kaczynski's cabin on the TV hanging over the bar. The damage had been done, and there was nothing further he could do.

With the bomb now out of the cabin, the team began bagging and tagging the evidence. "There was a second typewriter in the cabin," Webb said. "It was the last item on a multipage search warrant (inventory returned to the court). It was in the attic, it was a big ammo box, and that was the real UNABOM typewriter, the one with the twisted *W*."

Kathy Puckett and Jim Fitzgerald were flown in to Montana to deal with the nearly forty thousand pages of written documents found during the search of the cabin, much of which was in code, or in different languages. The FBI lab told Webb and the team that the code was based on mathematics and was more complicated than anything the experts had ever seen—including codes used by the KGB at the height of the Cold War. "If they hadn't had the two code books that we pulled out of the cabin, the guys in the lab wouldn't have been able to decipher it," Webb said.

Searchers also found a manila envelope with the word *autobiography* written across the front, which contained what appeared to be Kaczynski's autobiography. Once the cabin was rendered safe, Puckett and Fitz were permitted to enter so they could get a sense of the person they were dealing with.

Puckett would spend the next half of the year reading and analyzing Ted's writings, and she would later become part of the forensic psychiatric team the bureau hired for the prosecution phase of the case.

Agents learned that Ted had been faithfully following his case in the media. "He had a battery-powered radio," Webb recalled. "One of my regrets is that I never turned the radio on. Nobody ever did, so I cannot tell you what station it was tuned to; I can't tell you what he listened to. It is just one of those funny things, those missteps in life.

"But he was certainly a media hound and we know he followed the *Chronicle*, and he wrote to the *Chronicle* faithfully and to the *New York Times*. He had respect for the *New York Times*; it was the newspaper of record, and he took advantage of that."

After Kaczynski's arrest, investigators visited the little log cabin library in Lincoln. He lived three miles out of town, and he'd either walk in or he had a bicycle he'd ride into town on warm summer days. He would apparently sit at the library and read what he wanted to read.

"Kaczynski was job security for the librarian," Webb told me. "He was asking for these bizarre out-of-the-system books. She'd never filled so many interlibrary loans in her life."

"She had an affinity for him," Webb continued. "'He has always been such a nice man,' she told my people. Basically, Ted was just kind of a ghost impression, a guy who lived out in the hills somewhere. It's Montana; it is a very forgiving place, live and let live country.

"One thing we knew about him, the snowmobilers hated him," Webb chuckled. "There were a couple of places where he'd strung wire to decapitate snowmobilers—barbed wire between trees. Maybe he thought it would just keep him safe."

There is a bus station in Lincoln; the bus would either take you to Helena east or Missoula west. "He'd go to Helena, then Spokane, then Seattle via Greyhound. We interviewed every bus driver, and some people did remember him as just being a quiet, goofy guy on the bus."

On Webb's last night in Lincoln, he collected with his team. "We called the local steakhouse and said, 'Can we have a table for thirty?' And the whole crew went to the steakhouse.'"

Webb flew home to San Francisco in a Vicodin haze, and two FBI employees were there at the airport to meet his plane. The next morning, Webb's wife, Florence, took him to the doctor, where he learned he would have to have surgery on his shoulder.

So many years later, he remained convinced that had Kaczynski's brother not turned him in, the task force would have identified and arrested him. "My personal conviction is that we would have caught him eventually," he insisted. "In the manifesto, he cited some obscure text book, and we looked who had copies and where the copies were available. There were eight copies in libraries across the country. They would have been able to tell us who had requested them. Once we got the name of who ordered that book in Lincoln, Montana, we would have had him.

"It would have been a struggle and maybe I am fantasizing, but I think we would have gotten him through the grunt work. But it all stopped when his brother came forward."

CHAPTER 29

"I AM NOT MENTALLY ILL."

As investigators were executing the search warrant in Lincoln, Montana, Kathy Puckett, Lee Stark, and Jim Fitzgerald were pacing around the office in San Francisco. Word had gotten out that the FBI had arrested a suspect and Ted's name had been leaked. Kathy was eager to alert David to the latest development so the family could prepare for the media onslaught that would surely follow. In agreeing to speak with the FBI, David had asked that he be kept out of the story; it was important to him that no one knew he was the one who came forward. Above all else, he wanted to ensure that Ted never knew the role he played.

But headquarters made it clear that Puckett was not allowed to call David under any circumstances. The fear was that David would call or otherwise communicate with his brother, letting him know that the FBI was closing in on him.

Puckett said she did finally get a green light from headquarters to call David—but by then, it was too late, and the media had already descended on his house. Puckett had the radio on in the background as she made the call, and she heard a "live update" from a correspondent who announced that he was standing on David Kaczynski's front lawn.

277

David was furious with Kathy for what he perceived as a blatant violation of their trust.

"The only thing I asked you to do, you screwed up," David railed before hanging up on Puckett.

Upon learning what had happened with David, Agent Molly Flynn got in a car and drove to Schenectady to offer to David an apology. She parked some distance away and snuck through backyards to get to the house unseen. Once she arrived at the house, she knocked on the door and David let her in. She was so upset at the chaotic scene on the front lawn that she just burst into tears. David, Linda, and Wanda all embraced the agent. No one was happy with the way things went down. To this day, David, Linda, and Molly remain friends.

———

The two years leading up to Ted Kaczynski's criminal trial were fraught with legal twists and turns. Prosecutors charged him with a litany of offenses: four counts of transportation of an explosive with intent to kill or injure; three counts of mailing an explosive device in an attempt to kill or injure; and three counts of use of a destructive device in relation to a crime of violence. The charges were connected to the deaths of Hugh Scrutton and Gilbert Murray, and the injuries sustained by Charles Epstein and David Gelernter.

Kaczynski insisted he was not mentally ill and refused to go along with the insanity defense his federal defenders were pushing. Still, the court ordered that he undergo a psychological evaluation to determine whether he was competent to stand trial. Dr. Sally C. Johnson, chief psychologist and associate warden of health services for the Federal Correctional Institution in Butner, North Carolina, was retained by the court.

Dr. Johnson based her diagnosis on interviews with Kaczynski, his family, and his friends. She also administered psychological tests and was provided with copies of Ted's manifesto, journal entries, letters, and other writings found by investigators during a search of his cabin. She was also given medical records from his childhood hospitalization in Chicago, University Health Service records from Harvard University, and other records from Ted's various medical visits over the years.

At the onset of the interview, Ted indicated that he did not want to use a mental health defense in his case. He expressed his displeasure with having to speak to a psychiatrist, explaining that "science has no business probing the workings of the mind." He eventually came around, convinced that by taking the neuropsychological tests, he could prove that he was not mentally ill.

Dr. Johnson found Kaczynski to be a man whose early brilliance was ruined by paranoid schizophrenia. She concluded he had "an almost total absence of interpersonal relationships" and exhibited "delusional thinking involving being controlled by technology." She noted that he was "extremely sensitive to even minor criticism and tends to perceive this, or even an absence of encouragement or positive response from an individual, as a deliberate attempt at humiliation and harassment."

In spite of Dr. Johnson's diagnosis of schizophrenia, she found that Kaczynski was mentally competent to stand trial and a date was set for January 23, 1998, in US District Court for the Eastern District of California on I Street in downtown Sacramento.

US District Court Judge Garland Ellis Burrell, Jr. presided over the case. Judge Burrell, a former Marine who served in Vietnam, held a bachelor of arts degree from the University of California, Los Angeles (UCLA), a master of social work from Washington University in St. Louis, Missouri, and a juris doctor from California Western School of Law in San Diego. He held the positions of deputy district attorney of Sacramento, deputy chief of the civil division of the United States attorney's office for the Eastern District of California, and senior deputy attorney of Sacramento before his appointment to a newly created seat in the United States District Court for the Eastern District of California by President George H. W. Bush on August 1, 1991.

Judge Burrell had a reputation as a smart, no-nonsense administrator of the law. During jury selection in the UNABOM case, he surprised potential jury candidates when he stepped down from the bench to ask them questions face-to-face; this was a routine occurrence in Burrell's Sacramento courtroom, where he strove to put people at ease—but certainly not common in other courtrooms. But he was also stern. When Kaczynski submitted a request to act as his own attorney at trial, Burrell flatly denied his application, labeling the move "a deliberate attempt to manipulate the trial process."

David and Wanda Kaczynski were in the courtroom, as were a number of task force members, including Agent Kathleen Puckett, who was still reeling from what had transpired between her and David.

At the end of the proceeding, Puckett approached David's attorney, Anthony Bisceglie, who was seated with the family.

"How is David?" she asked.

"It has been really tough for him."

"Please tell him I am really sorry, and I am thinking about him."

Since Ted's arrest, David and Linda Kaczynski had been besieged by media, with television pundits debating David's decision to turn his brother in to the FBI on the nightly news. In his heart, David was convinced that Ted couldn't be the Unabomber. But both he and his wife just weren't sure, and they felt they needed to at least work with the FBI. David hoped that somehow things would work out and that Ted would be eliminated as a suspect. Unfortunately, the cards didn't fall that way.

Prosecutors had publicly praised David Kaczynski, calling him a "hero" for coming forward and preventing others from being harmed. Still, the toll on Ted's younger brother had been great.

That day Puckett finally got her chance to apologize in person. As she was making her way out of the courtroom, she and David locked eyes. After a brief exchange, the two hugged. "I am so sorry," Puckett told him.

"I understand, you did what you had to do," David replied.

Later that day, Ted tried to hang himself in his cell with his underwear, Puckett recalled. "I didn't think he was suicidal. A mental health defense was being forced on him, and it was most important that he not be seen as mentally ill. It was a feigned attempt to take back control. In that one day, he saw the writing on the wall, and they were going to make him take a mental health plea, not guilty by reason of insanity."

"Kaczynski kept insisting, 'I am not mentally ill. There is nothing wrong with my mind. I did what I did for a very justifiable reason,'" Puckett said.

"A lot of people agree with him," Puckett noted. "He is an underground hero to a lot of people. I think it is a measure of the absurdity of fame and notoriety that people are enchanted by, but I am always bemused by the number of women who make these guys heroes.

"His notoriety and just being associated with the case would make him attractive. He doesn't care that people venerate him or think his ideas are correct; he doesn't have a lot of regard for other people. How far did you get in school in math? He transcended society in his ideology and his campaign against technology by human beings; he rose above the lackies of civilization."

The following day, Ted Kaczynski further surprised everyone when he agreed to plead guilty to all the federal charges against him. His plea, which was unconditional and could not be appealed, carried a life sentence without the possibility of release. David and Wanda sat behind him in the courtroom, and he never once looked at them—his own brother and mother.

Jim Freeman retired and became director of security at Charles Schwab. Webb recalled that the next SAC who came to San Francisco didn't understand the culture.

"You guys have had a real great run here, a great success with UNABOM," he told agents in the San Francisco Division. "But it is time to get back to real work."

"This guy jumped up and laid into him," Webb recalled.

"We are so proud of what [UNABOM] means for the division," the agent railed, "and for you to demean the effort that was put on here is insulting." Then he just sat down.

Ted Kaczynski is now serving a life sentence at a maximum security "Supermax" prison, ADX Florence, in Colorado. "He is writing a lot of legal briefs," Webb said. "He doesn't come out of his cell anymore. He used to come out for an hour a day. He is on 'Bombers Row,' formerly alongside Timothy McVeigh and currently alongside the 'Shoe Bomber,' Richard Reid, and Ramzi Ahmed Yousef, who bombed the Twin Towers in New York in 1993. He lives in a ten-by-twelve room, which is about the dimensions of his cabin in Montana."

EPILOGUE

In the early years of the UNABOM investigation, the FBI clearly lacked coordination in their efforts to find their suspects. The agency offices simply did not communicate with each other. For years, leads were not shared between other federal agencies, let alone state law enforcement. I suspect this guarding of local jurisdictional fiefdoms and assuaging of individual agents' egos contributed to the glacial progress of the Unabomber investigation for nearly two decades.

I am deeply troubled thinking about September 11, 2001, where the FBI had tips and information about the potential of domestic terrorist attacks on New York, and yet that information was not communicated to New York, or to the CIA. One can only wonder if the attacks of 9/11 could have been thwarted had the FBI in one office communicated what they knew to New York and the CIA.

This lack of interagency communication has only become more pressing because domestic terrorism is on the rise since the days of the Unabomber. Federal law enforcement officials continue to warn about the growing threat of domestic terrorism, suggesting that these newly radicalized terrorists find their theology online and their hideouts in the dark web of social media. While rooting out Ted Kaczynski in his Montana cabin posed an almost insurmountable challenge, finding and prosecuting these modern-day domestic terrorists, extremists driven by racial and ethnic hatred, presents new obstacles.

One obstacle is the fact that there is no federal law labeling domestic terrorism a crime. Kaczynski was charged and pled guilty to charges of illegally transporting bombs and three counts of murder. He was not charged with domestic terrorism, because no such federal charge exists. If such a federal charge did exist, law enforcement would be able to attach an umbrella criminal charge to a defendant's criminal activity, and, as importantly, could be compelled to share information between state and even local agencies in the pursuit of domestic terrorists. This interagency information sharing is crucial to combat domestic terrorism as these extremists become even more radicalized.

Agent Webb and the others who hunted the Unabomber for years are unsung heroes, and they deserve our gratitude, as do Kacyzinki's brother and sister-in-law, who had the courage to do the right thing even when faced with their own doubts and internal struggles. We may never fully understand what set Ted Kaczynski off, or why he continued his deadly pursuit for so many years, but we do know he was hunted by brave men and women who were dogged in their pursuit.

The Unabomber still holds the infamous title of the "longest hunt" in FBI history. And the FBI did finally get their man. Now let's just pray that no one else takes a run for the title of the FBI's "longest hunt." If they do, the FBI of today will be ready.

AFTERWORD

After UNABOM, Terry Turchie, Kathy Puckett, and several others who had served on the UNABOM task force found themselves working the Eric Rudolph case. Rudolph—better known as the Olympic Park Bomber—was a serial bomber responsible for anti-gay and anti-abortion bombings in Atlanta, Georgia, and Birmingham, Alabama, which killed two people and injured hundreds of others. Rudolph's bombing spree commenced just as the UNABOM investigation was winding down, and Turchie's success on UNABOM led headquarters to tap him to join the bureau's effort to track down Rudolph. Turchie was promoted to inspector and appointed to lead the southeast bomb task force's fugitive hunt for Rudolph, who remained on the run until May 31, 2003, when a police officer in Murphy, North Carolina, spotted him rummaging through trash bins and placed him under arrest.

In March 2000, Turchie was promoted to deputy assistant director for the new Counterterrorism Division, and in April 2001 he retired from the bureau and became director of counterintelligence at Lawrence Livermore National Laboratory in San Francisco.

In 2001, FBI director Louis Freeh commissioned Kathleen Puckett to conduct a multijurisdictional risk assessment study concerning lone domestic terrorists, including Theodore Kaczynski, Timothy McVeigh, and Eric Rudolph, for the Counterterrorism Division of the FBI. Profilers at Quantico were furious when they learned Puckett had been given the assignment, believing that this was *their* purview.

Puckett looked at a subset of these "lone-wolf terrorists" and what set them apart; she was eager to understand how they chose their victims and also to identify any commonalities they shared. What she found was that they all came from different socioeconomic backgrounds; some came from intact families and some didn't; and they were all different ages. So what was it about them? What was going on in their heads that made them do large acts of societal-level aggression rather than petty attacks against people who might have aggravated them in some way?

Puckett observed that human beings are hardwired to connect with one another. "We evolve as social creatures; our brains are wired for communication and connection with each other. We don't have fangs or claws, we can't exist on our own, we rely on each other—we are social animals," she explained. "If you are an individual who grows and can't make the connection with people in a social way, you are still hardwired to connect." Ted Kaczynski, Timothy McVeigh, and Eric Rudolph were unable to make connections with other people, but they never lost their craving for it.

In reviewing the writings of Ted Kaczynski, Puckett found a passage in which he described a desperate longing to get married and have children. He even sought the help of a psychotherapist in Montana during his six-year bombing hiatus, spending $150 on his sessions. He told the doctor he wanted to learn how to rejoin society, get married, and have children, claiming he could "teach children" and "make them grow up right." He explained that he just needed to know the formula for being a functioning individual in society.

"He was profoundly isolated. Eric Rudolph was like this and so was Timothy McVeigh, because they couldn't make meaningful connections with other people that mattered," Puckett explained. "If you can't do it with people, you make a connection with nature or something else that doesn't have to do with human beings, because it is safer. It is always there for you; it is not going to reject you."

Puckett found that in Ted's case, he made the connection to an ideology. His revelation was that technology was pure evil, because it was keeping people away from each other. "If you are not a social human being, if you care about having a connection, but you can't have it, then how do you matter in the world? If you don't have a place in the social world, and you can't have a place in the social world because you can't fit in, how can you matter? That is why these guys have to take out a whole federal building. That is why they have to take out a whole island full of kids. That is why these isolated, unsocialized lone offenders, the casino shooter in Las Vegas with all his bump stocks, commit these acts; they want to matter in the world—they want to leave a legacy."

She explained that for most people, it is enough to matter to the people they love. They don't have to make history; they don't have to make a huge impression. But for the Kaczynskis, the McVeighs, the Rudolphs, who don't have a way to matter to anyone, they have to matter to everyone. "Basically, they are saying, 'I have been isolated my whole life, but I can show you the way because I need to be part of a social fabric that won't have me.'"

Remarkably, despite its many insights, Puckett's report ended up on a shelf at FBI headquarters collecting dust. "I finished it in September 2001, and 9/11 happened right before I turned it in," Puckett explained. The timing couldn't have been worse. The 9/11 tragedy forced the FBI to shift its focus to international terrorism; there simply wasn't any time for agents, or higher-ups, to even consider domestic terrorists like Kaczynski.

In 2001, Puckett retired from the FBI and joined Terry Turchie at Lawrence Livermore National Laboratory as the deputy director of counterintelligence and counterterrorism.

Supervisory Special Agent Webb retired from the FBI in 1999 after thirty-four years with the bureau. His next role was head of security for Lucasfilm and ILM, where, according to his daughter Eileen, he was tasked with "safeguarding Star Wars premieres and chasing down Ewok counterfeiters."

On December 17, 2018, at the age of seventy-three, Webb lost his battle with cancer. Sadly, he did not get to see the publication of this book, but his time and assistance with this project have been nothing short of invaluable and he will be sorely missed, not only by his family and his law enforcement colleagues, but also by my cowriter and me. Even as his condition worsened and he was placed on hospice care, he continued to contribute to the project and meet with us to help ensure a true telling of the nearly two-decades-long investigation. Most important to him was that people knew that this was an enormous interagency effort that was responsible for bringing Ted Kaczynski to justice. His chief concern was that the story reflect that no single individual should take credit for taking down the Unabomber; it could only have happened through the intense efforts of the hundreds of members that comprised the Unabomber task force and the contributions of dozens of law enforcement officials and support staff members. Webb's long work on this case, like that of the entire UNABOM team, is a testament to the dedication of the FBI, as well as the US Postal Inspection Service and the Bureau of Alcohol, Tobacco, Firearms and Explosives, to the cause of justice—and the importance of never giving up the hunt.

ACKNOWLEDGMENTS

When I took on the work of researching and writing about Ted Kaczynski, I wanted to pay particular attention to the details of the excruciatingly long hunt for this domestic terrorist. How had the FBI handled it internally? What were the battles within the FBI as the hunt languished between bombings? Was there tension, even discord among agents on how to proceed during the investigation and hunt for this terrorist who had alluded them for years? As a journalist, I could surmise from the outside but had no facts to back me up. That was until I came in contact with one retired Supervisory Agent Patrick Webb.

As I began my research in 2018, Agent Webb had long been retired with his wife, Florence, in a cozy existence in New Hampshire, quite a change from his days as the supervisory agent in San Francisco heading the Unabomber investigation.

I approached Agent Webb, opening the door with what I call the "federal family key," which is that I am a third-generation federal prosecutor and the daughter of an FBI agent. During our initial chat over the phone, Agent Webb and I discussed field agents that my father and he may both have known or come in contact with. I told him I wanted to write a book about the Unabomber. This initial contact was shortly after a miniseries had aired on TV about the Unabomber, in which one agent had been portrayed as almost singlehandedly solving the case, having met with the Unabomber several times over the course of the hunt and capture.

Pat (Agent Webb told me very quickly to dispense with the formality of calling him Agent Webb) said the miniseries had gotten it wrong, that the hunt was a team effort, and the agent portrayed in the show, while on the team, had not even met Kaczynski! Pat was upset by the miniseries. He said it painted a false narrative of how the FBI had really handled the case. Pat said that if people believe the series is the true story about what happened in the Unabomber case, then they don't know what really happened.

I told him I wanted to set the record straight, but I would need his help. I would need all his old files on the Unabomber, his photos, his contacts and connections to other agents who were on the case, and most of all, I would need his time to talk with me as I went through the process of writing this account.

Pat gave generously. Through Pat's introduction, I was led to all the other agents who gave their time and insight to tell the inside story of the hunt for the Unabomber. And, as for his time, that he gave most generously. Pat spent some of his final hours setting the record straight on the case he had pursued the most relentlessly.

Even now, after Pat is gone, his wife, Florence, has helped locate photos for the insert and has read the final manuscript. Thank you, Florence, for helping finish what Pat began.

Speaking of beginning and finishing, my editor Webster Younce can (and sometimes does) begin and finish my sentences with a few strokes of his pen. Thank you, Webb, for continuing this marvelous hunting journey with me. I am so lucky to have you!

And the team at Thomas Nelson/HarperCollins continues to shine, with Janene MacIvor at the helm as copy editor. Her eagle eye was invaluable during the many pass-through reads. And thank you to Kristen Andrews and Belinda Bass for their tireless work on getting the cover just right. Karen Jackson, thank you, my friend, especially now. And Claire Drake, welcome aboard.

ACKNOWLEDGMENTS

My many thanks to Laura Rossi Totten. And Sunil Kumar. Both of whom help make sure this book is seen far and wide.

And then there is a special place in my heart for Todd Shuster, my agent (Aevitas Creative) and friend for going on twenty years. I remember, Todd, that day when you told me I'd be a published author. Today, this book is number nineteen published. We did it! And, thank you, Justin Broukaert, also with Aevitas Creative, I really value your input and advice. Keep bringing it on.

And thank you to my coauthor, Lisa Pulitzer. She is an amazing pleasure to work with. She, too, was inspired by Pat's story. She had the thoughtful idea of sending him Florida grapefruits at Christmas. Florence said he really liked those grapefruits. They were one of the last things he enjoyed eating before he died of cancer.

I was inspired by Pat's courage to tell this story, even as he was dying. He wanted to set the record straight on what really happened with the hunt for the country's most notorious domestic terrorist.

There is inspiration all around us, if we look. I'm inspired every day by my children, Jacob and Dani, who are forging their own lives, telling their own stories, and making the world a better place just by being in it.

LIS WIEHL
February 2020

SOURCES AND METHODOLOGY

This book represents the culmination of many months and countless hours of research that included multiple, long interviews with some of the key individuals in the UNABOM investigation, the review of hundreds of pages of UNABOM investigative material, and numerous other sources ranging from books to newspaper articles and magazine stories and select television news programs. We sought to provide an accurate and articulate account that fairly summarized the work of more than one thousand dedicated individuals in the field, many of whom invested years of their lives to apprehend the unabomber.

NOTABLE IN-PERSON INTERVIEWS:

FBI SSA Patrick Webb
FBI Agent Kathleen Puckett
FBI ASAC Terry Turchie
US Postal Inspector Paul Wilhelmus

NOTABLE BOOKS:

Every Last Tie: The Story of the Unabomber and His Family, by David Kaczynski

Unabomber: How the FBI Broke Its Own Rules to Capture Ted Kaczynski, by Jim Freeman

Harvard and the Unabomber: The Education of an American Terrorist, by Alston Chase

Hunting the American Terrorist: The FBI's War on Homegrown Terror, by Terry Turchie and Kathleen Puckett

The Unabomber Manifesto: Industrial Society and Its Future, by Ted Kaczynski

NOTABLE RECORDS ACCESSED ONLINE OR THROUGH OTHER SOURCES:

Classified FBI UNABOM file.

The Ted Kaczynski Papers: FBI Files and Photographs, University of Michigan Library, by Rosemary Santos Pal, August 20, 2014.

M Library: Blogs.

Special Collections Library, University of Michigan, Ted Kaczynski Papers, 1996–2014, Bulk Dates (1996–2005).

48 Linear Feet.

Call No.: Labadie-Kaczynski.

United States v. Kaczynski, 262 F.3d 1034 (9th Cir. 2001).

Jim R. Freeman, interview by Brien R. Williams, Oral History Interview, National Law Enforcement Museum, September 19, 2014.

Daniel M. Noel, Former Special Agent of the FBI (1968–1999), interview by Brian Holstein, Society of Former Special Agents of the FBI, Inc., February 11, 2008.

Kathleen M. Puckett, PhD, Former Special Agent of the FBI (1978–2001), interview by Susan Wynkoop, Society of Former Special Agents of the FBI, Inc., October 8, 2008.

Society of Former Special Agents of the FBI, Inc., 2008.

Interview with Former Special Agent of the FBI James Freeman.

Court Ordered Psychological Evaluation of Theodore Kaczynzki by Sally C. Johnson, file:///unabomber%20/Psychological%20

Evaluation%20of%20the%20Unabomber:%20Theodore%20
Kaczynski.webarchive.

PRIMARY AND NOTABLE NEWS OUTLETS, MAGAZINES, WIRE
SERVICES, AND ARCHIVES:
Lengthy reporting published in:

Washington Post
San Francisco Chronicle
Chicago Tribune
Salt Lake Tribune
San Francisco Examiner
New York Times

"Unabomber Suspect Left Little Trace," by Marie Felde. UC Berkeley,
   Office of Public Affairs, April 10, 1996.
"What Is the Unabomber's Life Like Now?," by Meredith Worthen.
   Biography.com, August 19, 2019.
"Did Ted Kaczynski's Transformation into the Unabomber Start at
   Harvard?," by Brian Dunleavy. History.com, May 25, 2018.
Wikipedia, "Ted Kaczynski."
"Was the Unabomber Correct?," by Keith Ablow. Fox News,
   opinion, June 25, 2013.
"Unabomber Case and Trial," by Thomas Gale. Encyclopedia.com,
   2005.
"Retired FBI Agent Jerry Webb: The True Teamwork Involved
   in the Unabomber Case," by Jerry Webb. Tickle the Wire.com,
   September 5, 2017.
"Harvard and the Making of the Unabomber," by Alston Chase.
   Atlantic, June 2000.
"The Unlikely New Generation of Unabomber, Children of Ted," by
   John H. Richardson. *New York Magazine*, December 11, 2018.
"Defending the Unabomber." *New Yorker*, March 16, 1998.

"Harvard's Experiment on the Unabomber, Class of '62," by Jonathan D. Moreno. *Psychology Today*, May 25, 2012.

"Dead Letters," by Elizabeth Fernandez. *People Magazine*, November 15, 1993.

"Evil's Humble Home," by Richard Ford. *New York Times Magazine*, September 13, 1998.

"FBI Reveals Note of the Unabomber," *Journal Times* (Associated Press), October 7, 1993.

"Killer's Trail: Linguistics, Other Analyses Hint at Unabomber Type, Implying Long Search," by Mark Schoofs, Gary Fields, and Jerry Markon. *Wall Street Journal*, November 12, 2001.

"Excerpts from Unabomber's Journals," *New York Times*, April 29, 1998.

"In Unabomber's Own Words, a Chilling Account of Murder," by David Johnston. *New York Times*, April 29, 1998.

"He Came Ted Kaczynski, He Left the Unabomber," by Karl Stampfl. *Michigan Daily*, March 16, 2006.

"Prisoner of Rage," by Robert D. McFadden. *New York Times*, May 26, 1996, including the following:

    "The Child, Having Trouble Fitting In"

    "The College Student, Slamming His Door on the World"

    "The Graduate Scholar: Colleges Awed by His Brilliance"

    "The Professor: 'I Can't Recollect This Guy'"

    "The Hermit: An Austere Life in the Montana Woods"

    "The Rejected Suitor: A Good Mood After a Date"

    "The Correspondent: Letters of Friendship, Letters of Anger"

"Ex-FBI Agent: 'Manhunt Unabomber' Series Disrespects Heroes," by Greg Stejskal. *Detroit Deadline Media*, August 11, 2017.

"Matching Wits with the Unabomber: The Inside Story of How an Elite Bomb Squad Dismantled the Unabomber's Last Deadly Device," by Frank Vizard. *Popular Science*, April 1, 2013.

"Clue, $1-Million Reward Offered in University Bombings," by Ronald J. Ostrow. *LA Times*, October 7, 1993.

"Clue and $1 Million Reward in Case of the Serial Bomber," by Stephen Labaton. *New York Times*, October 7, 1993.

"5 Unabomber Suspects Under Constant Watch," by Michael Taylor. *San Francisco Chronicle,* November 22, 1995.

"FBI's 17-Year Search for Unabomber Often Seemed in Vain," by David Johnston. *New York Times*, May 5, 1998.

"Unabomber's Own Chilling Account of Murder," by David Johnston. *New York Times*, April 29, 1998.

New York Times, Letter to the Editor, October 5, 1995.

"Unabomber Misses College Reunion but Sends Update," by Michael Schwirtz. *New York Times*, May 23, 2012.

"BOOK OF THE TIMES: The Unabomber and the 'Culture of Despair,'" by Janet Maslin. *New York Times,* March 3, 2003.

"Portrait Unabomber, Environmental Saboteur Around Montana Village." *New York Times*, March 14, 1999.

"Publishing House Grapples with How to Publish Kaczynski's Book," by Doreen Carvajal. *New York Times*, October 11, 1999.

"Patrick C. Fischer, Unabomber Target, Is Dead at 75," by Paul Vitello. *New York Times*, August 21, 2001.

"Charles Epstein, Leading Geneticist Injured by Unabomber, Dies at 77," by Margalit Fox. *New York Times*, February 23, 2011.

"Personal Items of Unabomber Will Be Sold," by Jesse McKinley. *New York Times*, August 12, 2006.

"Unabomber's Kin Collect Reward of $1 Million for Turning Him In," by James Brooks. *New York Times*, August 21, 1998.

"17-Year Search, an Emotional Discovery and Terror Ends," by David Johnston. *New York Times*, May 5, 1998.

"*Times* and *The Washington Post* Grant Mail Bomber's Demand," by Robert D. McFadden. *New York Times*, September 19, 1995.

"Unabomber Lists Self as 'Prisoner' in Harvard Directory." *Boston Globe*, May 5, 2012.

"How Accurate Is Fitz in 'Manhunt: Unabomber'? Here's What the

Real James Fitzgerald Thinks of His Fictional Self," by Alaina Uruhart-White. *Bustle*, August 9, 2017.

"Flummoxing the Feds," by *Newsweek* staff. *Newsweek*, July 9, 1995.

"FBI Reveals Note of Unabomber." Associated Press, October 7, 1993.

"The Profile of a Loner," by Joel Achenbach and Serge F. Kovaleski. *Washington Post*, April 7, 1996.

"After Years of High-Profile Cases, Federal Prosecutor Takes Sacramento Judgeship," by Denny Walsh. *Sacramento Bee*, December 28, 2013.

"Did the FBI Ignore the 'Tafoya Profile?': An Eerily Accurate Unabomber Prediction," by Gordon Witkin. *U.S. News*, November 17, 1997.

"A Trail of Bombs: When Theodore Kaczynski Goes on Trial This Week . . ." *San Francisco Chronicle*, November 9, 1997.

"10 Years Ago, Unabomber Arrested," by Eve Byron. *Billings Gazette*, April 1, 2006.

"From 'Unabomber' to 'Mad Bomber,' A Look at Past Serial Bombers," by Linda Wang. NPR, March 21, 2018.

"The Unabomber Trial: The Manifesto." *Washington Post*, September 22, 1995.

TIMELINE AND
KEY PLAYERS

The hunt for the Unabomber was and remains the longest-running, most expensive, and most complex investigation in FBI history. Ted Kaczynski was responsible for sixteen attacks, a spree that began in May 1978 in Chicago, Illinois, and ended only with his capture in Lincoln, Montana, in April 1996. His reign of terror spanned nearly two decades in jurisdictions scattered across the United States, claiming the lives of three innocent people and harming twenty-three others—many of them suffering lifelong debilitating physical injuries. All told, more than one thousand federal and local law enforcement personnel and support staff contributed to the investigation.

To help readers navigate this complex story, we have created a detailed timeline of the bombing events and a list of key individuals who are referenced in the book.

TIMELINE OF UNABOMBER ATTACKS

Bomb Number One: May 25, 1978. On May 24, 1978, a passerby found a package in the parking lot of the University of Illinois, Chicago Circle Campus. The package was addressed to Professor E. J. Smith at Rensselaer Polytechnic Institute's School of Engineering in Troy, New York. The package included postage stamps but had not been dropped off at a post office or placed in a mailbox. Instead, it was left on the ground just yards from a public mailbox and near the main post office on campus. The package was picked up by campus police and returned to its supposed sender, Buckley Crist, a materials science professor at Northwestern University. Crist claimed to know nothing about the package and contacted campus police to alert them to its arrival. Public Safety Officer Terry Marker attempted to open the package and suffered minor injuries in the ensuing explosion.

Bomb Number Two: May 9, 1979. John Harris, a graduate student at Northwestern University, picked up what he thought was an empty cigar box from a table outside his office at the school's Technological Institute. Harris later recalled seeing a "bright flash" as he lifted the box, causing the detonator inside to go off. Luckily, the bomb did not explode, and Harris suffered only minor burns.

Bomb Number Three: November 15, 1979. American Airlines Flight 444 from Chicago to Washington, DC's Reagan International Airport made an emergency landing at Dulles Airport when a package exploded in the cargo hold, sparking a small fire. Twelve people suffered smoke inhalation and were treated by emergency personnel on the runway.

Bomb Number Four: June 10, 1980. Percy A. Wood, the president of United Airlines, was severely injured when a package sent to his Chicago-area home exploded, causing him to suffer burns over much of his body.

Bomb Number Five: October 9, 1981. Maintenance worker Robert Lockyer alerted campus officials after discovering what he deemed a suspicious package on a desk in a classroom at the University of Utah's School of Business in Salt Lake City. Federal authorities successfully defused the device in a woman's bathroom on the campus. No one was hurt.

Bomb Number Six: May 5, 1982. Janet Smith, a secretary at Vanderbilt University in Nashville, Tennessee, was gravely injured when she opened a package addressed to her boss, Patrick Fischer, a computer science professor, who was away lecturing in the Bahamas when the device detonated.

Bomb Number Seven: July 2, 1982. Professor Diogenes Angelakos, a computer science and electrical engineering professor at the University of California, Berkeley, suffered lasting damage to his right hand after he attempted to pick up an odd-looking device that had been left on the floor of a coffee lounge in Cory Hall, the school's engineering and technology building.

Bomb Number Eight: May 15, 1985. US Air Force pilot John Hauser, a graduate student at the University of California, Berkeley, was severely injured when he attempted to move what he thought was a notebook from a desk in a student computer room in Cory Hall. Hauser lost four of the fingers on his right hand in the explosion, forcing him to abandon his dreams of becoming an astronaut.

Bomb Number Nine: June 13, 1985. A mailroom employee at the Boeing Company's fabrication plant in Auburn, Washington, noticed a package that someone had left sitting on a shelf. He started to open the package but stopped when he suspected it might be a bomb. He alerted authorities, who were able to render the device safe. No one was injured.

Bomb Number Ten: November 15, 1985. A package arrived at the home of James McConnell, a professor at the University of Michigan. McConnell, a biologist and animal psychologist, was working at home with his research assistant, Nick Suino, who opened the package and triggered the device. Both men were injured in the explosion, with Suino sustaining burns and shrapnel wounds to his arms and abdomen, and McConnell suffering slight hearing loss.

Bomb Number Eleven: December 11, 1985. The Unabomber claimed his first fatality when computer store owner Hugh Scrutton attempted to move a dangerous-looking jumble of lumber lying on the ground near his car in the parking lot of his building in Sacramento, California. The ensuing blast ripped open his chest; life-saving attempts by two local servicemen who happened to be in the area failed to save him.

Bomb Number Twelve: February 20, 1987. Gary Wright, whose family owned a computer store in Salt Lake City, was severely injured by a device similar to the one that had killed Hugh Scrutton. Wright was returning to work from an off-site business meeting when he noticed what he thought was road debris in the parking lot just beside his coworker's rear tire. Concerned, he attempted to move it, causing the device to detonate and propel two thousand pieces of shrapnel into his nose, eyes, and forehead, permanently severing a nerve in his wrist.

Bomb Number Thirteen: June 22, 1993. Geneticist Charles Epstein, a professor emeritus of pediatrics at the University of California, San Francisco, was rushed to the hospital suffering from internal injuries, hearing loss, and severe injuries to his right hand after he attempted to open a package sent to his Bay Area home.

Bomb Number Fourteen: June 24, 1993. David Gelernter, a computer scientist and Yale University professor, lost several of his fingers and sustained permanent damage to his right eye as a result of an explosion that occurred when he attempted to open an envelope left on his desk in the school's Computer Science Department, Arthur K. Watson Hall.

Bomb Number Fifteen: December 10, 1994. Thomas Mosser, an advertising executive with Burson Marsteller, became Ted Kaczynski's second fatality. Mosser was seated at the kitchen table of his North Caldwell, New Jersey, home when he opened the Unabomber's package, detonating the bomb inside. His wife, Kelly, and the couple's fifteen-month-old daughter were only a few feet away when the device exploded, propelling nails through Mosser's heart and causing fragments of razor blades to rip open his stomach.

Bomb Number Sixteen: April 24, 1995. California Forestry
Association president Gilbert Murray was killed by a package bomb
sent to the company's headquarters in Sacramento. The force of the
explosion blew a hole in his chest and ripped off his jaw.

KEY PLAYERS

Special Agent in Charge James Freeman: the FBI Special Agent
in Charge of the bureau's San Francisco Division in 1992 when the
UNABOM task force was formed.

Assistant Special Agent in Charge Terry Turchie: appointed by
Freeman in 1993 to serve as head of the UNABOM task force,
which operated out of the bureau's San Francisco Division.
Turchie's unwavering dedication and leadership led the team to
identify and capture Ted Kaczynski.

Supervisory Special Agent Patrick Webb: one of the longest-
serving members of the UNABOM investigation, joining the case
as a junior bomb technician in 1982, when Kaczynski targeted the
University of California, Berkeley, campus. Webb spent much of
his career in the FBI's San Francisco Division and was on the scene
of three of Kaczynski's sixteen attacks. As supervisor of the San
Francisco Division, Webb oversaw the UNABOM investigation
before the multi-agency UNABOM task force was formed.

Special Agent Donald "Max" Noel: a highly trained bomb
technician who joined the UNABOM task force in 1992, making
him a member of the original multi-agency team. Noel was asked
to join the force for one year and promised he could return to his
post in counterterrorism. But his work on the case was deemed
too valuable and he was instructed to stay on, ultimately seeing
the case through to its conclusion. Noel was on the scene in
Montana for the arrest of Ted Kaczynski; he is the agent who
pulled him from his cabin and placed him under arrest. Noel is
one of only two members of law enforcement to interview the
Unabomber during his arrest.

Special Agent John Conway: the San Francisco case agent assigned to the UNABOM investigation and for a time the sole agent investigating the bombings, making him an important member of the UNABOM task force.

US Postal Inspector Paul Wilhelmus: joined the UNABOM task force in 1993, paired for much of his time on the investigation with FBI Special Agent John Conway.

FBI Director Louis Freeh: appointed to lead the bureau in 1993, making him responsible for overseeing the UNABOM investigation.

Special Agent Kathleen Puckett: a member of the behavioral analysis program in the bureau's national Security Division when she was tapped to join the UTF in 1993. She was a key member of the small team who counseled US Attorney Janet Reno and FBI Director Freeh on the importance of publishing the Unabomber's manifesto in the *Washington Post* in 1995 as a way of generating new leads in the case.

While it is impossible to name all those who worked on the investigation, we would like to extend our appreciation to those who shared their time and expertise with us. We would also like to acknowledge the innumerable law enforcement professionals who worked tirelessly to bring Ted Kaczynski to justice.

INDEX

ABOUT THE AUTHOR

Lis Wiehl is the former legal analyst for Fox News and the *O'Reilly Factor* and has appeared regularly on *Your World with Neil Cavuto, Lou Dobbs Tonight*, and the Imus morning shows. The former cohost of WOR radio's *WOR Tonight with Joe Concha and Lis Wiehl*, she has served as legal analyst and reporter for NBC News and NPR's *All Things Considered*, as a federal prosecutor in the United States Attorney's office, and was a tenured professor of law at the University of Washington. She appears frequently on CNN as a legal analyst. She lives near New York City.